M000223939

Liberal
Media
Industrial
Complex

Mark Dice

The Liberal Media Industrial Complex
© 2019 by Mark Dice
All Rights Reserved
Published by The Resistance Manifesto
San Diego, CA

No part of the text within this book may be reproduced or transmitted in any form and by any means, graphic, electronic, or mechanical, including photocopying, recording, taping, or by any information storage retrieval system, without the written permission of the author.

Printed in the United States of America

Visit www.MarkDice.com

ISBN: 978-1-943591-07-7

Cover images licensed from iStockPhoto
Logos for Google, Twitter, YouTube, Facebook, CNN, NBC, and the Washington Post are registered trademarks of their respective companies and are used in accordance with fair use statutes and case law.

Table of Contents

Introduction

Today, "media" doesn't just mean television, radio, newspapers, and magazines; since all of those industries have been swallowed up by the Internet (*convergence* as it's technically called). As you know, people now get most of their news and entertainment online where there is an endless supply of things to click on, scroll through, and stream. People carry TVs in their pockets and wear them on their wrists like the old science fiction films predicted. With the push of a button anyone can watch almost any show, access any newspaper or magazine article, and even send instant feedback about what they think. Everywhere you go people are constantly glued to their device, consuming an endless stream of "media." It's like a madhouse that's almost impossible to escape.

In our current mobile age, trying to keep up with the news is like running on a treadmill that's getting faster and faster. The longer you're on it, the more exhausting it gets, leading many to become so fatigued they decide to jump off and quit paying attention altogether. Many have become so stressed out, disgusted, and tired of the "news," that they basically boycott it and only follow sports or other forms of entertainment, but even there they can't escape being bombarded by political messages and cries for "social justice."

Those who wish to push political agendas know that movies, music, and TV shows are convenient vehicles to deliver their propaganda to millions under the cloak of "entertainment." Even some sports coverage on ESPN has become political in recent years, amplifying the messages of athletes involved in fringe causes or ones based on half-truths and out-right lies.[1]

Music, movies, and television shows are not just "entertainment." They shape and influence the culture by manufacturing iconic characters whose beliefs and behaviors are mimicked by millions. While art imitates life, life also imitates art, as President Obama admitted during an appearance via video at the 2015 Grammies where he told the audience, "Tonight, we celebrate artists whose music and message helps shape our culture... Artists have a unique power to change minds and attitudes and get us thinking and talking about what matters."[2] Celebrities have largely taken over the role that families, the Church, and national traditions used to play in molding and monitoring a society's attitudes and actions.

As Andrew Breitbart pointed out in his book *Righteous Indignation*, "Hollywood is more important than Washington. It can't be overstated how important this message is: pop culture matters. What happens in front of the cameras on a soundstage at the Warner Bros. lot often makes more difference to the fate of America than what happens in the back rooms of the Rayburn House Office Building on Capitol Hill."[3]

He continues, "As it stands, the Frankfurt School-taught Left is fighting the political battle on both the political and the cultural battlefields. Conservatives are

---

[1] Washington Post "'Hands up, don't shoot' was built on a lie" by Jonathan Capehart (March 16th 2015)

[2] NBC News "Obama Promotes #ItsOnUs Campaign At 2015 Grammy Awards (February 8th 2015)

[3] *Righteous Indignation: Excuse Me While I Save the World!* by Andrew Breitbart page 97

fighting it only on the political battlefield. That means that art, humor, song, theater, television, film, dance, are all devices used every day in order to influence the hearts and minds of the American people."[4]

He's talking about Cultural Marxism, which is the practice of waging a psychological war against America and all of Western civilization by relentlessly attacking every aspect of our culture, symbols, and institutions; hoping to gradually weaken society by subverting its foundations to the point where it becomes so dysfunctional it can be overthrown and replaced by a Marxist State.

To accomplish this, the supposed "news" media regularly engages in what's called Agenda Setting by hyping up certain stories and covering them ad nauseam to create the false impression that those stories are actually important because they're "what people are talking about." This provides a false justification for the extensive coverage, creating an artificial feedback loop where they hype up a story as if it's the talk of the town, and *then* everyone starts talking about it because they're inundated by reports about it, so the media keeps reporting on it, claiming that it's a relevant story *because* so many people are talking about it.

They carefully choose stories, oftentimes of rare and isolated incidences, and then amplify them hoping to give the impression that there's an epidemic and use the cherry-picked examples to promote or reinforce liberal ideologies. At the same time they act as gatekeepers, purposefully omitting other (actually important) stories and events which show a side of an issue they're hoping

---

[4] *Righteous Indignation: Excuse Me While I Save the World!* by Andrew Breitbart page 132

people don't hear about, or are trying to downplay the significance of.

The *Liberal Media Industrial Complex* uses their technology to influence rather than inform; to attack instead of educate; to promote certain events while pretending others don't exist. They always amplify salacious allegations that feed into the one-sided narratives they're pushing, and then completely ignore the facts when they later come out if they prove the initial reports to be false. They just carry on as if nothing happened and keep repeating the same pattern like clockwork — amplifying the allegation, and then ignoring the outcome.

The election of President Trump has resulted in the American mainstream media throwing all objectivity out the window and dedicating their existence to painting him as a mentally deranged dictator who needs to be impeached and imprisoned. They've gotten so bold in their attempts to overthrow our Republic that they now regularly engage in gaslighting and continue to repeat easily debunked falsehoods as if they are true, hoping to get people to start doubting their own memory, reasoning, and perception about what is actually going on. This is what gaslighting is.

By repeatedly lying with confidence, using misdirection and discounting contrary information, the media causes some people to begin questioning their own version of reality. The term *gaslighting* originates from an old 1938 play (later made into a movie in 1944) where a central theme of the plot involves a woman's husband who subjects her to all kinds of mind games trying to drive her insane, including dimming the gas lamps in their home while convincing her that she's just imagining it's getting darker.

The media insists that the name George Soros is a code word for anti-Semitism, as are "globalists" and "Hollywood liberals."[5]   The constant assertions that anyone who supports building a wall at the US-Mexico border is racist, and anyone who supports President Trump is a white supremacist are ridiculous, but are believed by gullible people who are susceptible to propaganda.   Television "news" anchors lie with such assurance and being accompanied by symbols of authority like their fancy studios and graphics, on the surface it appears as if they're legitimate news broadcasts.

The 2016 presidential election proved that the balance of power had shifted from the tight-knit group of mainstream media companies into the hands of everyday Americans who used Facebook, Twitter, and YouTube to spread their messages to others, whether it was a few hundred of their Facebook friends, or an audience of millions if their posts went viral.

So in order to regain control of the flow of information, the legacy media conglomerates began working closely with the Silicon Valley titans to rewrite the algorithms so these popular platforms would favor *their* content above that posted by ordinary people or popular social media personalities. It's an understatement to say that what's happening is a conspiracy between various sectors of the media industry which are working together to give traditional outlets the loudest voices online.

---

[5] Washington Post "Conspiracy theories about Soros aren't just false. They're anti-Semitic" by Talia Lavin (October 24th 2018)

Mix in Google and YouTube manipulating search results, Wikipedia being the number one source of "encyclopedia" articles, and social media companies systematically censoring prominent conservative accounts under the disguise of combating "hate speech," and you have a recipe for total information control. There is a reason that dictators throughout history have aimed to seize their country's media as one of their top priorities so they can use it to not only further their own aims, but prevent their opposition from using it for theirs.

Just two weeks after the shocking loss of Hillary Clinton to Donald Trump in the 2016 election, the war on "fake news" was launched as a smokescreen to suppress the reach of regular users' social media posts and artificially boost messages from the mainstream media. The Democrats became frantic about supposed "fake news" being shared on Facebook that they claimed had cast Hillary in a false light, and *that* was the reason they said, why so many people didn't trust her; and hence, didn't vote for her.[6]

While there were a few viral fake news stories smearing her, all the studies show they had no influence on people's votes and just reinforced beliefs they already held about her.[7]   There were also fake stories about Donald Trump that went viral during the heat of the campaign, but that fact is ignored and the "fake news" problem was framed as an issue that's only one-sided.

---

[6] CNBC "Read all about it: The biggest fake news stories of 2016" by Hannah Ritchie (December 30th 2016)

[7] The Washington Post "Real research suggests we should stop freaking out over fake news" by Christopher Ingraham (January 24th 2017)

In reality, the fake news scare was just an elaborate ruse to drastically alter the way social media functions by pressuring Big Tech companies to emphasize mainstream media outlets in people's feeds instead of showing organically what should be there based on who they were following and what was being posted.[8]

Barack Obama was the first "social media president," getting elected in 2008 when Facebook was first becoming a central hub in people's lives. He was the first president to have a Facebook page and a Twitter account, and his senior advisor David Axelrod admitted, "If not for social media, Barack Obama would never have been elected president [because] it gave us the ability to connect to a new generation of voters."[9]

At the time, social media was still kind of a novelty, but a few years later it would permeate most people's lives when everyone had to have an iPhone and the social media companies released mobile apps so people could "stay connected" wherever they were instead of having to wait until they got home from work or school to open up their laptop to see what's happening online.

But today, getting news online isn't just a novelty, it's the norm. A report from the Pew Research Center in 2018 showed that more Americans get their news from posts on social media than from newspapers.[10] Social media now starts revolutions, and overnight a single video clip can turn most of the world against a nation's leader, or

---

[8] Wired "YouTube Debuts Plan to Promote and Fund 'Authoritative' News" by Issie Lapowsky (July 9th 2018)

[9] David Axelrod interview in CNN's *The 2000s*

[10] TechCrunch "Pew: Social media for the first time tops newspapers as a news source for US adults" (December 11th 2018)

galvanize members of an entire political party to rally behind a cause.

Since the barriers to entry are now so low today with anyone being able to start a YouTube channel or create a Facebook page, we are seeing the legacy media frantically trying to stop their industry (and their influence) from slipping through their fingers. Liberals' favorite tactic today is silencing their opposition under the disguise of combating "hate speech" or stopping "right-wing extremists," and the ability to censor and manipulate information online rests in the hands of just a few gigantic corporations whose values are completely opposed to middle America and traditional family values.

Because of the emergence of social media, billions of people around the world communicate through Facebook, Twitter, and other online platforms which have largely taken the place of sending emails and talking on the phone. As you know, these social media apps can allow anyone's message to be spread just as far as something broadcast on the national news, or printed on the front page of the *New York Times*, but because of this massive redistribution of power, the *Liberal Media Industrial Complex* is scrambling to put the genie back in the bottle.

One doesn't even have to be a "social media star" to be a victim of the Left's censorship because average users have their Facebook posts, tweets, Instagram pics, and YouTube videos removed all the time for "violating community standards."

Big Tech's increasingly sophisticated artificial intelligence systems automatically scan every post for key words they have identified as sexist, racist, homophobic, transphobic, Islamophobic, anti-Semitic, or just generically "hateful" or "offensive;" and has them removed once discovered. Just a handful of these "violations" and your entire account is shut down for good and everything you've ever posted there deleted. Nothing is out of the reach of their AI, and anything can be deleted at any moment by the nameless and faceless moderators, leaving the victims with no recourse or appeal.

Total control of information is what they want, and they have hijacked the technology we all use to communicate in our modern age, but thankfully you were able to get this powerful tool into your hands before they could stop it — an old fashioned book! I commend you for picking one up and tuning out the noise relentlessly trying to make its way to your ears, and turning away from the millions of tweets, Facebook posts, and video clips all competing for your attention.

In the coming pages we'll do a deep dive into each of the major social media platforms and I'll detail their algorithm manipulation, double standards, liberal bias, and censorship. We'll also dissect the media's war on President Trump, their mission to destroy our culture by undermining traditional family values, and we'll look at the future of fake news.

While scrolling through tweets and Facebook posts is often like junk food for the brain, reading a book is a healthy and nourishing four-course meal in comparison. Sure, junk food is fine in moderation, but if it's all you eat then you're going to be very unhealthy. And the difference between reading through social media feeds (or watching the news) and reading a book is about the same as the difference between a good steak and eating a burger at McDonalds. One is quick, cheap, and poor quality; while the other is expensive, time consuming to make, and healthy to eat. And since we're dealing with a *very* important subject, it's best to do this right. So let's begin by taking a look behind the curtain of the monolithic *Liberal Media Industrial Complex* and start dismantling it piece by piece.

Censorship

There are several classic books that highlight the dangers of censorship and depict tyrannical governments that use their endless power to snuff out any opposition in hopes of maintaining their control over society. George Orwell's *Nineteen Eighty-Four*, which was first published in 1949, and *Fahrenheit 451*, published in 1953, are two of the most popular examples and weren't just written for entertainment. They were meant to serve as a warning of what giant bureaucracies could do if their growing power goes unchecked.

But today in America, it's not the government censoring what newspapers print or what airs on the evening news. It's the Silicon Valley titans — it's Mark Zuckerberg, Jack Dorsey, and Susan Wojcicki. In the marketplace of ideas they are losing, and so these industry leaders are silencing influential opponents who speak out against the Left's attempted revolution.

They're also trying to create a chilling effect by scaring people into not speaking out about certain issues or make us think twice before sharing certain information on social media out of fear we will be socially ostracized, or even fired from our job; so many people are self-censoring themselves in what's been called the "Spiral of Silence."[11] The fewer people who speak out about an issue due to fear of repercussions causes others who feel they should say something to be more apprehensive about

---

[11] http://www.pewinternet.org/2014/08/26/social-media-and-the-spiral-of-silence/

doing so because nobody else seems to be doing it, which in turn causes even more people to stay silent, causing the false impression that no one seems to be opposed to what's happening.

Thankfully, in the United States (at least today) the First Amendment is still intact, but in places like Canada,[12] Germany,[13] England,[14] Scotland,[15] and other supposedly "free" countries, people are being arrested and charged with "hate speech" crimes for posting things on their social media accounts that are critical of the "Islamization of Europe" from the mass influx of Muslim refugees and for voicing opposition to the LGBT agenda.[16]

But while Americans are still technically free to say these things without getting arrested, there are other serious consequences since we're living in an online world where most people rely on a handful of apps to communicate with others. Back in 1997, Harvard Law professor Larry Lessig wrote an article for *Wired* magazine titled "Tyranny in the Infrastructure" warning that, "Laws affect the pace of technological change, but the structures of software can do even more to curtail

---

[12] Huffington Post "Think Canada Allows Freedom of Speech? Think Again" by Tom Kott (December 19, 2012)

[13] BBC "Facebook, Google and Twitter agree German hate speech deal" (December 15th 2015)

[14] Associated Press "In UK, Twitter, Facebook rants land some in jail" by Jill Lawless (November 12, 2012)

[15] Breitbart "UK Police Arrest Man For 'Offensive' Facebook Post About Migrants" by Liam Deacon (February 16th 2016)

[16] Daily Caller "Mother Arrested, Spends Seven Hours In Jail For Calling Transgender A Man" by David Krayden (February 10th 2019)

freedom. In the long run the shackles built by programmers could well constrain us more."[17]

In his book *Cyber Ethics: Morality and Law in Cyberspace*, Richard A. Spinello expanded on this concern saying, "This notion that private code can be a more potent constraining force than public law has significant implications. The use of code as a surrogate for law may mean that certain public goods or moral values once protected by law will now be ignored or compromised by those who develop or utilize this code."[18]

We're seeing the very principle of free speech under attack like never before, with the *Liberal Media Industrial Complex* even claiming that freedom of speech is "dangerous" and saying that conservatives have "weaponized" the First Amendment.[19] There have always been restrictions on the First Amendment, for example you can't yell fire in a crowded theater, and you can't threaten to murder someone or encourage acts of terrorism; but today just insulting a person who believes there are 58 different gender identities or pointing out certain facts and statistics is considered "hateful" and "dangerous."

Democrat Congressman Ted Lieu from California says he's frustrated by the fact that the First Amendment is preventing him from silencing conservatives for Thought Crimes, so he's calling on the Big Tech

---

[17] Wired "Tyranny in the Infrastructure" by Larry Lessig (June 7th 1997 edition page 96)

[18] *Cyber Ethics: Morality and Law in Cyberspace* Second Edition by Richard A. Spinello page 5

[19] New York Times "How conservatives have weaponized the first Amendment" by Adam Liptak (June 30th 2018)

companies to do it on the government's behalf.[20] Meanwhile Jerry Nadler, a Democrat Congressman from New York, says it's just a "conspiracy theory" that the Big Tech companies have a liberal bias and, "The notion that social media companies are filtering out conservative voices is a hoax, a tired narrative of imagined victimhood."[21] Other Democrat members of Congress, like Jamie Raskin from Maryland, insist that it is an "entirely imaginary narrative that social media companies are biased against conservatives."[22]

Of course CNN repeatedly denies conservatives are being censored and claims that pushback from President Trump is, "exacerbating a longstanding paranoia from conservatives who have for years erroneously accused social media companies of bias and censorship."[23] It's just paranoia that conservatives are being censored, guys! Nothing to worry about!

CNN claims, "For years, the conservative media machine has pushed the flimsy narrative that conservatives are unfairly treated by social media companies, which they accuse of bias and censorship. When the claims often fall apart under a light touch of

---

[20] Washington Free Beacon "Lieu: 'I Would Love to Be Able to Regulate the Content of Speech' but First Amendment Stops Me" by David Rutz (December 12th 2018)

[21] Reuters "U.S. Congress spars over social media filtering; companies skip hearing" by David Shepardson (April 26th 2018)

[22] Jamie Raskin's opening statement at House Judiciary Committee hearing on Social Media Filtering the (July 17th 2018)

[23] CNN "Trump props up false claim that big tech is out to silence conservatives" by Oliver Darcy (August 24th 2018)

scrutiny, right-wing media outlets continue to advance the narrative, irrespective of the facts."[24]

After years of mounting evidence, Twitter CEO Jack Dorsey finally admitted that even conservatives who work at Twitter, "don't feel safe to express their opinions at the company" and that "They do feel silenced by just the general swirl of what they perceive to be the broader percentage of leanings within the company."[25]

With each new purge of conservative voices from the social media platforms, more and more people are seeing just how big of a threat these tech giants are to the principles of free speech and the massive implications of their monopoly on communication tools.

Donald Trump Jr., who obviously has the president's ear, has also been very vocal about the increasing censorship on social media, even writing an op-ed about it in *The Hill*, saying, "Our right to freely engage in public discourse through speech is under sustained attack, necessitating a vigorous defense against the major social media and internet platforms."[26]

In May 2019, the White House set up a new tool on WhiteHouse.gov for people to report instances of social media bias and censorship so the Trump administration could put together more thorough reports of what conservatives are facing online.[27] The page includes a

---

[24] Ibid.

[25] Recode "Twitter is so liberal that its conservative employees 'don't feel safe to express their opinions,' says CEO Jack Dorsey" (September 14th 2018)

[26] The Hill "Conservatives face a tough fight as Big Tech's censorship expands" by Donald Trump Jr. (March 17th 2019)

[27] The Hill "White House launches tool for reporting social media 'bias'" by Emily Birnbaum (May 15th 2019)

form for users to submit details about which post was taken down, what it said, and which platform removed it. "Social media platforms should advance freedom of speech. Yet too many Americans have seen their accounts suspended, banned, or fraudulently reported for unclear 'violations' of user policies," the website reads.[28]

In subsequent chapters I'll detail what's been happening on each of the major social media platforms, but rampant censorship isn't limited to just Facebook, Twitter, and YouTube.

Music Streaming Services

While politicians and news commentators have always had to watch what they say about certain subjects so they don't get fired, artists have always been seen as the bastions of free speech, and censoring art—no matter how provocative or offensive it is to some people—was always seen as something only a tyrannical government would do. Major music labels and movie studios always stood by their artists and vigorously resisted calls for censorship, championing the freedom of expression whether it was NWA's "Fuck the Police" or blasphemous anti-Christian films like *The Da Vinci Code* or Martin Scorsese's *The Last Temptation of Christ*.

But in August 2017 Spotify, the popular music streaming service, announced they would start censoring songs from "hate bands" including songs they claim "incite violence against race, religion, [or] sexuality."[29]

---

[28] https://whitehouse.typeform.com/to/Jti9QH

[29] The Independent "Spotify removes white supremacist bands from streaming service" by Roisin O'Connor (August 17th 2017)

How will they determine which bands and songs to censor? Whatever the Southern Poverty Law Center tells them to.[30] Not surprising, the SPLC got their tentacles wrapped around Spotify and other streaming services to "help" them keep a lookout for "hateful" content.[31]

Other streaming services like Apple and Pandora followed suit, banning supposed "white power" music, while allowing rap music that blatantly calls for the murder of police officers from people like Ice-T, NWA, and Snoop Dogg, who recently depicted himself murdering President Trump in one of his music videos.[32] As you know, it's common for rappers to diss "crackers" and "white boys" in their music, but that's just fine. Hating white people isn't considered to be racist to the Left.   And Jay Z's albums are okay, despite calling women "bitches" in (literally) 50% of his songs.[33]

About a year later Spotify announced another new policy, saying they were going to start banning songs from artists who have engaged in "harmful or hateful conduct" in their personal lives, like domestic violence or sexual abuse. That put songs by R. Kelly and Michael Jackson at risk of not being available anymore. But then just three weeks later they reversed their decision and apologized, saying they don't want to be the "moral

---

[30] Reason.com "Spotify Partners with the Southern Poverty Law Center to Purge 'Hate Content' from Its Music" by Christian Britschgi (May 14th 2018)

[31] Breitbart "Spotify Announces Partnership with Far-Left Groups Including SPLC to Police Platform" by Charlie Nash (May 22nd 2018)

[32] Rolling Stone "Watch Snoop Dogg Aim Gun at Clown-Trump in 'Lavender' Video" by Ryan Reed (March 13th 2017)

[33] Time "How Many of Jay-Z's Songs Contain the Word 'Bitch'?" by Claire Suddath (January 18th 2012)

police," but affirmed that they were still going to be censoring "hate speech."[34]

Guns 'N Roses song "One in a Million," which was released on their 1988 album *G N' R Lies,* includes a line about "immigrants and faggots" but when the studio released the Guns 'N Roses box set in 2018 they didn't include that song on the album because it's been deemed "racist" and "homophobic."[35]

It's probably only a matter of time before other songs like Aerosmith's "Dude Looks Like a Lady" will be banned for being "transphobic" as well. Once you give liberals an inch, they demand a mile, and since they smell blood in the water they will continue their quest to eliminate everything they find offensive.

Netflix and Prime Video

Even movie streaming services like Netflix and Amazon's Prime Video are showing signs of liberal bias and censoring "controversial content" that had once been available on the platforms for years. Netflix won't allow *The Red Pill,* a popular documentary about the Men's Rights Movement produced by Cassie Jaye, to be streamed. Through the course of producing the film she found that claims about the "patriarchy" and supposed "male power" were extremely warped and that many of

---

[34] Rolling Stone "Spotify Admits Its R. Kelly Ban Was 'Rolled Out Wrong'" by Amy X. Wong (May 31st 2018)

[35] The Guardian "Guns N' Roses remove song with homophobic and racist language from reissued album" by Ben Beaumont-Thomas (May 8th 2018)

the burdens men typically bear in society are overlooked and often discounted by feminists.[36]

Cassie Jaye herself was a feminist when she started making the film and expected to find the Men's Rights Movement would be full of misogynists and losers who had no luck with women, but learned they have very legitimate points about gender roles and unfair treatment in child custody cases, and by the end of the film she admitted they weren't a bunch of women-haters as she had previously thought, and decided that she could no longer call herself a feminist because "feminism is not the road to gender equality."[37]

When the trailer was released on YouTube it reached over a million views in 24 hours and was the number one purchased movie on YouTube (which streams movies on-demand for 4 or 5 dollars) beating *Guardians of the Galaxy* and *Rogue One: A Star Wars Story*.[38] But Netflix wouldn't allow the film to be streamed on their platform because when it was released in selected theaters it had generated some negative publicity from feminists protesting it, calling it "misogynistic propaganda."[39]

In March 2019 Democrat Congressman Adam Schiff sent a letter to Amazon CEO Jeff Bezos pressuring him to censor "anti-vaccination" documentaries from Amazon

---

[36] Breitbart "Netflix Declines Streaming Hit Documentary 'The Red Pill'" by Lucas Nolan (May 8th 2017)

[37] Evening Standard "Feminist filmmaker Cassie Jaye: women's rights have gone too far are now silencing men" by Chloe Chaplain (December 1st 2016)

[38] Ibid.

[39] The Sydney Morning Herald "Melbourne's Palace Cinemas cancel screenings of MRA documentary 'The Red Pill' after petition" by Jenny Noyes (October 25th 2016)

Prime after seeing a report on CNN claiming that "Anti-vaccination conspiracy theories thrive on Amazon."[40] Within hours of Schiff sending his letter, the streaming service pulled at least five documentaries including the popular *Vaxxed: From Cover-Up to Catastrophe*,[41] which had been promoted by Robert De Niro when it first came out because one of his children is autistic which he suspects may have been caused by the MMR vaccines.[42]

Others included: *We Don't Vaccinate!;" Shoot 'Em Up: The Truth About Vaccines*, *The Greater Good*; and *Man Made Epidemic*, which investigated the alleged connections between the autism epidemic and the preservative Thimerosal used in vaccines. Many have long suspected a link between Thimerosal and autism, including Robert F. Kennedy Jr., who has tried to bring awareness to the dangers of vaccines for years.[43]

CNN then celebrated the censorship with a follow-up story touting, "Anti-vaccine movies disappear from Amazon after CNN Business report."[44] During a segment on CNN in 2009 Dr. Oz was talking with host Campbell Brown about the H1N1 (swine flu) vaccines, encouraging people to get them, but was put on the spot by the host

---

[40] CNN "Anti-vaccination conspiracy theories thrive on Amazon" by Jon Sarlin (February 27th 2019)

[41] Variety "Amazon Pulls Anti-Vaccination Documentaries From Prime Video After Congressman's Inquiry to Jeff Bezos" by Todd Spangler (March 1st 2019)

[42] Sky News "De Niro offers $100k reward to media for 'truth' about controversial children's vaccine" by Duarte Garrido (February 17th 2017)

[43] Rolling Stone "Deadly Immunity" by Robert F. Kennedy Jr. (July 14th 2005)

[44] CNN "Anti-vaccine movies disappear from Amazon after CNN Business report" by Jon Sarlin (March 1st 2019)

about her concerns that they may not be safe. He responded, "I'm going to get it, if that helps at all, but I'll tell you my wife is not going to immunize our kids. Cuz I've got four of them and when I go home I'm not Dr. Oz, I'm Mr. Oz."[45]

So he went on television encouraging people to take the vaccine and give it to *their* children, but admitted that he's not going to give it to his own children because his wife didn't think it was safe; and despite him being a famous doctor, he couldn't convince her otherwise and allowed his children to go unvaccinated.

Netflix also censored an episode of comedian Hasan Minhaj's show, blocking it for customers in Saudi Arabia at the request of the government there because in it he talked about Saudi Arabia's role in the 9/11 attacks and the murder of *Washington Post* columnist Jamal Khashoggi at the hands of Saudis.[46]

Netflix will not stream the 1980s classic *Dukes of Hazzard* because that's too "racist" today. Reruns of the show were pulled from TV Land and other cable networks in 2015 after growing sentiment that the Confederate Flag is a "white supremacist" symbol, and since the Duke boys' car (The General Lee) has one painted on the roof, networks now deem the TV show too offensive to air.[47] Other classic TV shows and movies will likely slowly and quietly disappear from the streaming services and cable

---

[45] The New Yorker "The Operator: Is the most trusted doctor in America doing more harm than good?" by Michael Specter (January 27th 2013)

[46] NBC News "Netflix pulls episode of 'Patriot Act with Hasan Minhaj' after Saudi complaint" by Saphora Smith (January 2nd 2019)

[47] Vanity Fair "*The Dukes of Hazzard* Pulled Off TV Following Confederate-Flag Controversy" by Julie Miller (July 1st 2015)

TV because they're deemed too "insensitive" for our modern age. Owning DVDs may be the only way to ever see them again.

A growing number of activists are upset about *Ace Ventura: Pet Detective* for what they call its "contempt" for LGBT people because the main suspect in the movie later started living as a woman and after catching him and realizing this, Jim Carrey goes into convulsions vomiting while having flashbacks to when "she" had kissed him earlier in the film. Or other comedies like *Mrs. Doubtfire* or Tyler Perry's "Medea" character may be banned for being "transphobic" as well. Or films like *Idiocracy*, *The Breakfast Club*, or *Bill and Ted's Excellent Adventure* because characters call people fags. Or maybe even *The Sand Lot* since one boy tells another that he plays baseball like a girl. That's sexist!

In 2018, Barack and Michelle Obama signed a deal with Netflix to produce several documentaries, scripted series, and full-length feature films through a production company they started called Higher Ground.[48] "Touching on issues of race and class, democracy and civil rights, and much more, we believe each of these productions won't just entertain, but will educate, connect and inspire us all," said Barack.[49]

The couple's debut documentary *American Factory* was hailed as their "first big anti-Trump statement of 2020" by Politico, although it didn't mention him by

[48] The New York Times "The Obamas and Netflix Just Revealed the Shows and Films They're Working On" by John Koblin (April 30th 2019)

[49] Rolling Stone "Barack, Michelle Obama Unveil Initial Slate of Netflix Projects" by Althea Legaspi (April 30th 2019)

name "it's message is clear."[50]   Others called it "lefty propaganda" and an attack on Trump.[51]

Netflix has also produced various liberal "comedy" shows called Netflix Originals which have included hosts like skank Chelsea Handler, Michelle Wolf, and other insufferable and non-funny Leftists.   Similarly, Hulu produced a show hosted by Sarah Silverman called "I Love You America" which got canceled after two seasons, calling into question the streaming services ability to tap into the late-night talk show genre.[52]   They also produced a documentary following the Congressional campaign of Alexandria Ocasio-Cortez.

After Georgia's controversial "heartbeat" abortion bill was signed by the governor in May 2019 which bans abortions after six weeks into the pregnancy, Netflix announced they may quit using the state as a production location because several of their shows like "Stranger Things" and "Ozark" are shot there. They even vowed to help fight the bill in court.[53] It certainly is strange for a major corporation to take a stance on abortion, but that's where we're at.

---

[50] Politico "The Obamas' First Big Anti-Trump Statement of 2020" by Ted Johnson (August 20th 2019)

[51] Fox News "Obamas' debut Netflix documentary slammed as 'lefty propaganda,' an attack on Trump" by Brian Flood (August 20th 2019)

[52] The Hollywood Reporter "Hulu Cancels 'I Love You, America With Sarah Silverman'" by Lacey Rose (January 9th 2019)

[53] Bloomberg "Netflix Threatens to Leave Georgia If Abortion Law Stands" by Nick Turner (May 28th 2019)

Amazon Banning Books

Banning books was once seen as the ultimate sin, and something only the Nazis would do, but today we're seeing a growing number of books disappearing down the memory hole in the name of political correctness and stopping "hate speech." 65% of all books are sold through Amazon and they have a virtual monopoly over the entire industry.[54] They are the reason Borders, Walden Books, and B. Dalton went out of business. Amazon advertises themselves as the world's largest bookstore where you can find practically any book, new or used, since if they don't stock it, they (supposedly) allow anyone to list used copies for sale themselves.

For over twenty years since Amazon was launched in 1995 they would sell any book new or used, but recently that all changed. In July 2018 a children's book titled *No Dress for Timmy* was banned for being "transphobic." It was written by Shefflorn Ballantyne and is described as, "A story of a little boy who found himself in a perplexing situation where he was forced to choose between speaking the truth and cheering on a friend who thinks of himself as a girl."[55] The young protagonist basically wouldn't support a transgender classmate.

After an LGBT advocacy organization called Family Rhetoric discovered it when searching for LGBT-themed children books, they launched a campaign to pressure Amazon to ban the book, which they did. The group later celebrated on their Facebook page saying, "We did it.

---

[54] TheAtlantic "Amazon Has Basically No Competition Among Online Booksellers" by Polly Mosendez (May 30th 2014)

[55] ShefflornBallantyne.com (the author's website) So far no major media outlets have reported on Amazon banning the book.

You did it friends! The link to *No Dress for Timmy* is not working. Amazon took down the book. It's gone!"[56] And indeed it is.

Amazon banned almost all of pickup artist Roosh V's books just days after his latest one was released, titled *Game: How to Meet, Attract, and Date Attractive Women.*[57] They wouldn't even give him a reason, just that they "violated" their policy and "can't offer any additional insight or action on this matter."[58] Roosh had come to the attention of various radical feminist groups who see him as a huge "misogynist" for his views on women and feminism, and they most likely lobbied Amazon to pull his books.

Juanita Broaddrick's book about Bill Clinton allegedly raping her was removed in June 2018, and then later restored.[59] It appears that Amazon keeps testing how far they can push the envelope by gauging the backlash, but not everyone is so lucky to have their books re-listed after media reports denounce the censorship.

In August 2018 Amazon banned a book that contained plans to build a 3D printed gun called *The Liberator Code Book: An Exercise in Freedom of Speech*, which had been listed by the publisher just a few weeks earlier. An Amazon spokesperson said it violated their guidelines.[60]

---

[56] Family Rhetoric by Amer Leventry on Facebook (July 10th, 2018)

[57] RooshV.com "Amazon Has Banned 9 Of My Books Without Explanation (UPDATE)" by Roosh (September 10th 2018)

[58] Ibid.

[59] PJ Media "Juanita Broaddrick's Book about Alleged Clinton Rape Disappears from Amazon" by Jeff Reynolds (June 12th 2018)

[60] FreeBeacon "Amazon Bans Gun Book" by Stephen Gutowski (August 23rd 2018)

Yet they sell the *Anarchist's Cookbook* and other bomb-making manuals (at least at the time this book was first published in November 2019). *The Anarchist's Cookbook* author William Powell later denounced his terrorist manual which he wrote in 1971 when he was just nineteen-years-old.[61] But he does not own the rights to the book; the publisher does (now Ozark Press), which keeps it in print, and which Amazon still sells.[62]

The Columbine school shooters, who planted bombs in the school aside from shooting and killing twelve students and one teacher, owned a copy of the *Anarchist's Cookbook* and used it to manufacture their bombs.[63] When members of the Black Liberation Army were arrested in the 1970s for murdering several police officers, they had a copy in their possession and are believed to have planted a bomb in a San Francisco church during the funeral of a police officer who died in the line of duty.[64]

Thomas Eugene Spinks, who bombed ten abortion clinics in the 1980s, used the *Anarchist Cookbook* to build his bombs.[65] Many others have used it as well, including Timothy McVeigh, who carried out the 1995 Oklahoma City bombing, and the radical Islamic terrorists who

---

[61] The Guardian "I wrote the Anarchist Cookbook in 1969. Now I see its premise as flawed" by William Powell (December 19th 2013)

[62] As of November 2019 when this book was first published.

[63] NBC News "After latest shooting, murder manual author calls for book to be taken 'immediately' out of print" by Tony Dokoupil (December 17th 2013)

[64] Wired "THE ANARCHIST COOKBOOK TURNS 40" by Matthew Honan (January 31st 2011)

[65] Newsweek "Sorry About All The Bombs" by Tony Dokoupil (February 20th 2011)

committed the July 2005 bombings on the London public transportation system used the book as their instruction manual too. So *No Dress for Timmy* is too "transphobic" to be sold, but a literal bomb-making manual used by terrorists in numerous high-profile bombings is okay.

Jared Taylor, a leader in the white identitarian [pro-white] community, had several of his books censored from Amazon in February 2019, including *White Identity*, despite having been sold on the site since 2011.[66] The following month Tommy Robinson's book *Mohammed's Koran* was banned from Amazon just days after Facebook and Instagram banned him (in response to Tommy posting a documentary critical of the BBC on his YouTube channel).[67] His book was deemed "Islamophobic."[68]

Then in March 2019 they banned David Duke's autobiography *My Awakening* and another one of his books titled *Jewish Supremacism* where he details what he believes is a Jewish supremacist belief system within Judaism.[69] The books had been available on Amazon since they first came out, one in 1998, and the other in 2004, but were removed shortly after a no-name freelance writer "inquired" about why Amazon was selling books

---

[66] American Renaissance Press Release "Amazon Now Banning Books Based on Political Content" (February 27th 2019)

[67] The Sun "Amazon stops selling Tommy Robinson's book on Islam the day after he was booted off Facebook and Instagram – but he can still broadcast on YouTube" by Annabel Murphy (February 27th 2019)

[68] Independent "Amazon bans book co-written by Tommy Robinson from their website" (March 7th 2019)

[69] The Script "Amazon Removes David Duke's Books After Inquiry By The Script [UPDATED with Amazon response]" (March 18th 2019)

written by a "white supremacist."[70]   They're not just shown as out of stock or unavailable; the entire listings for the books have been deleted, and it appears Amazon is also prohibiting any 3rd party sellers from listing used copies as well.

They also banned several books published by the Nation of Islam which were critical of Jews,[71] as well as a few written by Christian pastor Texe Marrs, including *Holy Serpent of the Jews*, for being "anti-semitic."[72] This is especially interesting because Amazon still sells Adolf Hitler's *Mein Kampf* (for now).[73]

After CNN successfully pressured Amazon to censor various popular documentary films from their Prime Video streaming service in March 2019 that question the safety of some vaccines, they went on to lament that Amazon still sold "anti-vaccine" books, saying, "while some anti-vaccine videos are gone from the Prime streaming service, a number of anti-vaccine books were still available for purchase on Amazon.com when CNN Business reviewed search results on Friday afternoon, and some were still being offered for free to Kindle Unlimited subscribers."[74]   Amazon soon banned several "anti-vax"

---

[70] https://twitter.com/JerylBier/status/1107675822377316352

[71] Nation of Islam Research Group "Amazon Bans the Secret Relationship Between Blacks & Jews" (March 16th 2019)

[72] TexeMarrs.com "Amazon Bans Texe Marr's Book for 'Content.'"

[73] As of November 2019 when this book was first published.

[74] CNN "Anti-vaccine movies disappear from Amazon after CNN Business report" by Jon Sarlin (March 1st 2019)

books for promoting what they called "vaccine misinformation."[75]

In July 2019 they banned books by Dr. Joseph Nicolosi, who is best known for advocating conversion therapy for homosexuals. Two of his most popular books on the subject, *Healing Homosexuality* and *A Parent's Guide to Preventing Homosexuality* were taken down after sustained pressure from LGBT activists.[76] Perhaps Amazon will ban some of Sigmund Freud's books next because he believed that homosexuality was caused by a disruption in a child's development due to a dysfunctional relationship with their parents in terms of the role those parents fill in their lives.[77]

For several years now Amazon has banned sales of all Confederate flags because they're considered to be symbols of "white supremacy" these days.[78] They have also banned the sale of various Halloween costumes liberals consider to be offensive, like the "Tranny Granny" costume that's "transphobic,"[79] a Chinese dress for being "cultural appropriation," and a "sexy burka" costume for being disrespectful to Islam. In January 2019

---

[75] NBC News "Amazon removes books promoting autism cures and vaccine misinformation" by Brandy Zadrozny (March 12th 2019)

[76] NBC News "Amazon removes controversial books by 'father of conversion therapy'" by Gwen Aviles (July 3rd 2019)

[77] *Basic Freud: Psychoanalytic Thought for the 21st Century* by Michael Kahn, Ph.D pages 78-79

[78] USA Today "Amazon, eBay join other retailers to pull Confederate flag" by Gregg Zoroya and Hadley Malcolm (June 23rd 2015)

[79] Fortune "Walmart and Amazon Pull 'Tranny Granny' Halloween Costume From Their Sites" by Michelle Toh (October 7th 2016)

Amazon removed dozens of other products that were said to be offensive to Muslims as well.[80]

Meanwhile, an album by a band called Marduk titled "Fuck Me Jesus" is allowed, which shows a naked woman using a crucifix as a dildo on the cover.[81] Amazon also sells a song titled "Fuck White People" which has a noose on the album cover.[82] They also stock various black supremacist books that promote hate groups like the Black Hebrew Israelites.

Twitch.TV

Twitch.TV (which is owned by Amazon) is a website where people livestream themselves playing video games (I know this seems strange to anyone over 40) and they can have a large number of viewers who enjoy watching them play. Like YouTube livestreams, there is a chat box on Twitch where viewers can post comments and even tip the player.

While it's mostly for video games, sometimes the gamers will talk politics during their streams, and the Thought Police are watching in case they say something "racist," "sexist," "homophobic," etc., etc. One gamer was recently banned from Twitch for simply saying there

---

[80] CNN: Complaints prompt Amazon to remove products that are offensive to Muslims" by Alaa Essar (January 8th 2019)

[81] Newsbusters "Amazon Removes 'Islamophobic' Products But Sells 'F**k Me Jesus'" by Corinne Weaver (January 8th 2019)

[82] https://www.amazon.com/Fuck-White-People-Explicit/dp/B07HXDG3JL/ref=sr_1_2?ie=UTF8&qid=1543984803&sr=8-2&keywords=fuck+white+people

are only two genders.[83]   The email informing her of the ban read, "Your recent behavior has proven your lack of understanding of what hateful speech is and how it may affect your community on your channel...Several of your statements have been found offensive towards the transgender community, and we don't tolerate this kind of behavior."[84]

In a YouTube video discussing the ban she said, "I specifically said, it's okay if a man wants to be a woman, and a woman wants to be a man, you cannot be anything in between," referring to the odd "gender fluid," "pan gender," and the dozens of other "genders" liberals have invented.

A popular DJ named Deadmouse (stylized Deadmau5), who also streamed on Twitch for fun was banned for "hate speech" after he called another streamer a dreaded "homophobic slur."   He issued a statement saying, "It was intended to insult a fuckin asshat who was being a fucking asshat...it wasn't 'directed at an entire group of people who have a sexual orientation that differs from my own.' Fuck off with that shit. I know who I am, and I don't have to fucking sit here and cry and defend my fucking self with the obligatory 'I'M NOT THAT PERSON, I AM SORRY" reflex...The sane people who knew what it was in the heat of the moment knew the purpose of the statement, and the people that think

[83] Newsweek "Streamer HelenaLive Speaks Out After Being Banned From Twitch For Saying 'There Are Only Two Genders'" by Steven Asarch (February 12th 2019)

[84] News.com.au "Gamer reportedly banned from Twitch for claiming there are only two genders" by Nick Whigham (February 7th 2019)

otherwise, I'm better off not even fucking knowing and they can just keep the fuck clear of me."[85]

It was great to see someone of his celebrity push back against this PC nonsense, but he soon backtracked and issued an apology, along with apologizing for his previous "non-apology" in response to the ban, saying, "I know what I said was wrong, and my hastily composed non-apology was an insult to injury."[86]

Many other Twitch streamers have had their accounts suspended and banned for just uttering what moderators *thought* were "slurs" out loud in a fit of anger when something went wrong on the game they're playing when they actually said something that just sounded similar to one.[87]   So even while players are virtually "mass murdering" people in a video game, the Thought Police are carefully monitoring them to make sure their off-the-cuff commentary doesn't happen to offend someone in the LGBTQ community or other "protected group."   One streamer was even given a 30-day suspension for calling another player a "mongoloid," because Twitch considers that "hate speech" too.[88]

Like YouTube and Facebook Live, Twitch uses real-time voice recognition systems to analyze what people are saying in order to lookout for any words that are flagged

---

[85] Business Insider "deadmau5 accuses Twitch of censorship after being suspended for using homophobic language during a live stream" by Kevin Webb (February 13th 2019)

[86] Newsweek "DeadMau5 Apologizes For Homophobic Slur After Twitch Ban" by Steven Asarch (February 14th 2019)

[87] The Verge "League of Legends streamer banned from Twitch for slur says he was misheard" by Julia Lee (April 24th 2019)

[88] Dexerto.com "Twitch streamer banned for 30 days for using word he didn't know was offensive" by David Purcell (March 19th 2019)

as being inappropriate. Monitoring livestreams using AI is one of the top priorities of the tech companies due to the bad press they get when someone livestreams something completely ridiculous (or criminal) so they are putting enormous resources into being able to detect what is being said in real-time, and even what is being shown so they can take down a stream if their algorithm deems the broadcast includes anything "inappropriate." Twitch, however, like all the other major platforms turns a blind eye when liberals flagrantly violate their rules.

A popular streamer who goes by "Destiny" (real name Steven Kenneth Bonnell II) has explicitly called for violence against conservatives on at least one occasion. When he was asked during a stream, "You genuinely do hate conservatives, don't you?" he answered, "Very much so. I've moved full-on to the political violence level or the real violence level when it comes to conservative people. I feel like they need to be fucking excised from my fucking country. I think they're demonstrably evil people."[89] He remains on the platform and his channel is still monetized.

Alex Jones "Unpersoned"

One of the scariest aspects of censorship isn't a few songs, movies, or books disappearing from the Internet, but a person being deleted. An "Unperson" is a term from George Orwell's *Nineteen Eighty-Four* that describes someone whose very existence has been erased from society, and this basically happened to radio talk show host Alex Jones in August 2018.

---

[89] Newsbusters "Still on YouTube: Lefty Who Calls for Violence, Purge of Conservatives" by Alexander Hall (May 31st 2019)

Within the course of just a few days he was banned from YouTube, Facebook, iTunes, the TuneIn radio app, Spotify, Stitcher, Pinterest, and even LinkedIn! Years of archived shows and interviews just disappeared. PayPal also closed his account, preventing his website Infowars.com from accepting payments through the service,[90] and numerous credit card processors also refused to allow him to have an account, making it difficult to accept debit and credit cards for the products he sells.

Liberals were thrilled with the actions, including Democrat Senator Chris Murphy from Connecticut who said, "Infowars is the tip of a giant iceberg of hate and lies that uses sites like Facebook and YouTube to tear our nation apart. These companies must do more than take down one website. The survival of our democracy depends on it."[91]

Many conservatives, even those who think Alex Jones is a raving lunatic, were quite concerned about his sudden "disappearance" from the Internet. Even Senator Ted Cruz defended Alex, tweeting, "Am no fan of Jones — among other things he has a habit of repeatedly slandering my Dad by falsely and absurdly accusing him of killing JFK — but who the hell made Facebook the arbiter of political speech? Free speech includes views you disagree with."[92]

Others came to his defense as well, including Bill Maher who said despite Jones telling "lies" about him, "if

---

[90] Bloomberg "PayPal Is Latest Tech Company to Ban Alex Jones and InfoWars" by Julie Verhag (September 21st 2018)

[91] https://twitter.com/ChrisMurphyCT/status/1026580187784404994

[92] https://twitter.com/tedcruz/status/1023207746454384642

you're a liberal, you're supposed to be for free speech. That's free speech for the speech you hate. That's what free speech means. We're losing the thread of the concepts that are important to this country. You care about the real American shit or you don't. And if you do, it goes for every side. I don't like Alex Jones, but Alex Jones gets to speak. Everybody gets to speak."[93]

The ACLU [American Civil Liberties Union] even warned his ban could set a dangerous precedent and expressed concerns that the pendulum could swing the other way some day, and groups like Black Lives Matter could be shut down under the same pretense.[94]

President Trump appeared to reference the unpersoning of Alex Jones which had made national headlines, saying, "I won't mention any names but when they take certain people off of Twitter or Facebook and they're making that decision, that is really a dangerous thing because that could be you tomorrow."[95]

Alex Jones Was Just the Beginning

Many people who were quite concerned about Alex Jones getting unpersoned overnight were afraid to speak out against it because they didn't want to appear as if they supported Jones because of some of the outlandish things he has said over the years, but Big Tech coordinating with

---

[93] The Hill "Bill Maher criticizes social media bans: 'Alex Jones gets to speak'" by Jacqueline Thomsen (August 18th 2018)

[94] The Hill "ACLU: Alex Jones ban could set dangerous social media precedent" by Megan Keller (August 21st 2018)

[95] Reuters "Exclusive: Trump says it is 'dangerous' for Twitter, Facebook to ban accounts" by Steve Holland and Jeff Mason (August 20th 2018)

each other to ban him was just a test case and the beginning of what was to come.

The editor in chief of *The Verge*, one of Vox Media's online properties, started calling for Fox News to be taken off the air next, saying, "I feel like we should be just as comfortable asking Comcast and Verizon and Charter why they continue to offer Fox News on their networks as we are about Facebook and Alex Jones."[96]

Immediately after Jones was universally deplatformed PBS did a report about it and in that report complained that he had inspired countless "imitators" who "sell merchandise" and then showed a clip of me from one of my YouTube videos promoting my popular t-shirts.

Apple CEO Tim Cook then said it's a "sin" for social media platforms not to ban people the Left deems "hateful" and "divisive." He was given the first "Courage Against Hate Award" from the Jewish ADL, and during his acceptance speech said, "We only have one message for those who seek to push hate, division, and violence: You have no place on our platforms. You have no home here."[97] He went on to say, "and as we showed this year, we won't give a platform to violent conspiracy theorists on the app store," referring to banning Alex Jones. "Why? Because it's the right thing to do," Cook concluded.[98]

Even conservative darling Ben Shapiro is technically in violation of their terms of service for "hate speech" by

---

[96] http://archive.fo/xb693

[97] Washington Times "Apple CEO Tim Cook: Hateful views have 'no place on our platforms'" by Jessica Chasmar (December 4th 2018)

[98] Ibid.

saying transgenderism is a mental illness.[99]   They could drop the hammer on anyone at anytime for things they've said years ago, and even "off platform," meaning things said in interviews or speeches that didn't even directly involve social media.

Just voting for Donald Trump is considered "hate speech" by the Silicon Valley titans, and it won't be long now before they include negative tone of voice, contorted facial expressions or even supposed "code words" and "dog whistles" into their terms of service as things that are not allowed.

For example, if someone is reporting on a new television commercial featuring two gay men who are raising a child they adopted and react with a disgusted look on their face, or a sarcastic, "I'm sure the child will grow up to be totally normal."   That will likely be a violation of their policies.   George Orwell even warned about such things in his classic novel *Nineteen Eighty-Four*, saying, "to wear an improper expression on your face (to look incredulous when a victory was announced, for example) was itself a punishable offense.   There was even a word for it in Newspeak: facecrime, it was called."[100]

They'll start claiming that certain words or phrases are "code words" for something else just like they've done with the "okay" hand sign, and soon nobody will be safe from being smeared as a "white supremacist," "Islamophobe," "homophobe," "xenophobe," etc.

The Left are now engaged in a Maoist-style attempted overthrow of our culture and our country, and are

[99] https://twitter.com/benshapiro/status/890824543522226178

[100] George Orwell in *Nineteen Eighty-Four*

systematically purging influential dissenting voices from social media. Get ready, because this is just the beginning. They don't just want prominent vocal opponents of the liberal agenda silenced; they want our lives destroyed.

Some people believe censorship amplifies extremism by forcing people to descend into the dark corners of the Internet where their ideas aren't challenged or debunked by onlookers who disagree with them, and so they fester in an echo chamber that fuels and radicalizes them. Censoring someone who's not calling for violence can also be seen as confirmation that they are being persecuted and cultivate a sense that they feel justified fighting back in a more extreme way. By having their voice taken away for what was perfectly legal speech, they may be compelled to act out in other ways in order to "be heard."

The liberal Establishment is working tirelessly to take down any independent social media personalities who organically gain sizable followings, and if they're truly independent, meaning not working for a major media outlet then they are extremely vulnerable because they don't have a legal department behind them that can push back on their behalf. They have developed a formula to take us down. First, a few unscrupulous liberal online outlets like the Huffington Post, BuzzFeed, and Vox label certain conservatives "Alt-Right" or "right-wing extremists" and then the editors at Wikipedia update those people's pages to claim they are a white nationalists or neo-Nazis and use those dubious reports as "sources" to solidify the smear.

And since Wikipedia is the go-to place for information for most people and one of the top search results on

Google, anyone looking those people up from that point on will be presented with information claiming they're a racist or far-right extremist. Then, even more outlets repeat the false claims, thus generating even more news articles from mainstream sources parroting the smear which are then used to add even more citations to the Wikipedia articles to reinforce their false narrative.

These liberal outlets know that most people don't have the vast resources necessary to sue for defamation, and so they are forever branded a "racist." Then the self-referencing Wikipedia page is used as the justification to demonetize their YouTube channels and suspend their PayPal accounts to cutoff their revenue streams in order to crush them into silence. In our current political climate, especially as the 2020 election is approaching, I wake up every morning wondering if today will be the day that it happens to me.

What's Next?

How far will this fascism go? Will Visa, MasterCard, or American Express deactivate certain accounts because the banks don't like what some people say or believe? Will Bank of America and Wells Fargo start closing people's checking accounts because they don't like their politics? Some banks are already doing just that. Chase Bank issued a letter to Proud Boys (a pro-Trump men's fraternity) leader Enrique Tarrio that they would be closing his account and he had until the end of the month to move all his money somewhere else.[101]   Then Joe Biggs, a former reporter for Infowars who banks at Chase,

---

[101] BigLeaguePolitics "Chase Bank Shuts Down Proud Boys Leader's Personal Bank Account" by Waldo Crane (February 8th 2019)

got the same notification. Others did as well, including Martina Markota who works for the conservative news site Rebel Media.[102]

After word spread of the shocking move, outraging many veterans groups because Joe Biggs is an Iraq vet, Chase re-activated his account, but wouldn't give him a reason as to why they had initially banned him.[103] PayPal has already banned Alex Jones, Laura Loomer, Milo Yiannopoulous, Lauren Southern, Tommy Robinson, Gavin McInnes, Roosh V, Faith Goldy, as well as Twitter alternative Gab, and YouTube alternative BitChute because they support free speech and won't ban users for posting things that hurt others feelings.[104]

A senior software engineer at Google recommended the company delete Donald Trump's G-mail account, and that of everyone working in his administration. He even suggested they "brick" Donald Trump's cell phone.[105] A "bricked" phone, if you're not familiar with the term, means one that is completely deactivated and won't even turn on. So the engineer was literally recommending Google remotely disable Donald Trump's phone, since they are the owners of the Android operating system which it uses.

---

[102] Breitbart "Financial blacklisting: Chase bank withdraws service from independent and conservative figures" by Allum Bokhari (February 27th 2019)

[103] One America News "Chase Bank suspends account of pro-Trump Iraq vet" (February 20th 2019)

[104] Breitbart "PayPal Blacklists Free Speech YouTube Alternative 'BitChute'" by Charlie Nash (November 14th 2018)

[105] Breitbart "Google Lawsuit: Senior Engineer Alon Altman Wanted to Sabotage Trump's Android Phone, Ban His Gmail Account" by Allum Bokhari (April 19th 2018)

We only know about this because the proposal was included in a series of documents obtained as part of a lawsuit filed by former Google employee James Damore who was fired after circulating a memo explaining how the company's obsession with "diversity" is misguided.

While the company didn't authorize those radical actions, who's to say in the future they (or Apple) won't ban certain people from using their phones? When you activate a smartphone you "agree" to the terms and conditions, even though hardly anyone actually reads them. Those terms also say the manufacturer can change the terms at any time, so what's to stop them from adding a clause that says they reserve the right to brick your phone (or computer) if they feel you're engaging in certain kinds of behavior or speech that they find objectionable? Perhaps Google didn't want the publicity and the backlash of sabotaging the President of the United States' cellphone, but what's to stop them from doing it to people who aren't as powerful or well known?

How far will the Silicon Valley titans go to stamp out vocal critics of the radical Leftists' agenda? Will video editing software companies deactivate their software on people's computers if they don't like the content people are creating? Will Photoshop not sell their software to artists who are making the "wrong" kind of memes? Or will Microsoft and Apple refuse to license their operating systems on the computers (or smartphones) of political activists, social media personalities, or authors they consider racist, sexist, homophobic, transphobic, Islamophobic, etc.?

Or maybe their local ISP [Internet Service Provider] won't even allow them to have an Internet connection or

41

will start blocking certain websites.[106]   What if Priceline or Orbitz decides not to sell you a plane ticket because they refuse to do business with "hateful" people? Or if Enterprise decides they won't rent you a car. Or a popular gas station chain won't sell you gas?   What if a major grocery store chain decides they won't sell you any food? If Visa or Mastercard blacklist you, then you won't even be able to have a debit card. If no banks will allow you to have an account, how can you cash your paycheck?

In the Bible, a prophecy in the Book of Revelation says that one day "no man might buy or sell, save he that had the mark, or the name of the beast, or the number of his name," warning that people who don't worship the counterfeit Christ will be completely cut off economically from the modern world.   It appears we are beginning to see the justifications for such widespread bans by those who control the backbone of the financial system.

Section 230 of the CDA

Technically, private companies can ban people from their platforms as long as it's not because of their race, sex, sexual orientation, age, disability, country of origin, or other legally "protected" class. But political affiliation is not a protected class, and companies could legally ban all Republicans if they wanted to.   Laws and regulations are always many years behind innovation, and the framers of the legislation governing our communication infrastructure could have never imagined the emergence

---

[106] Major Internet Service Providers in Australia and New Zealand completely blocked the video sharing site BitChute in March 2019 for supposedly not promptly removing re-uploads of the Christchurch mosque shooting which was originally livestreamed on Facebook.

of social media, let alone how instrumental of a role it would come to play in our lives.

The Telecommunications Act of 1996 was passed by Congress and signed into law by President Clinton in order to overhaul the rules and regulations governing communication systems in response to the development of the Internet. Within the Act was a subsection called the Communications Decency Act, and Section 230 of the law granted immunity to Internet Service Providers, Domain Registrars, and website hosting services so if customers use these services in ways that violate copyright laws (or criminal statutes), the companies themselves are not liable for the legal consequences because they are not deemed publishers, but platforms, and are not responsible what their customers are posting.

In other words, if someone posts an episode of *The Big Bang Theory* television show on their YouTube channel, YouTube is not responsible for that person violating CBS's copyright (as long as YouTube would promptly remove the infringing video if notified by CBS.) Because YouTube provides a service (i.e. the "platform") to the public, they can't necessarily prevent people from using that service to post copyrighted material, so they are given "safe harbor" and are immune from any civil or criminal penalties when their users break the law.

Section 230 of the CDA also granted immunity to Internet Service Providers and interactive websites if third party users post defamatory information about someone,[107] death threats,[108] or even if they sell fake

---

[107] Green v. AOL and Blumenthal v. Drudge and Zeran v. AOL

[108] Delfino v. Agilent Technologies Inc.

merchandise on eBay, meaning eBay is not responsible, only the person posting the fake listing is.

Today, many Big Tech companies are abusing their immunity granted to them by Section 230 of the Communications Decency Act by censoring certain users and posts and deciding themselves what to delete from their platforms, when that content is not violating any laws. They are now acting as publishers, not platforms, because they are making editorial decisions about what will and will not be allowed. If a person posts something that doesn't violate any laws, then why should the social media companies have the right to take it down if they are in the business of offering a platform for (supposedly) anyone to use?

Currently there is a loophole in section 230 that allows for what it calls "Good Samaritan" blocking and screening of "obscene, lewd, lascivious, filthy, excessively violent, harassing, or otherwise objectionable content."[109] So they interpret "objectionable" content as being facts or opinions that hurt people's feelings or undermine the liberal agenda.

Further evidence that section 230 of the CDA is outdated and unfair can be seen by the fact that a court ruled that President Trump can't block people on Twitter after several trolls who he had blocked found a law firm that sued the President on their behalf.[110] The court ruled that Trump can't block people on social media because it "deprives them of access to official Presidential statements," and his feeds are considered a "public square." This begs the question, why is Facebook, Twitter

[109] CDA Section 230(c)(2)(A) Protection for Screening.

[110] New York Times "White House Unblocks Twitter Users Who Sued Trump, but Appeals Ruling" by Charlie Savage (June 5th 2018)

and YouTube allowed to deprive citizens access to that same public square?

If the President of the United States can't "deprive" someone of access to his statements on social media, why should the tech companies be allowed to do that to ordinary citizens? Facebook and Twitter are basically the modern day equivalent of a telephone, or post office. They've become an intimate and crucial part of billions of people's lives. It's how friends and families communicate with each other, and share photos and videos. It's where they send out party invitations and look up old childhood friends or family members they've lost touch with. It's how they get their news and see what the President is saying.

Imagine the phone company canceling your service because they didn't like what you and your friends talked about. That's essentially what Facebook and other social media platforms are doing today when they suspend people, delete their posts, or ban them completely because of what they say when their statements are not crimes, but just a "controversial," "divisive," or "hateful" point of view.

The power these mega corporations have over how billions of people on the planet communicate with each other is staggering. And the fact that they are working in concert together to enforce their arbitrary and bias "terms of service" to silence certain people and points of view is beyond horrifying. As George Washington said, "If the freedom of speech is taken away then dumb and silent we may be led, like sheep to the slaughter."[111]

---

[111] BrainyQuote.com "George Washington Quotes"

Author's Note: Please take a moment to rate and review this book on Amazon.com, or wherever you purchased it from if you're reading the e-book, to let others know what you think. This also helps to offset the trolls who keep giving my books fake one-star reviews when they haven't even read them.

Almost all of the one-star reviews on Amazon for my last two books "The True Story of Fake News" and "Liberalism: Find a Cure" are from NON-verified purchases which is a clear indication they are fraudulent hence me adding this note.

It's just more proof that liberals are losers and can't play fair, so if you could help me combat them as soon as possible since you actually bought this book, that would be great!

Thank you!

The Memory Hole

Censorship encompasses much more than people getting their posts and accounts deleted from social media platforms. It involves the mainstream media self-censoring stories and certain issues as well. They lie by omission and purposefully ignore events and individuals they don't want to give publicity to, even when what's happening fully warrants extensive coverage.

They spent years chasing after "Russian agents" who are supposedly around every corner trying to infiltrate every aspect of America, while ignoring that the National Security Agency actually considers Israel to be the top espionage threat against the United States.[112] While regularly portraying Muslims and Jews as poor minorities who are constantly persecuted by Islamophobes and anti-Semites, the American media never reports that Christians are actually the most persecuted religion in the world, and are being murdered at such a rate in the Middle East that it is considered to be "near genocide levels" according to human rights groups.[113]

When a reporter for Reuters learned that Beto O'Rourke was a member of the infamous Cult of the

---

[112] Newsweek "Israel Flagged as Top Spy Threat to U.S. in New Snowden/NSA Document" by Jeff Stein (August 4th 2014)

[113] BBC "Christian persecution 'at near genocide levels'" (May 3rd 2019)

Dead Cow hacking group when he was a teenager, he promised Beto he wouldn't reveal that information until after the 2018 midterm election when Beto was running against Ted Cruz for his Senate seat.[114]   During the campaign Beto was already being haunted by his past for leaving the scene of an accident he caused while driving drunk, and if word got out that he was also committing computer crimes as well, it certainly wouldn't have looked good.

PBS edited out a part of *Finding Your Roots*, a documentary series that traces celebrities' ancestry, after Ben Affleck discovered that his ancestors owned slaves and then pressured the network to cut that part out of the episode, which they did, so it wouldn't hurt his image.[115] We only know about the censorship because hacked emails from Sony were posted on Wikileaks, including one between *Finding Your Roots* host Henry Louis Gates Jr. and the CEO of Sony Entertainment discussing Affleck's request.[116]

In our digital world, news outlets can alter an article or a headline after something is published without most people even noticing, covering up falsehoods and mistakes, or even changing the overall message of the story. This often results in an inflammatory article going viral and whipping people into a frenzy, only to later have key points quietly changed in response to the backlash.

---

[114] Reuters "Backstory: How Reuters uncovered Beto O'Rourke's teenage hacking days" by Jame Lee (March 15th 2019)

[115] New York Times "Citing Ben Affleck's 'Improper Influence,' PBS Suspends 'Finding Your Roots'" by John Koblin (June 24th 2015)

[116] CBS 5 KPIX "WikiLeaked Sony Emails Reveal Ben Affleck Told Producers Not To Reveal His Slave-Owning Ancestor On PBS 'Roots' Show" (April 19th 2015)

Sometimes outlets have other reasons for dumping things down the memory hole.

For example, the popular New Zealand news website Stuff.co.nz quietly deleted an article about how a local resident had allegedly been "introduced to radical Islam at the Al-Noor mosque in Christchurch," immediately after a white supremacist walked into the same mosque and livestreamed his mass-murder of 50 Muslims inside.[117] It appears the website was trying to prevent word from getting out that the attacker appeared to have targeted that particular mosque because it had allegedly been linked to Muslim extremists.

Project Censored

Have you heard of Project Censored? Most people have not, which is the ultimate irony because it's an organization that highlights important under-reported or censored stories that mainstream media buries. Each year they publish a list of the top 25 censored or under-reported stories in America hoping to give them the attention they deserve. "Under-reported" meaning that they may have been mentioned in some mainstream outlets, but weren't front page stories or didn't dominate the news cycle for a week as they should have due to their importance.

In our fast paced world, if a story isn't one that happens to get circulated in the news cycle non-stop for a week, it is almost immediately forgotten by most people who are swept up in the next wave of reporting about

---

[117] http://archive.is/phtxU

mass shootings, fires, floods, celebrity gossip, health scares, and political scandals.

Project Censored was founded in 1976 at Sonoma State University by a professor who wanted to expose censorship and propaganda in mainstream media. It has been praised by many media analysts around the world. Whistleblower Daniel Ellsberg, who leaked the Pentagon Papers which showed that the Johnson administration lied to the American people and Congress about the reasons for getting involved in the Vietnam War, said Project Censored, "shines light in the dark places of our government that most need exposure."[118]

Even Walter Cronkite, who anchored the *CBS Evening News* for almost twenty years and who was considered to be "the most trusted man in America" said, "Project Censored is one of the organizations that we should listen to, to be assured that our newspapers and our broadcasting outlets are practicing thorough and ethical journalism."[119]

The Los Angeles Times once admitted that Project Censored, "offers devastating evidence of the dumbing-down of mainstream news in America" and said their annual book of the top 25 most censored and under-reported stories was, "Required reading for broadcasters, journalists, and well-informed citizens."[120]

---

[118] ProjectCensored.org "What Some People Been Saying About Project Censored Over The Past Decades"

[119] Ibid.

[120] Ibid.

New York Times Best Seller List

When the *New York Times* learned the NSA was illegally spying on tens of millions of Americans they sat on the story for over a year and only published it after the reporter who got his story killed by the editors decided to write a book about the spying since the paper couldn't stop him from publishing that.[121]   But that's not the only censorship the *New York Times* has engaged in.   They even censor books from their prestigious "best seller" list.

Ted Cruz's book *A Time for Truth* was excluded from their list in 2015 when it qualified to be number three on the list.[122] They claimed it was because most of the sales were from bulk orders, which they say was evidence that an author is ordering their own book to artificially inflate the numbers, but the publisher HarperCollins issued a statement saying they investigated the sales patterns and found no evidence of any such bulk orders.[123]

Cruz's campaign tweeted "The New York Times is lying — they should release their evidence or issue a formal apology."[124]   A few days later, the book was then finally included on the best seller list.[125]

---

[121] The Washington Post "At the Times, a Scoop Deferred" by Paul Farhi (December 17th 2005)

[122] The Daily Signal "The New York Times Leaves Ted Cruz's Book Off Bestseller List" by Kate Scanlon (July 13th 2015)

[123] BuzzFeed "HarperCollins Refutes New York Times Claim That Ted Cruz Tried To Game Bestseller List" by McKay Coppins (July 10th 2015)

[124] https://twitter.com/TeamTedCruz/status/619585464144519168

[125] Mediaite "New York Times Finally Adds Ted Cruz Book to Bestsellers List" by Alex Griswold (July 16th 2015)

Bill O'Reilly's book *Legends & Lies: The Patriots* was included on *The New York Times* best sellers list when it came out in 2016, but was only ranked number six despite being number one on the *Wall Street Journal's* best seller list, as well as number one on the *Publisher's Weekly* list. At the time the Nielsen organization reported Bill O'Reilly's book sold 24,348 copies that week, while the number one book on *The New York Times* best seller list, *The Gene*, sold only 9,781 copies.[126]

The New York Times also omitted a bestselling book about the Philadelphia abortionist Dr. Kermit Gosnell who killed babies that were born alive during his attempted abortions and was found to have kept baby body parts in jars around his office. He was later convicted of three counts of murder and one count of involuntary manslaughter but the liberal media paid little attention to the trial because it cast abortion in such a horrific light.[127]

The book's co-author Ann McElhinney said it is "shocking that the cover-up of the Gosnell story is continuing...It's clear that this is a blatant fake list in a fake news newspaper...It's not only an insult to the people who have bought this book, but an insult to the readers of *The New York Times* who buy the newspaper and think they are getting the truth about book sales across America but instead get false facts disguised as a neutral list."[128]

---

[126] Fox News "The O'Reilly Factor" (June 8th 2016)

[127] Washington Times "Kermit Gosnell's abortion trial draws little media coverage, much outrage on Twitter" by Douglas Ernst (April 12th 2013)

[128] Washington Examiner "NYT snubs top-selling book on abortionist Gosnell" by Paul Bedard (February 2nd 2017)

In October 2018 when Stormy Daniels' book came out detailing her alleged affair with Donald Trump, the *New York Times* included it on their top 10 best seller list but not Fox News' Jeanine Pirro's book *Liars, Leakers, and Liberals*, or David Limbaugh's *Jesus is Risen*, both of which had actually sold more copies than Stormy's.[129]

In June 2019, CNN's Jim Acosta released a book about President Trump titled *The Enemy of the People: A Dangerous Time to Tell the Truth In America* that didn't even make it into the top 50 on Amazon's best seller list and completely dropped off the top 100 list after just two days. But the *New York Times* placed Acosta's book at number ten on their "best seller" list, proving once again it's not an accurate ranking of the week's best-selling books, but really just a favorites list of the editors.

Books are so powerful that today liberals even protest companies which decide to publish certain authors. Simon & Schuster came under tremendous fire when it was revealed they had signed a deal with right-wing provocateur Milo Yiannopolous, causing the publisher to become one of the top trends on Twitter from triggered liberals calling for people to boycott not just Milo's book (which they weren't going to read anyway), but every book Simon and Schuster publishes![130]

Hollywood producer Judd Apatow tweeted support of the boycott, saying, "I am in! In these times we can not let hatemongers get rich off of their cruelty. Shame on

---

[129] Washington Examiner "NYT bestseller list ignores 'Jesus' for porn star Stormy Daniels" by Paul Bedard (October 12th 2018)

[130] Huffington Post "Critics Threaten Boycotts Of Simon & Schuster Over Milo Yiannopoulos Book Deal" by Claire Fallon (December 30th 2016)

Simon (and) Schuster."[131] Former Governor of Vermont Howard Dean tweeted, "This is an embarrassment for [Simon & Schuster] and their owner CBS which is already on record putting their company ahead of the USA."[132] The publisher eventually canceled their contract with Milo and he later had to self-publish it.

Illegal Immigration

The facts about illegal immigration are rarely allowed into the news cycle because the American people would learn just how big of a crisis it is, and the damage illegal aliens are doing to our country. In 2015 over 50% of *legal* immigrant households received some form of government welfare—including food stamps, housing assistance, school lunch programs, or Medicaid.[133] A 2018 report by the Center for Immigration Studies found that 63% of non-citizens use at least one form of welfare.[134] While the liberal media loves to report that they're just coming here to work, the fact is millions of them are sucking off our tax dollars.

Many illegal immigrants come infected with diseases as well, including ones that had been previously eradicated from the United States, like measles—resulting in new "mysterious" outbreaks (at places like Disneyland)

---

[131] https://twitter.com/JuddApatow/status/814658578174935040

[132] https://twitter.com/GovHowardDean/status/814969506615455749

[133] CNBC "Report: More than half of immigrants on welfare" by Alan Gomez (September 2015)

[134] Center for Immigration Studies "63% of Non-Citizen Households Access Welfare Programs" by Steven A. Camarota and Karen Zeigler (December 2nd 2018)

because the diseases are imported by illegal aliens and those claiming to seek asylum.[135]

Just in the last few years there have been thousands of murders committed by illegal aliens.[136] Lives stolen and families shattered by people who should have never been in our country in the first place. Every day there are headlines in local papers about violent illegal aliens ("undocumented workers," as liberals call them) being arrested, and the stories may get a 15-second sound bite on the local news, but that's it. The number of drunk driving arrests, thefts, burglaries, rapes, and other crimes they commit on a daily basis is staggering. One study shows that illegal aliens commit crimes at double the rate of native-born citizens.[137]

In June 2018 when President Trump met with Angel Families at the White House (people whose family members have been killed by illegal aliens), both MSNBC and CNN abruptly cut their live feed and began talking about how the Trump administration isn't treating illegal immigrant families who sneak into our country good enough. Ironically, during the meeting a woman who lost her son to an illegal alien drunk driver began telling the president, "The mainstream media does not let you know what is really happening."[138]

---

[135] Breitbart "Six Diseases Return To US as Migration Advocates Celebrate 'World Refugee Day'" by Michael Patrick Leahy (June 19th 2016)

[136] Breitbart "Fact Check: Yes, Thousands of Americans Have Been Killed by Illegal Aliens" by John Binder (January 8th 2019)

[137] Washington Times "Illegals commit crimes at double the rate of native-born: Study" by Stephen Dinan (January 26th 2018)

[138] Washington Times "CNN, MSNBC cut away from Trump event with 'Angel Families'" by S.A. Miller and Stephen Dinan (June 22nd 2018)

Democrats say the flood of illegals entering our country isn't a national emergency, as President Trump declared, meanwhile in a recent four-month period Border Patrol agents apprehended 136,000 people crossing from Mexico into the U.S. illegally.[139] In February 2019 alone over 66,400 people were arrested trying to cross the border, the most detained in a single month in over ten years.[140]

During one live feed on MSNBC when their reporter was down at the border talking about the prototypes for Trump's proposed new wall, in the background a group of illegal aliens climbed over the current short and inadequate fence that's only a few feet high, right in the middle of his report.[141]

The Left go so far when denying and defending the crimes of illegal aliens that when Donald Trump called MS-13 gang members "animals" the Democrats and their mouthpieces in the media began claiming that he was referring to immigrants in general! "Trump calls immigrants animals" was their new talking point which was repeated for years as a deceptively edited video of his statement continues to circulate as the "proof."[142] MS-13 is widely considered to be the most sadistic and vicious

---

[139] The Wall Street Journal "Record Immigration Surge at the Border" by Alicia A. Caldwell and Louise Radnofsky (March 5th 2019)

[140] Ibid.

[141] Town Hall "Ha: Illegal Immigrants Jump Border Fence During MSNBC Report on Trump's Wall" by Leh Barkoukis (October 24th 2017)

[142] Politifact "In Context: Donald Trump's comments about immigrants, 'animals'" by Miriam Valverde (May 17th 2018)

street gang in the world by law enforcement agencies.[143] Their motto is "rape, control, kill" and they are known for torturing and dismembering people.[144]

Democrats all used to support expanding the border wall and were tough on illegal immigration, until Donald Trump became president.[145] You've probably seen the video compilations of Chuck Schumer, Hillary Clinton, Barack Obama, and other top Democrats all previously supporting the wall and saying we need to stop the influx of illegals crossing the border—but that has changed.

It appears the Democrats don't support the blue collar working class any more. President Trump has won most of them over to his side, so now the Democrats are hoping to build a new base of future voters consisting of Americans who are too lazy to work and want free handouts from a Socialist government, and 20 million illegal aliens who they are hoping to grant citizenship to.

Transgender Crimes

Transgender people have an extremely high rate of mental illness,[146] so it should be expected that they also have a high rate of crime. But because they're part of a legally "protected class" and liberals see them as having

---

[143] Newsweek "MS-13: How an FBI Informant Risked Death to Bring America's Most Brutal Gang to Justice" by Michele McPhee (June 14th 2018)

[144] Fox News "What is MS-13, the violent gang Trump vowed to target?" by Kaitlyn Schallhorn (May 23rd 2018)

[145] Washington Post "Trump says Democrats used to be for new border barriers. He's right" by JM Rieger (January 19th 2019)

[146] Medical News Today "Mental health risk higher for transgender youth" by Honor Whiteman (April 16th 2018)

achieved the next phase in human evolution, the media always ignores the dangers they pose to society. While their crimes may be reported briefly in local outlets where they occurred, the national conversation regarding transgender people is always framed as if they are amazing and special people who are being treated unfairly by society because they are different.

A 30-year-old transgender "woman" in Wyoming was convicted of raping a ten-year-old girl in a bathroom in 2017 but nobody really heard about this story except for maybe some locals.[147] Another transgender "woman" sexually assaulted a ten-year-old girl in a grocery store bathroom in Scotland but avoided jail and was just given community service.[148]

A 52-year-old transgender "woman" was arrested for raping (an actual) woman in 2016 and then once placed in a female jail "she" sexually assaulted four female prisoners within the first few days.[149] This story spread through social media because people found it so disturbing, but some were in denial and thought it was a hoax, causing Snopes to post an article asking "Did a Male Rapist Who Identifies as Female Transfer to a

---

[147] Christian Post "Transgender Woman Convicted of Raping 10-Y-O Girl in Bathroom, Faces Up to 70 Years in Prison" by Leonardo Blair (October 20th 2017)

[148] The Sun "Transgender woman, 18, sexually assaulted girl, 10, in female toilets in Morrisons" by Gemma Mullin (March 15th 2019)

[149] The Telegraph "Transgender person accused of rape is remanded into female prison and sexually assaults inmates within days" by Martin Evans, Kate McCann, and Olivia Rugard (September 6th 2018)

Women's Jail and Assault Female Inmates?" and rated the claim "True."[150]

In March 2019 a black transgender "woman" in New York was arrested for hate crimes after targeting random white women walking along the sidewalk near subway stations in Harlem and the Upper West Side and spraying them in the face with pepper spray. Police believe 37-year-old Thomas Herd, a black man who identifies as a woman, was behind almost a dozen other similar attacks in the area.[151]

A transgender "woman" in Sydney, Australia was captured on surveillance cameras inside a 7-Eleven walking into the convenience store in January 2019 with an ax, and then randomly smashing two customers in the face after getting upset about a bad Tinder date.[152]

In 2015, a 30-year-old man dressed as a woman was arrested for secretly videotaping women in a mall's bathroom in Virginia.[153] A 37-year-old man in Toronto was arrested after he claimed to be a transgender "woman" and was allowed inside a women's shelter, where he then assaulted four women.[154] These are just a few of many examples.

---

[150] Snopes "Did a Male Rapist Who Identifies as Female Transfer to a Women's Jail and Assault Female Inmates?"

[151] CBS New York "Police Arrest Transgender Woman In Bronx Pepper Spray Attack, Links To More Hate Crimes Being Investigated" (March 9th 2019)

[152] BBC "Sydney axe attacks: Woman jailed for wounding 7-Eleven customers" (January 18th 2019)

[153] NBC Washington "Man Dressed as Woman Arrested for Spying Into Mall Bathroom Stall, Police Say" (November 17th 2015)

[154] Toronto Sun "Predator who claimed to be transgender declared dangerous offender" by Sam Pazzano (February 26th 2014)

Aside from ignoring the transgender Peeping Toms, rapes, and hate crimes that transgender "women" commit, the liberal media also ignores the rapes that gay men commit, and try to portray rape as something that only a man does to a woman, but the reality is that gay men raping other men occurs far more frequently than people know, particularly in the U.S. military since Barack Obama lifted the ban on gays being allowed in.[155]

Black Crime

The liberal media always portrays black people as being "racially profiled" by police and cite figures about black people being arrested at exponentially higher rates than whites as some kind of "proof" that the police are racist, but the reality is that black people per capita commit significantly more violent crimes than whites, so it only makes sense that they would get arrested more!

Since liberals don't know anything about math, when you mention that black men commit murder at approximately ten times the average of whites, they may lookup the statistics and claim that's not true, but they are only comparing the *total* number of murders committed by whites to the *total* number committed by blacks, and don't factor in that blacks are only about 13% of the U.S. population.[156]

The figures are *per capita*, meaning the average per person, and since less than 20% of murders in Chicago

---

[155] Washington Times "Victims of sex assaults in military are mostly men" by Rowan Scarborough (May 20th 2013)

[156] U.S. Department of Justice "Homicide Trends in the United States, 1980-2008" by Alexia Cooper and Erica L. Smith (November 2011)

are actually solved,[157] the number of murders committed by black people is likely much higher than the FBI and Department of Justice records show, which again, reveal that black people commit murder at close to ten times the average of whites. Not twice as many per capita, or three times as many—*ten times*, or 1000% more murders per capita!

Unfortunately many black Americans have embraced the identity of a thug, and see gangster rappers as role models, and view going to jail as a badge of honor. Local TV news in Chicago, Detroit, Milwaukee, and Baltimore cover the day's murders, stabbings, and robberies for a few minutes each night, and it's almost the same story the next night, and the night after that, but the black crime problem in America is never addressed as part of our national discussion.

Memorial Day weekend of 2016 in Chicago ended with 69 people shot, every one of them from black on black crime.[158] And while the story may have gotten a fifteen second segment on some of the national broadcast news networks, the horrifying weekend was forgotten by the next day. There was no CNN Town Hall special to discuss the violence problem there. No endless panelists brought on air to discuss it with Anderson Cooper or Don Lemon. It's like it never even happened.

---

[157] USA Today "Chicago police solved fewer than one in six homicides in the first half of 2018" by Aamer Madhani (September 21st 2018)

[158] Chicago Tribune "Memorial Day weekend closes with 69 shot in Chicago, many of them on West Side" by Peter Nickeas, Grace Wong, Alexandra Chachkevitch and Joe Mahr (May 31st 2016)

The following year 52 people were shot in Chicago over the same holiday weekend.[159]   36 people were shot the year after that over Memorial Day weekend.[160]   All black victims and black perpetrators. Over the Fourth of July holiday and Labor Day weekends the same thing happens every year.   It's total carnage in the black communities in Chicago.

It's especially sad that the emergence of the Black Lives Matter movement was built upon a foundation of lies. The list of armed and dangerous perpetrators justly shot and killed by police and then labeled "victims" of "police brutality" is long.   In fact, convicted cop killer Assata Shakur, who fled to Cuba which granted her "political asylum," is considered to be an inspiration for starting the Black Lives Matter movement.[161] She was a member of the domestic terrorist organization the Black Liberation Army which stated their goal was to wage war against the United States government, and they carried out a series of bombings and assassinations of police officers in the 1970s.[162]

Many Black Lives Matter supporters carried on the philosophy of the Black Liberation Army and see themselves in a war against police. During their marches

---

[159] Chicago Tribune "52 shot in Chicago over Memorial Day weekend, nearly half on final day" by Peter Nicheas and Elvia Malagon (May 30th 2017)

[160] USA Today "36 people shot in Chicago over Memorial Day weekend, marking a reduction in gun violence" by Aamer Madhani (May 29th 2018)

[161] Town Hall "Exposing The Black Lives Matter Movement For What It Is: Promotion of Cop Killing" by Katie Pavlich (September 2nd 205)

[162] Politico "The Untold Story Behind New York's Most Brutal Cop Killings" by Bryan Burrough (April 21st 2015)

they would sometimes chant "What do we want? Dead cops! When do we want them? Now!"[163] In June 2015 two black men were arrested for plotting to blow up a police station in Ferguson, Missouri to get revenge for an officer shooting Michael Brown (after Brown attacked him and tried to take his gun).[164] In July 2016 a black man ambushed a group of police officers during a Black Lives Matter march in Dallas, Texas, killing five of them and injuring nine others.[165]

In 2017 when groups of black youth were robbing people of their cellphones at a train station in San Francisco, police refused to release security footage of the crimes "to avoid racial stereotypes."[166] Debora Allen, who works for the Department of Transportation, gave an interview with the local news and explained the police told her that, "To release these videos would create a high level of racially insensitive commentary toward the district. And in addition it would create a racial bias in the riders against minorities on the trains."[167] Police wouldn't release video footage of the perpetrators because they were concerned it would make black people look bad!

---

[163] Real Clear Politics "Last Week: NYC Protesters Chant 'What Do We Want? Dead Cops! When Do We Want It? Now!'" by Tim Hains (December 22nd 2014)

[164] St. Louis Post-Dispatch "Two admit plot to blow up police station, St. Louis County prosecutor and Ferguson police chief" by Robert Patrick (June 2nd 2015)

[165] NBC News "Dallas Police 'Ambush':12 Officers Shot, 5 Killed During Protest" by F. Brinley Bruton, Alexander Smith, Elizabeth Chuck and Phil Helsel (July 7th 2016)

[166] KPIX CBS SF Bay Area "BART Withholding Surveillance Videos Of Crime To Avoid 'Stereotypes'" by Melissa Caen (June 9th 2017)

[167] Ibid.

The media regularly tries to ignore or downplay most instances of anti-white hate crimes committed by black people. For example, after a black man walked into a predominately white church in Nashville, Tennessee in 2017 and opened fired, killing one woman and wounding seven others, a judge sealed most of the evidence for almost two years, and then during the trial it was revealed, as many had suspected, that he specifically went there to kill white people.[168]

Meanwhile, if you're concerned about white farmers being murdered in South Africa by the racist mobs of blacks who believe it's their rightful land, you are called a racist conspiracy theorist for promoting what the *Liberal Media Industrial Complex* calls the "white genocide conspiracy theory."[169]

In recent years, white farmers in South Africa (called the Boers) have been facing persecution by vicious black gangs who raid their homes and slaughter them to get "revenge" against the "imperialists" who benefited from the Apartheid.[170] And God forbid you point out the anti-white hate crimes that occur in the United States at the hands of disgruntled blacks who blame white people for all of their personal and cultural failures. That's a guaranteed way to get labeled a "white supremacist."

---

[168] Associated Press "State: Man in church shooting aimed to kill 10 white people" by Jonathan Mattise (May 20th 2019)

[169] Newsweek "Organization Candace Owens Represents Shares, Then Deletes, Photo Promoting White Genocide Conspiracy Days After Her Testimony" by Daniel Moritz-Rabson (Aril 12th 2019)

[170] Newsweek "A White Farmer is Killed Every Five Days in South Africa and Authorities Do Nothing About it, Activists Say" by Brendan Cole (March 19th 2018)

Fake Hate Crimes

Since a large part of our culture has come to celebrate victimhood instead of personal achievement, we have seen a staggering increase in the number of hate crime hoaxes where mostly black people, gays, Muslims, and Jews report fake hate crimes to the police after vandalizing their own property with racial slurs, or claim they were physically attacked by some evil white people. The initial reports air on local and national news and go viral on social media, sparking outrage at the "racist" white people and "Trump supporters" who allegedly keep carrying out these attacks.

But oftentimes when police get involved and interview the "victim" and gather evidence, the supposed "hate crime" turns out to be a hoax and it's quietly forgotten about. Just after the 2016 election an 18-year-old Muslim woman in New York claimed that Trump supporters harassed her on the subway, chanting "Trump!" while trying to steal her hijab, but after police launched their investigation *she* was arrested for making the whole story up in an attempt to distract her father from the fact that she had been out getting drunk with her friends that night.[171]

A Muslim student at the University of Texas-Arlington said she was threatened at gunpoint by a group of white men in a pickup truck only to later admit she fabricated the whole story too.[172]

---

[171] USA Today "NYPD arrest Muslim woman who claimed attack by Trump supporters" by Melanie Eversley (December 14th 2016)

[172] Dallas News "UT-Arlington student admits making up claim that gunman followed her to campus, threatened her" by Matt Peterson (February 13th 2015)

Hate crime hoaxes are a specialty in LGBT communities and have been used to further their cause and gain sympathy for years, and in some cases defame a neighbor they're feuding with.[173] Since LGBT people are treated like an endangered species by the liberal media, every time a claim is made that one of them has been harassed, assaulted, or had their property vandalized with anti-gay "slurs," the activist media is more than happy to amplify their claims. But when the police discover, as they often do, that the "victim" made the whole thing up, the story is dropped like a hot potato and the media just moves on to cover something else.

For example, after a transgender "man" who was a prominent LGBT "rights" activist in Michigan had "his" home burned down, killing five pets, the FBI investigated it as a hate crime and the incident was used as leverage by the "man" to help pass a local ordinance that prohibited the discrimination of gays, but authorities later arrested "him" for the crime and said the motive was to create publicity to help pass more gay "rights" legislation.[174]

It seems every "protected" group engages in these kinds of false flags. A Jewish freshman at George Washington University reported someone had drawn swastikas on her dorm room door, but a security camera actually captured her doing it.[175] At the same school another student posted a swastika on a community bulletin board that belonged to a Jewish fraternity and it

---

[173] ABC News "Lesbian Couple Charged With Staging Hate Crime" by Alyssa Newcomb via Good Morning America (May 19th 2012)

[174] Detroit News "Jackson gay rights leader accused of burning down own home" by Francis X. Donnely (February 25th 2019)

[175] National Review "George Washington University's Swastika Problem" by Kevin D. Williamson (April 26th 2015)

was later discovered that the perpetrator, a Jew, was a member of that same fraternity.[176]

An African American community center in Seattle was vandalized with racist graffiti including "Nigger Babies" and "Vote Trump," and as you can guess, an African American was arrested for the crime.[177]

A 44-year-old black man in Colorado was arrested after it was discovered he was the one who hung racist flyers outside of a predominantly black church that caused the local community to be understandably outraged.[178]

A black man reported that while his car was parked near Kansas State University it had been vandalized by someone painting "Go home nigger boy" on it. A photo of the damage went viral on social media only to later be exposed as another false flag and the man admitted that he defaced his own car and filed a false police report.[179] The FBI was even brought in to help investigate the case, which turned out to be another hoax.

The following year a black student at the same school posted a photo of a note on his Twitter account that he claimed had been put on the door of his apartment, reading "Beware Niggers Live Here!!!" But when the

---

[176] Daily Caller "Jewish Student Admits Swastika Hoax in Jewish Frat Dorm at George Washington U" by Eric Owens (March 19th 2015)

[177] Seattle PD Crime Blotter "Burglary, Bias Crime Investigation at Africatown Center, Arrest Made" by Detective Mark Jamieson (March 26th 2016)

[178] CBS Denver "Black Suspect Arrested After Racist Message Discovered Outside Predominately Black Church" (June 30th 2015)

[179] The Wichita Eagle "Kansas man said he defaced his own car with racist slurs" by Kaitlyn Alanis (November 6th 2017)

police got involved he admitted that he made the note and put it there himself.[180]

And of course the most popular hate crime hoax in decades involves actor Jussie Smollett, who claimed that two men wearing MAGA hats attacked him in the streets of Chicago in subzero weather and tied a noose around his neck, poured bleach on him, and yelled "This is MAGA country, nigger." His story was so absurd that many were skeptical from the start, and as the investigation went on, police discovered he staged the whole thing hoping to become a social justice hero.[181]

Aside from a lot of fake hate crimes being fabricated by black people, they also hallucinate that there are hate crimes committed against them. The black mayor of a small South Carolina town called police thinking she was the victim of a hate crime after she found a "yellow, sticky substance" covering her car in March 2019 which was parked in the driveway of her home. She assumed someone had spray-painted it, but police investigated and discovered it was just pollen.[182]

Black college students at the University of Mississippi freaked out when someone saw a banana peel hanging over a tree branch outside a cabin at a fraternity's weekend retreat. It caused such a concern that the retreat was canceled because some black students were afraid it

---

[180] The Witchita Eagle "For second time in two years, racist slur at Kansas State was a hoax, police say" by Jason Tidd (November 8th 2018)

[181] Variety "Jussie Smollett Indicted on 16 Counts in Attack Hoax Case" by Gene Maddaus (March 8th 2019)

[182] Newsweek "S.C. Mayor Says 'Yellow Sticky Substance' on Her Car Was Sprayed by Vandals, Police Say It's Just Pollen" by M.L. Nestel (March 1st 2019)

was meant as a warning or to harass them, but it turns out a student who had finished eating the banana hung it on the tree because there were no garbage cans nearby and he didn't want to just throw it on the ground where someone may end up stepping (or slipping) on it.[183]

The list of recent hate crime hoaxes from "protected groups" like gays, lesbians, and black people could fill an entire book.[184] If you want to learn more about the issue there's a whole chapter in my previous book, *The True Story of Fake News* which details these kinds of incidents.

Good News Ignored

Aside from burying bad news that will cause audiences to question the liberal narrative of how the world works, the *Liberal Media Industrial Complex* also ignores good news that undermines the agenda they're trying to push. If it's not completely ignored, it might be mentioned for 15 or 30 seconds on the broadcast news or published in newspapers or online articles but won't be included in the lengthy discussions on cable news or the weekend talk shows like *Meet the Press* (NBC), *Face the Nation* (CBS), or *This Week* (ABC).

Good news about President Trump is just a tiny blip on the radar, and then drowned out by the endless whining and moaning about minor issues and pundits' latest paranoid delusions about what Trump "may do." Despite reporting that if Donald Trump won the 2016 election the

---

[183] National Review "Frat Retreat Ends Early after Students 'Frightened' by a Banana Peel" by Katherine Timpf "August 31st 2017)

[184] Hate Crime Hoax: How the Left is Selling a Fake Race War by Wilfred Reilly (2019)

stock market would tank, it has skyrocketed largely in part due to him repealing countless burdensome business regulations and scrapping various awful trade deals previous administrations had gotten us into such as the Trans Pacific Partnership and NAFTA. In the first two years of his presidency the S&P 500 rose 28%[185] The Dow Jones Industrial Average later reached a record high, closing above 27,000 for the first time ever.[186]

Black unemployment hit an all-time record low in May 2018 of just 5.9 percent.[187] In Trump's first two years as president he was able to do more for African American communities than Barack Obama did in eight. Hispanic unemployment has fallen to its lowest level on record, down to 4.8%.[188] The unemployment rate for veterans also fell to an all-time low as well.[189] The average unemployment rate for the country dropped to 3.7% in October 2018, the lowest in almost 50 years.[190] The average American's salary is also increasing at record rates.[191]

---

[185] Reuters "Two years in, Trump holds stock market bragging rights" by Noel Randewich (November 5th 2018)

[186] NBC News "Dow notches record high, closing above 27,000 for first time" by Lucy Bayly (July 11th 2019)

[187] CNBC "Black unemployment rate falls to 5.9%, ties record low hit earlier this year" by Kate Rooney (December 7th 2018)

[188] Bloomberg "Black and Hispanic Unemployment in America Reach Record Lows" by Randy Woods (May 4th 2018)

[189] Fox Business "US veteran unemployment rate hits all-time low in 2018" by Brittany De Lea (January 14th 2019)

[190] NPR "U.S. Unemployment Rate Drops To 3.7 Percent, Lowest In Nearly 50 Years" by Avie Schneider (October 5th 2018)

[191] New York Post "Average US salaries on the rise thanks to booming economy" by John Aidan Byrne (May 18th 2019)

President Trump signed the Veterans Affairs Choice program to dramatically speed up the amount of time that it takes U.S. veterans to get their healthcare claims processed by enabling them to use private doctors and health care facilities instead of just the government-run VA hospitals.[192] The VA, like the DMV, the Post Office, and almost every other government-run program, was a disaster and it had taken months for veterans to see doctors and get the treatment they need. Trump's reforms were a much-needed and long-overdue upgrade to how our veterans are taken care of.

When Trump first took office ISIS controlled about 20,000 square miles of territory in Iraq and Syria, which contained a population of several million people.[193] However a year later they were driven out of their last outpost in Syria, crippling their organization and expelling them from their "Islamic State."[194] While there are many Muslims in the Middle East who still adhere to the radical Islamic ideology of ISIS, they lost their territory and precious caliphate under President Trump.

The *ABC Nightly News* spent literally 18 seconds on the story the day the Department of Defense announced the news that ISIS' once planned Islamic State had fallen.[195] The *CBS Evening News* spent one minute and

---

[192] USA Today "Trump signs VA law to provide veterans more private health care choices" by Donovan Slack (June 6th 2018)

[193] Washington Post "Under Trump, gains against ISIS have 'dramatically accelerated'" by Karen DeYoung (August 4th 2017)

[194] NPR "U.S.-Backed Forces Declare Defeat Of ISIS 'Caliphate'" by Ruth Sherlock (March 23rd 2019)

[195] Newsbusters "ABC Yawns as ISIS Stripped of All Territory, CBS Declares 'ISIS Is Done'" by Nicholas Fondacaro (March 20th 2019)

twenty three seconds on the event.[196]   Admitting that, despite his abrasive style and personality flaws, President Trump's policies have been great for America is the last thing the Establishment will do. Instead they are trying to misdirect people's attention and occupy their minds with issues of little significance and artificial controversies they drum up to smear him.

---

[196] Ibid.

The War on Trump

Because politicians on the Left and the Right have been screwing us over for years and using the mechanisms of government to fulfill their own selfish desires for power and wealth, the election of Donald Trump shook the very foundation of the Washington D.C. Establishment. The lifelong bureaucrats knew the gravy train was going to come to a halt. For decades millions of Americans had felt a businessman, not a politician, would be the only one who could begin to fix the broken system —and the opportunity had finally come.

Trump's arrival to Washington was like parents who came home early from a long vacation, and now the kids (who were running around unsupervised breaking the rules) have to end the party and be held accountable for their actions. In 1988 on Oprah Winfrey's show he was asked if he would ever run for president and he responded probably not, but added that he wouldn't rule it out in the future because he was tired of seeing what's happening in America.[197] And that's why he thought about running in 2012, but felt his sons needed a few more years of experience before they were ready to take over the family business.

---

[197] Washington Examiner "Flashback: Trump and Oprah discuss presidential run in 1988 interview" by Melissa Quinn (January 8th 2018)

In 2016 he felt it was the right time, and the rest is history, but the Establishment immediately struck back because they needed to destroy him before he started cleaning up the mess that decades of corruption had created. He was the ultimate roadblock to their globalist agenda, and long-awaited New World Order. They were so upset about Trump's victory they counterattacked by kicking off the "fake news" scare hoping to regain control of the flow of information.

The Big Tech companies then started changing their algorithms and suppressing posts about certain topics and artificially favoring content from "authoritative" [liberal] mainstream sources. Even Tim Berners-Lee, the "founder of the World Wide Web" and the man who basically created HTML, said, "[People] are all stepping back, suddenly horrified after the Trump and Brexit elections, realizing that this web thing that they thought was that cool is actually not necessarily serving humanity very well."[198]

Nonstop Negative Coverage

They began fabricating fake stories like the supermarket tabloids that invent scandals based on their own imaginations to smear President Trump and keep him constantly on the defense. "Our source says" and "if true" are littered throughout reports that endlessly speculate about Trump being engaged in a massive conspiracy to steal the election and work as a Russian

---

[198] Newsweek: World Wide Web Inventor on 30th Anniversary: People Horrified by Trump Election Realize Web Is Not 'Serving Humanity'" by Jason Murdock (March 12th 2019)

"Manchurian candidate." Nothing President Trump does is good in the eyes of the mainstream media.

Everything he says is twisted and taken out of context in order to paint him as an incompetent racist who is destroying America. Journalist critic Anthony Brandt once said, "Members of the press sometimes print gossip as truth, disregard the impact they have on people's lives, and are ready to believe the worst about people because the worst sells...We in the media have much to answer for."[199]

The week President Trump was inaugurated, Democrat operative David Brock, founder of Media Matters, a Leftist "media watchdog group," launched a new plan to "kick Donald Trump's ass" which included handing out a 50-page document marked "private and confidential" that outlined how they were going to use their resources to push for impeachment, bog down his administration by continuously filing lawsuits, and use their new proxy "media outlet" Shareblue to attack conservative media personalities and harass their advertisers to pull out.[200]

The city of West Hollywood even voted to remove Donald Trump's star from the Walk of Fame. "Earning a star on the Hollywood Walk of Fame is an honor," the mayor said. "When one belittles and attacks minorities, immigrants, Muslims, people with disabilities or women

---

[199] Quoted in Media/Impact: An Introduction to Mass Media (12th Edition) by Shirley Biagi page 312

[200] Washington Free Beacon "David Brock's Shareblue to Be 'Nucleus' of Multi-Platform Anti-Trump Media Entity" by Joe Schoffstall (January 24th 2017)

— the honor no longer exists."[201]   The city has no problem with accused underage sexual predator Kevin Spacey having a star, or convicted rapist Bill Cosby, or accused pedophile Michael Jackson.   But they were determined to have Trump's removed.   So far, the star remains, since the Walk of Fame is considered a historic landmark and run by the Hollywood Chamber of Commerce which said "as of now" they have no plans to remove it.[202]

A Pew Research study found that the media's coverage of President Trump's first 60 days in office was three times more negative than that of President Obama.[203]   Even NPR admitted, "Compared to other recent presidents, news reports about President Trump have been more focused on his personality than his policy, and are more likely to carry negative assessments of his actions."[204]

Another study from the Media Research Center showed that 89% of the broadcast news reports from President Trump's first 100 days in office were negative.[205]   Newsbusters, a website run by the Media

---

[201] PJ Media "Trump May Lose Star on Walk of Fame, But Kevin Spacey Won't" by Tom Knighton (August 8th 2018)

[202] The Wrap "Why Trump Won't Lose His Star on the Hollywood Walk of Fame Anytime Soon" by Itay Hod (August 8th 2018)

[203] Washington Times "As first 100 days in office approaches, media coverage of Trump is 89% negative: Study" by Jennifer Harper (April 19th 2017)

[204] NPR "Study: News Coverage Of Trump More Negative Than For Other Presidents" by Danielle Kurtzleben (October 2nd 2017)

[205] NewsBusters "Honeymoon from Hell: The Liberal Media vs. President Trump" by Rich Notes and Mike Ciandella (April 19th 2017)

Research Group, declared 2017 "The year the news media went to war against a president."[206]

A poll by Politico showed that 46% of Americans believe the media just makes up fake stories about President Trump.[207]   And ethics scholar John Hulteng previously warned, "It may be well that if journalism loses touch with ethical values, it will then cease to be of use to society, and cease to have any real reason for being."[208]   But unfortunately that ship sailed a long time ago.

"He'll Crash the Economy"

Just a few weeks before the 2016 election, CNN reported that, "A Trump win would sink stocks."[209] Politico said that, "Wall Street is set up for a major crash if Donald Trump shocks the world on Election Day and wins the White House."[210]   CNBC warned that, "it probably won't be a pretty picture for stocks if he does."[211] *New York Times* economist Paul Krugman wrote

---

[206] Newsbusters.org "2017: The Year the News Media Went to War Against a President" by Rich Noyes and Mike Ciandella (January 16th 2018)

[207] Politico "Poll: 46 percent think media make up stories about Trump" by Steven Shepard (October 18th 2017)

[208] Media/Impact: An Introduction to Mass Media (12th Edition) by Shirley Biagi page 312

[209] CNN "A Trump win would sink stocks. What about Clinton?" by Heather Long (October 24th 2016)

[210] Politico "Economists: A Trump win would tank the markets" by Ben White (October 21st 2016)

[211] CNBC "This is what could happen to the stock market if Donald Trump wins" by Patti Domm (November 2nd 2016)

a column the day after the 2016 election saying, "So we are very probably looking at a global recession, with no end in sight," adding that, "a terrible thing has just happened."[212]

Instead, the stock market kept reaching all-time highs,[213] black unemployment soon reached the lowest in history,[214] and countless Americans were getting bonuses and taking more money home each week in their paychecks because of his new tax reforms,[215] but still the liberal media kept nitpicking every little thing he did or said, trying to spin it as if it was the end of the world.

People's tax refunds were technically "lower" under Trump's new tax code because less money was being taken out of their paychecks; money that would have been returned to them once they filed their taxes at the end of the year. Headlines from *NBC News* read, "Under new Trump tax code, average refund is 8.4 percent smaller," and they reported, "Frustrated taxpayers are using the hashtag #GOPTaxScam to vent about their smaller than expected tax refunds."[216] All the major news outlets piled on with similar reports, but this was only half of the story. The other half would put things into perspective.

---

212 New York Times "Paul Krugman: The Economic Fallout" by Paul Krugman (November 11th 2016)

213 CNBC "S&P 500 and Nasdaq close at record highs after strong GDP report" by Fred Imbert (April 26th 2019)

214 Washington Post "Black unemployment falls to lowest level on record" by Heather Long (January 5th 2018)

215 Money.com "Check Your Paycheck: You Probably Just Got a Surprise Pay Bump" by Katie Reilly (February 2nd 2018)

216 NBC News "Under new Trump tax code, average refund is 8.4 percent smaller" by Alyssa Newcomb (February 11th 2019)

An executive at the Tax Foundation, a think tank that studies U.S. tax policies, told a New Jersey PBS station, "What the Treasury Department did is they adjusted the amount of taxes that were withheld from your paycheck every time you got paid, say every two or three weeks. And so you actually saw a little bit more in every paycheck in terms of less taxes withheld, but that means your refund at the end of the year might be a bit smaller than you actually expected."[217]

Why would you want to give the government more money than is required each paycheck and then wait until the end of the year to get it back? Taking less money from each paycheck is much more efficient, but since many people are too dumb to grasp this simple concept the media spun the news about lower refunds as if people were somehow having to pay more taxes to the government, when the complete opposite is true!

"Trump is Hitler"

We've never seen the American media be so slanderous, vicious, and dangerous when reporting on a president. They sound worse than a raving lunatic you would find standing in the streets ranting about the end of the world. CNN and MSNBC hosts regularly say that President Trump is acting like a dictator and often compare him to Adolf Hitler. Not even in the months and years after the weapons of mass destruction hoax fell apart did the liberal media stoop so low when criticizing President George W. Bush for the disaster that the Iraq War had become.

---

[217] NJTV News "Here's why your tax refund may be disappointing this year" by Raven Santana (February 18th 2019)

Just two days after Donald Trump was inaugurated, CNN's Brian Stelter gave the impression that the country had just been hijacked by a dictator. "These are uncomfortable questions, especially these last ones, but it's time to ask them," he began. "Do citizens in dictatorships recognize what's happening right here, right now? Are they looking at the first two days of the Trump administration and saying, 'that's what my leader does.' What should we learn from them today?"[218]

Don Lemon opened his broadcast one night by declaring "This is CNN Tonight. I'm Don Lemon. The President of the United States is racist,"[219] and often insinuates the President supports neo-Nazis and could become the next Hitler.[220]

In response to Trump's speech at CPAC 2019 where he highlighted his America First agenda, CNN analyst Sam Vinograd said she felt "sick" after hearing it, because Trump talking about "preserving our heritage" to her, "sounds a lot like a certain leader that killed members of my family, and about six million other Jews in the

218 CNN's Brian Stelter (January 22nd 2017)

219 Washington Post "'This is CNN Tonight. I'm Don Lemon. The president of the United States is racist.'" by Samantha Schmidt (January 12th 2018)

220 RealClear Politics "CNN's Don Lemon Says Trump Could Become Like Hitler: 'It Starts With Little Lies'" by Tim Hains (June 19th 2019)

1940s."[221]   Another CNN panelist said that President Trump has radicalized more people than ISIS ever did.[222]

The *New York Daily News* ran a headline reading, "Trump, Not ISIS is America's Greatest Existential Threat," and went on to say "This is not some bit of clickbait," and claimed, "Trump can wreak far more havoc on America, its vaunted institutions and its people than a terror group on the other side of the world."[223] Keith Olbermann later said that Donald Trump and his family have done more damage to America than Osama Bin Laden and ISIS combined.[224]

MSNBC's Donny Deutsch has said Trump is a dictator on several occasions and people need to hit the streets and start a "revolution" to overthrow him.[225] Fellow MSNBC host Christ Matthews even compares Ivanka Trump and her husband Jared Kushner to Saddam Hussein's two murderous sons, Uday and Qusay.[226] In his

---

[221] Mediaite "CNN Analyst: Trump CPAC Speech Looked Scripted by Putin, 'Reclaiming Our Heritage' Talk Sounded Like Hitler" by Josh Feldman (March 2nd 2019)

[222] Real Clear Politics "GQ's Julia Ioffe: 'This President Has Radicalized So Many More People Than ISIS Ever Did'" by Ian Schwartz (October 29th 2018)

[223] NY Daily News "Trump, Not ISIS is America's Greatest Existential Threat" by Gersh Kuntzman (February 17th 2017)

[224] Real Clear Politics "Olbermann: Osama Bin Laden Did Less Damage To America Than Donald Trump" by Ian Schwartz (November 4th 2017)

[225] Free Beacon "MSNBC Panel Says Trump Is a 'Dictator' Who's Owned by Putin: 'We Need a Revolution'" by Paul Crookston (February 2nd 2018)

[226] Fox News "Chris Matthews Compares Ivanka, Jared Kushner to Saddam Hussein's Sons" (March 28th 2017)

commentary about President Trump's inauguration speech Matthews said it sounded "Hitlerian."[227]

Just before the 2018 midterms an MSNBC legal analyst hoping the Democrats would take back control of the House and the Senate said, "We're going to see if this reign—that [Republicans] now have control over all three branches of government—we're going to see if this reign lasts for 30 days or two years, or a thousand-year Reich."[228] The "thousand-year-Reich" was the Nazi's name for their planned global empire.

In the past, if an unhinged guest on cable news would make such outrageous statements they would never be invited back and the host would apologize for their behavior, but it is a common occurrence in the Trump era to compare him to Hitler, and it's not just guests who aren't affiliated with the networks, it's people on the payroll, from regular contributors, to the hosts themselves!

Calls to Assassinate Trump

The endless streams of fake news painting President Trump as a Russian agent or the reincarnation of Hitler have incited countless unhinged whack jobs to publicly make assassination threats against him on social media.[229] There have also been numerous arrests of individuals who

---

[227] Real Clear Politics "Chris Matthews: Trump's Inauguration Speech Had 'Hitlerian' Tone To It" by Ian Schwartz (January 20th 2017)

[228] Washington Free Beacon "MSNBC Panelist: Kavanaugh Appointment Supports GOP's Goal of 'Thousand-Year Reich'" by Paul Crookston (October 8th 2018)

[229] Breitbart "Twitter Explodes with Donald Trump Assassination Fantasies" by Patrick Howley (November 10th 2016)

have made such threats (and taken specific action towards their goal), but the vast majority of them go unpunished.

Just a few weeks before he was elected, a Secret Service agent said she wouldn't protect Donald Trump if someone tried to assassinate him.[230] After word spread of her treasonous statements she was forced to retire. *The New York Times* even published several fictional stories by various novelists imagining how the Mueller investigation may end, and one of them depicted President Trump getting assassinated with the help of a Secret Service agent.[231]

The anti-Trump mania has even resulted in numerous high-profile celebrities uttering threats of violence or wishing violence against him. Madonna famously declared she "thought an awful lot about blowing up the White House," but that was just the beginning. Johnny Depp asked an audience, "When was the last time an actor assassinated a president?" answering, "it's been awhile and maybe it's time," referring to John Wilkes Booth (who was an actor) killing Abraham Lincoln.[232]

Jim Carrey said he had a dream about killing President Trump with a golf club.[233] Mickey Rourke said

---

[230] Real Clear Politics "Anti-Trump Secret Service Agent Leaving With Pay, Pension" by Susan Crabtree (March 1st 2019)

[231] The Washington Examiner "New York Times publishes fictional story on Trump assassination" by Caitlin Yilek (October 25th 2018)

[232] NBC News "Johnny Depp: 'When Was the Last Time an Actor Assassinated a President?'" (June 23rd 2017)

[233] World Net Daily "Jim Carrey defends Griffin: I dreamed of beating Trump with golf club" by Chelsea Schilling (June 1st 2017)

he wanted to beat him with a baseball bat.[234] And Robert Di Niro said he wants to "punch him in the face."[235]

Rapper Big Sean did a free style on a popular radio show about how he wanted to "murder Trump."[236] Snoop Dogg released a rap video depicting himself shooting Donald Trump in the head.[237] Marilyn Manson made a video titled "Say 10" (a play on words to sound like "Satan") which depicted him decapitating Donald Trump with a large knife.[238] Green Day singer Billie Joe Armstrong shouted "Kill Donald Trump!" at one point when performing the song "American Idiot" at a concert in Oakland, California.[239] And of course Kathy Griffin posted that infamous photo of herself holding Trump's bloody decapitated head.[240]

Never before have there been so many threats to assassinate a president of the United States, and it's

---

[234] Breitbart "Mickey Rourke: Donald Trump 'Can S*ck My F**king D*ck,' Threatens to Beat GOP Candidate With Baseball Bat" by Daniel Nussbaum (April 7th 2016)

[235] Associated Press "De Niro: I'd Like to Punch Trump In the Face" (October 8th 2016)

[236] Rolling Stone "Hear Big Sean Threaten Donald Trump in New Freestyle" by Daniel Kreps (February 3rd 2017)

[237] Rolling Stone "Watch Snoop Dogg Aim Gun at Clown-Trump in 'Lavender' Video" by Ryan Reed (March 13th 2017)

[238] Independent "Marilyn Manson 'beheads Donald Trump' in new music video" by Jack Shepherd (November 8th 2016)

[239] Multiple people recorded video of the incident and posted it on YouTube the next day, although it went unnoticed by major media outlets unlike most of the other incidents of celebrities making similar threatening statements.

[240] USA Today "Kathy Griffin says she doesn't regret Trump photo despite backlash, death threats" by Sara M. Moniuszko (March 24th 2019)

utterly shocking to see that there have been little to no repercussions for the high profile celebrities who have done so. Previously such reckless and dangerous statements would completely end someone's career and gotten their movies and music pulled from store shelves and streaming services, but today these celebrities have been mostly immune from any consequences.

The Red Scare

The Democrat conspiracy theory that Donald Trump "colluded" with Russians to "steal" the 2016 election caused the greatest case of mass hysteria in America since the Salem witch trials. As you know it completely consumed the news cycle for over two years, and every night the speculation and imagination about "what really happened" got more and more out of control. "Donald Trump now sits at the threshold of impeachment," MSNBC's Lawrence O'Donnell once declared with glee.[241] "The worst case scenario that the president is a foreign agent suddenly feels very palpable," Rachel Maddow concluded one night.[242]

He was certainly going to not only be impeached, but led out of the White House in handcuffs for committing "treason" and "undermining our Democracy," they thought. Those who hadn't succumbed to the madness were skeptical of these wild allegations from the start, and when the "bombshell" reports kept turning out to be

---

[241] Newsbusters "MSNBC's O'Donnell Claims Trump Will Get Impeached for 'Ignorance'" by Kristine Marsh (May 17th 2017)

[242] RealClear Politics "Rachel Maddow: "Worst-Case Scenario That The President Is A Foreign Agent Suddenly Feels Very Palpable" by Tim Hains (July 22nd 2018)

completely false, the mainstream media became increasingly discredited and desperate.

Alan Dershowitz, a rare liberal who still maintained his sanity though all of this, summed it up pretty well when he said that "hope over reality" fueled their delusions.[243]   When the Robert Mueller investigation finally cleared Trump and everyone connected to him of conspiring with the Russians in any way, the Democrats and their mouth pieces in the media still couldn't admit they were wrong (and completely insane), and instead kept concocting new conspiracy theories about a "cover-up."   Since they took control of the House of Representatives in the 2018 midterm election, they kept "investigating" Trump's business records trying to find "something."

As President Trump once noted, "If it was the goal of Russia to create discord, disruption and chaos within the U.S. then, with all of the Committee Hearings, investigations and party hatred, they have succeeded beyond their wildest dreams. They are laughing their asses off in Moscow."[244]

LGBT "Rights"

President Trump supports gay "marriage" unlike every previous Republican president (and all Democrat presidents too, except for Obama when he flip-flopped during his second term).   But the media still portrays Trump as anti-gay.   At a campaign event before he was

---

[243] Washington Times "Dershowitz: 'Hope over reality' delusion fuels obstruction of justice claims against Trump" by Douglas Ernst (December 4th 2017)

[244] https://twitter.com/realDonaldTrump/status/965212168449941505

elected, Donald Trump held up a big gay pride rainbow flag and waved it around stage after seeing someone in the audience holding it.[245] He even said Caitlyn Jenner can use whatever bathroom "she" wants to in Trump Tower.[246] But the radical LGBT activists are still convinced that he "hates" gay people because the mainstream media ignores his pro-LGBT positions.

After President Trump announced a plan to work with the United Nations to prevent countries from enforcing laws banning homosexuality, *Out Magazine*, a popular American gay publication, attacked him, publishing a story titled, "Trump's Plan to Decriminalize Homosexuality Is an Old Racist Tactic," and claimed, "The Trump administration is set to launch a global campaign to decriminalize homosexuality in dozens of nations where anti-gay laws are still on the books," which you would think they would be happy about, but they denounced the move, saying, "Rather than actually being about helping queer people around the world, the campaign looks more like another instance of the right using queer people as a pawn to amass power and enact its own agenda."[247] You can't make these lunatics happy!

---

[245] The Washington Times "Donald Trump holds high the flag for gay equality" by Richard Grenell (November 2nd 2016)

[246] ABC News "Donald Trump OK With Caitlyn Jenner Using Any Bathroom in His Tower" by Candace Smith and Jessica Hopper (April 21st 2016)

[247] Out Magazine "Trump's Plan to Decriminalize Homosexuality Is an Old Racist Tactic" by Matthew Rodriguez (February 19th 2019)

They Sided with North Korea

The liberal media hates Trump so bad, they basically sided with North Korea out of spite when President Trump was trying to help broker peace between the North and the South. When he was trying to incentivize Kim Jong Un to dismantle his nuclear program, NBC News complained about it, reporting that, "Trump's North Korea policy could trigger famine," because of new sanctions he threatened to put in place if they didn't comply with the U.S. demands.[248] How else was he supposed to apply pressure to them without launching a full-out war? Applying sanctions to cutoff imports is a basic tactic when dealing with rogue regimes!

Comedian Michelle Wolf (who had recently bombed at the White House Correspondents Dinner) polled her Netflix audience, asking them, "Are you sort of hoping we don't get peace with North Korea so you wouldn't have to give Trump credit?" and 71% agreed that they didn't want peace in North Korea because it would make President Trump look good.[249]

When Michael Moore was talking with MSNBC's Chris Hayes, the cable news host admitted that he was "genuinely rooting for him to handle the Korean situation well," at which point Michael Moore cut him off and replied, "I don't know if I agree with that." A stunned Hayes responded, "You're not rooting for him to deal with North Korea well?!" Michael Moore continued his explanation with a ridiculous analogy trying to justify his

---

[248] NBC News "Trump's North Korea policy could trigger famine, experts warn" by Alexander Smith December 9th 2017)

[249] Herald Sun "Leftists: Rather War with North Korea Than Peace with Trump" by Andrew Bolt (June 17th 2018)

hope that President Trump fails at helping negotiate a peaceful resolution between North and South Korea.[250]

The two countries joined together during the 2018 Winter Olympics to form a unified Korean hockey team which was an incredible sign that relations were improving. Kim Jong Un later crossed over the DMZ (demilitarized zone—the border between the North and South) to meet personally with the leader of South Korea, marking the first time leaders of the two countries had met since Korea split apart after World War II.[251]

Families have been allowed to reunite with each other for the first time since the separation, and President Trump himself was invited to step over the DMZ where he was greeted by Kim Jong Un in a historic moment giving more hope for peace in the region, but Trump doesn't get any credit for that, and the media kept claiming his tactics were going to start World War Three.

Trump Derangement Syndrome

Conservatives began joking about liberals being afflicted with Trump Derangement Syndrome when it became obvious that they weren't able to cope with the fact that he is the president, but as time went on many psychologists said they were actually treating patients for

---

[250] Mediaite "'I'm Not Rooting for the 6-Year-Old': Michael Moore Not Sure He Wants Trump to Succeed on North Korea" by Justin Baragona (April 28th 2017)

[251] ABC News "North Korea's Kim Jong Un crosses DMZ line for historic meeting with South Korea" by Joohe Cho, Hakyung Kate Lee, and Tara Fowler (April 26th 2018)

what they called Trump Anxiety Disorder.[252]   A therapist at the Washington D.C. Counseling and Psychotherapy Center admitted that they were getting a lot of patients who had anxiety, fear, and hopelessness about the Trump administration.[253]

The shock on election night 2016 when Hillary Clinton lost was like nothing the country had ever seen. Reporters couldn't hold back their horror and Democrats across the country were in tears, but after a week the shock still hadn't worn off. And then a month went by and they were still in denial that Trump was going to be our next president and were getting increasingly distraught. But the months dragged on, and then it was a year, and then two years since he won the election, and instead of gaining their composure and getting back to business, they continued to get more unhinged with every passing week.

When a *New York Times* reporter was asked about why Hillary Clinton wrote her *What Happened* book, she responded, "I think that the intention of the book was two things. One, it was to really, I think, just to vent and get it out there because there are so many people like Hillary Clinton who are still writing about this, who are still thinking about this, who are still in therapy frankly,

---

252 Newsweek "Therapists Coin New Term: Trump Anxiety Disorder" by Emily Zogbi (July 28th 2018)

253 CBC "In a divided U.S., therapists treating anxiety are hearing the same name over and over: Donald Trump" by Matt Kwong (July 28th 2018)

sources that I know who are still really upset about the election."[254] In therapy!

On the one-year anniversary of the 2016 election, anti-Trump protesters gathered in Boston to "scream helplessly at the sky."[255] Over 4000 people RSVP'd to the event on Facebook which was literally titled, "Scream helplessly at the sky on the anniversary of the election," and hundreds of them actually showed up and did just that![256]

Rosie O'Donnell later admitted that she had been seeing a therapist and it took her a year to be able to compose herself enough to go out into public again.[257] Chelsea Handler also opened up a few years after the election and admitted she too had been seeing a psychiatrist because she had a "mid-life identity crisis once Trump won the election."[258] Model Chrissy Teigen, who's married to singer John Legend, admitted that she asked her doctor to up her medication because Trump was causing her "crippling anxiety" and had to get a Botox

---

[254] Real Clear Politics "New York Times' Yamiche Alcindor: 'Sources' 'Still In Therapy' Because Clinton Lost" September 14th 2017)

[255] Newsweek "Thousands of Americans Will Scream Helplessly at the Sky on Trump's Election Anniversary" by Chris Riotta (October 23rd 2017)

[256] Fox News "Anti-Trump protesters 'scream helplessly at the sky' to demonstrate on election anniversary" by Caleb Parke (November 9th 2017)

[257] The Daily Caller "Rosie: Trump's Presidential Victory Made Me 'Physically Sick,' Took a Year to Recover" by Benny Johnson (October 19th 2018)

[258] CNS News "Trump Win Sent Chelsea Handler to a Psychiatrist: 'I Just Wanted to F***king Fight People'" (April 8th 2019)

injection in her jaw to relieve tension because she kept grinding her teeth, which she blames Trump for.[259]

Since Democrats always project, meaning they imagine others doing what they themselves are doing, they started saying that President Trump was "mentally unfit" for office, and kept floating around the idea that the 25th Amendment could soon be enacted to remove him. But to actually invoke the 25th Amendment and get him removed it would take the vice president, his entire cabinet, and two-thirds of both the House and the Senate to achieve it. Democrats are so delusional that they are regularly accusing the president of being crazy, while being completely unaware of the irony of their own activities.

One MSNBC guest even said that President Trump's strong warnings to North Korea were the result of him having, "profound sexual and masculine insecurities" that "are literally threatening to annihilate the planet."[260] Shortly before he died, Stephen Hawking warned that since President Trump is not very concerned about man-made global warming he may, "push the Earth over the brink, to become like Venus, with a temperature of 250 degrees, and raining sulfuric acid."[261]

One way liberals regularly vent their hatred of President Trump is by obsessively replying to his tweets,

[259] The Independent "Chrissy Teigen says Donald Trump's election victory has damaged her mental health" by Maya Oppenheim (May 4th 2017)

[260] Newsbusters "MSNBC Analyst: Trump's 'Profound Sexual and Masculine Insecurities' Threaten to Kill Us All" by Tim Graham (January 3rd 2018)

[261] BBC "Hawking says Trump's climate stance could damage Earth" by Pallab Ghosh (July 2nd 2017)

and it's become a game for them to see who can reply first and whose reply can get the most "likes." Some Twitter activists, like the odd Krassenstein brothers whose obsession with trolling President Trump's tweets have become "Twitter famous." (They were later banned for allegedly using fake accounts to artificially amplify their tweets).[262]

As one writer in the London *Guardian* pointed out, it appears that liberals "worst nightmare" is actually a successful Donald Trump presidency.[263] The mainstream media would have to admit that they were wrong about everything and had been stringing along their audience for years under the false pretense that they were reporting news, when in reality they were just throwing an endless temper tantrum and lost every ounce of their integrity.

---

[262] Variety "Twitter Permanently Bans Anti-Trump Krassenstein Brothers, Who Deny They Broke Platform's Rules" by Todd Spangler (May 24th 2019)

[263] The Guardian "Your worst nightmare: a successful Donald Trump presidency" by David Smith (July 3rd 2017)

The War on Trump Supporters

The oldest trick in the Democrats' playbook is to call Republicans racist. When the Tea Party movement emerged in 2009 as a response to Barack Obama's massive government expansion and increasing taxes, supporters were smeared as a bunch of old racist white people. The same tactic has been deployed against popular social media personalities today who have built up large followings in recent years and are often smeared as members of the alt-right in attempts to derail their careers and get their accounts shut down.

Online media outlets and self-proclaimed journalists on Twitter often call conservatives Nazis and alt-right even if they're Jewish! Laura Loomer (who is Jewish) has been smeared as a member of the white nationalist "alt-right"[264] As has Trump advisor Stephen Miller, who is also Jewish.[265] And even Ben Shapiro, a devout Orthodox Jew who wears a yarmulke in every one of his public appearances, is considered to be a member of the

---

[264] Vox "Far-right protester interrupts Dorsey hearing. Auctioneer-turned-congressman drones her out." by Emily Stewart (September 5th 2018)

[265] The Jerusalem Post "Ilhan Omar Defends Calling Stephen Miller a White Nationalist" by Ron Kampeas (April 11th 2019)

alt-right by these morons.[266]　　Instead of defending conservative Jews smeared by the liberal media, Jonathan Greenblatt, the head of the Jewish ADL [Anti-Defamation League], adds fuel to the fire by saying that the words "caravan," and "open borders" are "literally white supremacist phrases."[267]

Alex Jones has been called an "alt-right" radio host by *Forbes* magazine, which you would think would be a credible publication.[268]　　YouTuber Steven Crowder was smeared by *Newsweek* as becoming popular by "touting an alt-right ideology."[269]　　And immediately after Trump won the 2016 election various outlets defamed me with the same smear, even though I had never expressed any support whatsoever for white nationalism and am just an ordinary Constitutional Conservative.　　Several publications issued retractions or removed my name from such articles after I sent them cease and desist notices.[270]

Psychology Today published an article titled, "An Analysis of Trump Supporters Has Identified 5 Key Traits," and said we have "Authoritarian Personality Syndrome, social dominance orientation, prejudice, lack

---

[266] The Hill "Shapiro rips Economist after it labels him alt-right" by Joe Concha (March 28th 2019)

[267] Council on Foreign Relations event "The Rise of Global Anti-Semitism (February 26th 2019)

[268] Forbes "Alex Jones: The Preposterous Poster Boy For Bitcoin" by Billy Bambrough (February 28th 2019)

[269] Newsweek "Steven Crowder Incites Homophobic Harassment of Voc Reporter, YouTube Slow to React" by Steven Asarch (May 31st 2019)

[270] The Guardian "Former Ku Klux Klan leader and US alt-right hail election result" by Esther Addley (November 9th 2016)

of intergroup contact (contact with minorities), and relative deprivation." [271]

Actor Rob Reiner (who played "Meathead" in the 1970s show *All in the Family*) told MSNBC that "20 to 30 percent" of Trump supporters "are hardcore racists."[272] And guests on MSNBC and CNN often declare that a huge number of Donald Trump supporters are white nationalists and only support building the wall to "keep the brown people out."[273]

Don't forget the mainstream media's vicious smears against Nick Sandmann, the high school student from Covington Catholic who was pestered by an old Native American man who beat a drum in the kid's face when he and his classmates were visiting Washington D.C. on a school trip. CNN then declared that MAGA hats "have become a potent symbol of racism."[274] Sandmann then filed lawsuits against the *Washington Post,* CNN, and NBC for $250 million dollars each for defamation.[275]

A reporter that CNN gave their "Journalist of the Year" award to was later fired in disgrace after it was

[271] Psychology Today "An Analysis of Trump Supporters Has Identified 5 Key Traits" by Bobby Azarian Ph.D (December 31st 2017)

[272] Newsbusters "Rob Reiner and Wife Liken 'Evil' Trump to Hitler, Supporters Are 'Hardcore Racists'" by Brad Wilmouth (June 24th 2018)

[273] International Journal Review "MSNBC Guest Claims That 'Everything' Trump Says Is Racist, Says POTUS 'Is a White Nationalist'" by Madison Dibble (April 28th 2019)

[274] CNN "Why Trump's MAGA hats have become a potent symbol of racism" by Issac Bailey (January 21st 2019)

[275] Fox News "Trump supporter, 76, blames 'fake news' CNN for threats following reporter ambush" by Brian Flood (February 23rd 2018)

discovered he had fabricated numerous stories including claiming he saw a "Mexicans Keep Out" sign at the city limit of a small Minnesota town when he was reporting "from Trump country."[276]

The *Daily Beast* published an article just before the 2019 Super Bowl titled, "Tom Brady's New England Patriots Are Team MAGA, Whether They Like It or Not," and declared, "Their star quarterback, coach, and owner all supported Trump," and then called them "the preferred team of white nationalists."[277]   It went on to attack quarterback Tom Brady because he was pictured previously with a MAGA hat in his locker which the *Daily Beast* says is, "a symbol of white nationalism in America."[278]

The article concluded that the Patriots "are the official team of American White Nationalism" and "When you root for the Patriots, you are associating yourself with a virulent and revolting strain of politics that seeks to Make America Great Again—which is to say, white, European, English-speaking."[279]   It also said the Covington Catholic kids are "entitled little shits being racist."

CNN is so despicable they even sent a reporter to an elderly woman's home to confront her about sharing something on Facebook that had allegedly been originally

---

[276] Washington Post "A Reporter's dispatch from Trump country featured a 'Mexicans Keep Out' sign. But he made it all up" by Antonia Noori Farzan (December 21st 2018)

[277] The Daily Beast "Tom Brady's New England Patriots Are Team MAGA, Whether They Like It or Not" by Corbin Smith (February 1st 2019)

[278] Ibid.

[279] Ibid.

posted by a Russian troll farm.[280]   She was ambushed while doing yard work in the front of her home and had a microphone stuck in her face and was accused of being a pawn of the Russians. The woman, who is 76-years-old, said after CNN aired the segment confronting her she was relentlessly harassed online and her phone rang off the hook from strangers calling her.[281]

Denial of Basic Services

An increasing number of reports keep circulating about instances where people wearing red MAGA hats have been kicked out of bars and restaurants for just wearing the hats.   After attending a Trump rally in Richmond, Virginia during the summer of 2016 a family stopped into a local Cook Out burger joint for lunch but were turned away by staff because they were wearing Trump t-shirts and hats.[282]   After a man wearing his MAGA hat was kicked out of a bar in New York City, he sued the owner for discrimination, but a judge threw out the lawsuit.[283]

A 9-year-old boy in California who is a big fan of the President wanted a Trump birthday cake, but his mother

---

[280] Real Clear Politics "CNN Reporter Confronts Trump Supporter: Your Pro-Trump Group Was Infiltrated By Russians" by Ian Schwartz (February 21st 2018)

[281] Fox News "Trump supporter, 76, blames 'fake news' CNN for threats following reporter ambush" by Brian Flood (February 23rd 2018)

[282] Fox News "'Hell No!' Cashier refuses to serve Trump backers" by Todd Starnes (June 17th 2016)

[283] The Hill "Judge rules bar was allowed to kick out Trump supporter" by Luis Sanchez (April 25th 2018)

said she couldn't find a bakery that would make one for him.[284] Gays want bakeries sued into bankruptcy if they refuse to bake a special cake for a gay "wedding" but think it's okay for them to deny service to Trump supporters.

White House Press Secretary Sarah Huckabee and her family were kicked out of a restaurant in Lexington, Virginia after the owner recognized her and made them leave.   When word of the incident spread, liberals celebrated it. *The Washington Post* even ran a headline saying, "Chasing White House officials out of restaurants is the right thing to do."[285]

Congresswoman Maxine Waters then encouraged more harassment, saying, "If you see anybody from that cabinet in a restaurant, in a department store, at a gasoline station, you get out and you create a crowd, and you push back on them, and you tell them they're not welcome anymore, anywhere."[286]   Soon after this, activist Laura Loomer confronted Maxine Waters in the halls of the Capitol on camera, asking her, "Where can a conservative eat at a restaurant in D.C.? Do you think it's civil to call for the harassment? Are we supposed to sit at the back of the bus?"[287]   Maxine scurried away to a "members only"

---

[284] Washington Times "Bakers refused to make pro-Trump birthday cake for 9-year-old boy: Report" by Bradford Richardson (August 7th 2017)

[285] Washington Post "Chasing White House officials out of restaurants is the right thing to do" by Tom Scocca (June 26th 2018)

[286] Time "'They're Not Welcome Anymore, Anywhere.' Maxine Waters Tells Supporters to Confront Trump Officials" by Jennifer Calfas (June 25th 2018)

[287] Daily Wire "WATCH: Activist Confronts Waters Publicly. Here's How Waters Responded." by Hank Berrien (June 26th 2018)

elevator in shock from getting a taste of her own medicine.

The *Boston Globe* published an op-ed that began describing how one of the writer's "biggest regrets" of his life was not pissing in political commentator Bill Kristol's food when he ate at a restaurant the writer worked at. He went on to urge people to tamper with Trump supporters' food by doing what he was afraid to do, saying members of the Trump administration "have to eat," and while the person may lose their job, (tampering with someone's food is actually a crime) "you'd be serving America," he said. "And you won't have any regrets years later."[288]

The *Boston Globe* actually published this filth, but after a growing backlash changed parts of the op-ed and added a note saying, "A version of this column as originally published did not meet Globe standards and has been changed. The *Globe* regrets the previous tone of the piece."[289] Even with the alterations, the title was, "Keep Kirstjen Nielsen unemployed and eating Grubhub over her kitchen sink," and the overall message of the piece was still that people should run members of the Trump administration out of any restaurant they're seen in. After growing shock and outrage that a major paper would publish such garbage, the *Globe* later deleted the article.[290]

---

[288] RedState "Toxic Masculinity: 'Journalist' Writes Boston Globe Column Urging Waiters to Pee, Bleed On Kirstjen Nielsen's Food" by Sister Toldjah (April 10th 2019)

[289] Boston Globe "Keep Kirstjen Nielsen unemployed and eating Grubhub over her kitchen sink" by Luke O'Neil" (April 10th 2019)

[290] The Washington Times "A column suggested waiters could 'tamper' with Trump officials' food. Amid backlash, the Boston Globe pulled it" by Allyson Chiu (April 12th 2019)

The Left Encouraging Violence

In the Trump era political rhetoric from the Left has sunk to levels never before seen in modern American history. Not only are they insistent on smearing all Trump supporters as racists, but they are encouraging people to physically attack anyone seen wearing a MAGA hat in public.

During the 2016 election season many peaceful Trump supporters were assaulted as they were leaving events by rabid protesters who had gathered outside. At a San Jose rally one woman was pelted with eggs and water balloons by an angry mob and others were punched and hit with bottles as they left.[291]

After a 16-year-old Trump supporter was assaulted in a Whataburger fast food joint by having a drink thrown on him and had his MAGA stolen, CNN's Marc Lamont Hill said, "I actually don't advocate throwing drinks on people. Not at all. But yes, I think MAGA hats (deliberately) reflect a movement that conjures racism, homophobia, xenophobia, etc. So yes, it's a little harder to feel sympathy when someone gets Coca Cola thrown on him."[292] Vox's Carlos Maza encouraged assaulting right-wing figures as well, and hopes to make them "dread" being in public.[293]

Breitbart News compiled a list of violent acts against Trump supporters and detailed mainstream media reporters and pundits who approved of them and counted

[291] NBC News "Protesters Assault Trump Supporters With Eggs, Bottles, Punches After Rally" by Jacob Rascon and Ali Vitali (June 3rd 2016)

[292] https://twitter.com/marclamonthill/status/1014904101988167685

[293] https://twitter.com/gaywonk/status/1130862813713502210

639 incidents between September 2015 and November 2018.[294]

Just wearing a red MAGA hat in public can put you in danger of getting assaulted by some random lunatic who happens to see it. An MSNBC host even said wearing one is "an invitation for confrontation" and considers them "the modern day version of the Confederate battle flag."[295] The *Huffington Post* reported that, "Searching for MAGA symbolism is one of the easiest ways to notice online extremists and members of hate groups."[296] CNN's Angela Rye said that MAGA hats are "just as maddening and frustrating and triggering for me to look at as a KKK hood."[297]

An 81-year-old man in New Jersey was attacked inside a grocery store by a 19-year-old teen because the old man was wearing a Make America Great Again Hat.[298] A couple shopping at a Sam's Club in Kentucky had a gun pulled on them by a man who got triggered

---

[294] Breitbart "Rap Sheet: ***639*** Acts of Media-Approved Violence and Harassment Against Trump Supporters" by John Nolte (July 5th 2018)

[295] Washington Times "MSNBC host, Princeton professor discuss MAGA hats as an 'invitation' to confrontation" by Douglas Ernst (January 23rd 2019)

[296] HuffPost "How Far-Right Extremists Abroad Have Adopted Trump's Symbols As Their Own" by Nick Robins-Early (April 6th 2019)

[297] Washington Free Beacon "CNN Commentator Angela Rye Compares MAGA Hat to KKK Hood: I'm 'So Triggered' by the 'Hatred' It Represents" by Nic Rowan (January 22nd 2019)

[298] NBC New York "Teen Arrested for Attack on 81-Year-Old Man Wearing MAGA Hat: Prosecutors" (February 27th 2019)

after seeing their MAGA hats.[299]   A man eating at a restaurant in Massachusetts was assaulted by a woman who spotted him wearing the hat. She was arrested for assault and it turns out was an illegal alien, so a few days after her initial arrest, she was arrested again by ICE.[300] A legal immigrant from Africa living in Maryland was beat down by two other black men because he was spotted walking down the street wearing a MAGA hat.[301]

A group of five Asians walking down the street in Washington D.C., all wearing MAGA hats, were harassed by two black men who videotaped themselves stealing two of the hats and posted the video on Twitter to brag about what they had done. The group happened to be North Korean defectors who had escaped the country and proudly wore their MAGA hats because President Trump was making progress facilitating peace between the North and the South.[302]

A young woman wearing a red hat reading "Make Bitcoin Great Again" in the style of the MAGA hat was pepper sprayed right in the face by a member of Antifa while she was in the middle of doing a television interview on the campus of UC Berkeley during an event at the school.[303]

---

[299] WTSP "Man accused of pulling gun on couple wearing MAGA hats at Sam's Club" by 10News Staff (February 18th 2019)

[300] CBS Boston "Woman Charged With Attacking Falmouth Man Wearing MAGA Hat Taken Into ICE Custody" (February 26th 2019)

[301] New York Post "Men accused of beating, robbing African immigrant because of MAGA hat" by Max Jaeger (April 17th 2019)

[302] Washington Times "North Korean defectors wearing MAGA hats harassed in D.C." by Jessica Chasmar (May 6th 2019)

[303] ABC7 News "VIDEO: Trump supporter pepper sprayed at Milo protest" by Wayne Freedman (February 1st 2017)

A man in the back of a pickup truck leaving a Trump rally in Arizona was sucker punched in the head by a protester as the truck pulled away.[304] A customer eating at a Cheesecake Factory in Miami was harassed and threatened by several employees of the restaurant because he was wearing a MAGA hat.[305]

When Hillary Clinton was asked about civility returning to America, she endorsed the growing angry mobs saying, "You cannot be civil with a political party that wants to destroy what you stand for, what you care about. That's why I believe, if we are fortunate enough to win back the House and or the Senate [in the 2018 midterms], that's when civility can start again."[306]

Barack Obama's former attorney general Eric Holder went even further saying, "Michelle [Obama] always says, you know, 'When they go low, we go high.' No. When they go low, we kick them! That's what this new Democratic Party is about."[307]

Two days after the 2018 midterm election a fascist mob gathered right outside the home of Fox News host Tucker Carlson and with a bullhorn shouted, "Tonight you are reminded that the people have a voice. Tonight, we remind you that you are not safe," adding, "We know

[304] Mediaite "Black Trump Supporter Punched While Fleeing Arizona Melee" by Aidan McLaughlin (August 23rd 2017)

[305] USA Today "Cheesecake Factory apologizes to black man reportedly harassed for wearing Trump cap" by Eli Blumenthal (May 15th 2018)

[306] USA Today "Hillary Clinton: You 'cannot be civil' with Republicans, Democrats need to be 'tougher'" by William Cummings (October 9th 2018)

[307] Washington Post "Eric Holder: 'When they go low, we kick them. That's what this new Democratic Party is about.'" by Aaron Blake (October 10th 2018)

where you sleep at night."[308]   Facebook didn't even suspend the Antifa page that organized the event.[309]

The *Huffington Post* published an op-ed calling for violent resistance against Trump and denounced those on the Left who were saying violence isn't the answer. It's titled "Sorry Liberals, A Violent Response To Trump Is As Logical As Any," and starts off saying "there's an inherent value in forestalling Trump's normalization. Violent resistance accomplishes this."[310]

It went on to say, "Assuming anti-Trump protests should be strictly focused on electoral politics and not these broader goals would be a detrimental oversight. Understanding European anti-fascists' use of violent tactics to shut down large rallies from White Supremacists can be illustrative here. Because while Trump isn't leading full bore White Supremacist rallies, there is value in making it clear that even his fascism-lite has no place in civilized society."[311]

The liberal media has been engaging in what's called stochastic terrorism, which is when the widespread demonization of an individual or a group incites lone wolf political extremists or members of an extremist group to attack them in what appears to be a random act of violence but was actually inspired by inflammatory

---

[308] The Hill "Activists converge on home of Fox's Tucker Carlson: 'You are not safe'" by Joe Concha (November 8th 2018)

[309] Townhall "Chilling Details: Tucker Carlson's Terrified Wife Hid in the Pantry As Antifa Thugs Damaged Her Home" by Guy Benson (November 8th 2018)

[310] Huffington Post "Sorry Liberals, A Violent Response To Trump Is As Logical As Any" by Jesse Benn (June 6th 2016)

[311] Ibid.

rhetoric being aimed at that individual or the group they belong to.

In April 2019 the CBS show *The Good Fight* posted a teaser video on their official Twitter account showing one of the main characters engaging in a diatribe about how "some speech" deserves "enforcement" and that "It's time" to physically attack American citizens "unprovoked" who are engaging in speech that social justice warriors perceive as "racist."[312]

Anti-White Racism

Part of the war on Trump supporters involves painting a large percentage of white people as racists in hopes of preventing more blacks and latinos from joining the Trump train. The *Liberal Media Industrial Complex* now regularly paints white people as the enemy, blaming "systemic racism" for the problems in black communities, and depicts anyone who wants to stop the flood of illegal aliens into America as members of the KKK.

While Martin Luther King wanted everyone to judge their fellow man by the content of their character—not the color of their skin, the Liberal Establishment uses identity politics to pit the different races against each other and are trying to create a culture where white people should be ashamed of being white and atone for their "white privilege" by paying reparations to black people and giving blacks special perks in America just because of their race.

Online outlets like Salon.com and BuzzFeed are notorious for their anti-white articles. Salon has posted

---

[312] RedState "Is CBS Inciting Violence In The Latest Episode Of 'The Good Fight'" by Jennifer Van Laar (April 13th 2019)

articles titled, "White men must be stopped; The very future of mankind depends on it,"[313] "10 ways white people are more racist than they realize,"[314] and "White guys are killing us: Toxic, cowardly masculinity, our unhealable national illness,"[315] just to name a few.

One of BuzzFeed's racist articles links to various Power Point presentations with titles like "White People Are a Plague to the Planet," and "White People are Crazy."[316] They've also published articles titled "17 Foods That White People Have Ruined," "17 Deplorable Examples of White Privilege," and "22 Reasons Why Straight White Boys Are Actually The Worst."

Vice News calls whiteness "toxic"[317] and black publications like *The Root* regularly attack white people as "useless."[318] MTV did a whole documentary titled "White People" that depicts the entire race as a group whose very existence is based on oppressing black people and other "people of color."[319]

---

313 Salon.com "White men must be stopped: The very future of mankind depends on it" by Frank Joyce (December 22nd 2015)

314 Salon.com "10 ways white people are more racist than they realize" by Kali Holloway (March 5th 2015)

315 Salon "White guys are killing us: Toxic, cowardly masculinity, our unhealable national illness" by Chauncey Devega (December 17th 2015)

316 BuzzFeed "19 School Powerpoint Presentations That Give Zero Fucks" by Hattie Soykan and Rachael Krishna (December 5th 2016)

317 Vice "Want to Heal Yourself from 'Toxic Whiteness'? This Class Can Help" by Shahirah Majumdar (October 15th 2016)

318 The Root "Polite White People Are Useless" by Damon Young (August 29th 2017)

319 The Independent "MTV's White People documentary succeeds in making viewers 'uncomfortable'" by Emily Shackleton (July 23rd 2015)

Hollywood constantly complains about white people with campaigns like the "Oscars are too white" and always cries about how there isn't enough "diversity" in leading roles.   When hosting *Saturday Night Live* to promote his new movie *Django Unchained*, actor Jamie Foxx bragged, "I kill all the white people in the movie! How great is that!?"[320]

Rapper Jay-Z has been photographed at an NBA game wearing a medallion from the 5% Nation, a black power group that believes white people are the Devil.[321]   Many rappers admire Nation of Islam leader Louis Farrakhan who has taught that white people are "the Devil" and "deserve to die."[322]

CNN's Don Lemon says the biggest terrorist threat in America are white men.[323] The network also claims that, "The Internet is radicalizing white men" and urges Big Tech to censor YouTube videos and change the algorithms even more to hide certain ideas on the Internet.[324] CNN contributors and other cable news pundits go so far as to say blacks can't be racist and justify their racism against white people as "payback" for slavery in the 1800s. Just pointing out anti-white racism is enough for the *Liberal*

---

[320] Ebony "Jamie Foxx Defends 'I Kill All the White People' Joke" by The Grio (December 14th 2012)

[321] New York Post "Jay Z's bling from 'whites are devils' group" by Gary Buiso (April 6th 2014)

[322] The Daily Caller "Seven Louis Farrakhan Quotes on Jews, Gays, and White People" by Peter Hasson (January 26th 2018)

[323] The Washington Post "CNN's Don Lemon doubles down after saying white men are 'the biggest terror threat in this country'" by LIndsey Bever (November 1st 2018)

[324] CNN "The internet is radicalizing white men. Big tech could be doing more" by Alex Koppelman (March 17th 2019)

Media Industrial Complex to label you a "white supremacist," so most people are afraid to talk about it.

Demonizing Black Conservatives

While it appears that black people can do no wrong in the eyes of liberals and that all their shortcomings, bad decisions, and crimes are the fault of white people; there is one thing that black people aren't allowed to do in America today without severe criticism and backlash—and that's be conservative.

Black conservatives like Larry Elder, David Webb, Sheriff David Clark, Pastor Daryl Scott, Ben Carson, and others are constantly smeared by the media as "traitors" to their race, or "uncle Toms" and "house niggers" who have sold out to white people.

After Diamond and Silk appeared at CPAC 2019, CNN's Oliver Darcey insinuated they were "grifters," meaning con artists.[325] Rolling Stone magazine called Candace Owens an "Alt-Right Provocateur" once she became a star.[326] After posting a few YouTube videos about being a black conservative she was thrust into the spotlight when Kanye West tweeted about her, jumpstarting her career and turning her into one of the most popular young black conservative women in the country.

When Candace spoke at a college in Utah, protesters gathered outside, which is common at her events, but this time they had a huge banner that read "End White

---

[325] https://twitter.com/oliverdarcy/status/1102248695989325825

[326] Rolling Stone "Kanye West Distances Himself From Alt-Right Provocateur" by Brendan Klinkenberg (October 30th 2018)

Supremacy."[327]   When visiting Philadelphia in August 2018 a group of protesters surrounded the cafe she was eating breakfast at and shouted with a megaphone "fuck white supremacy."[328]

Georgetown University professor and regular MSNBC guest Michael Eric Dyson attacked Kanye West after he met with President Trump in the Oval Office (while wearing his MAGA hat), saying, "This is white supremacy by ventriloquism. A black mouth is moving, but white racist ideals are flowing from Kanye West's mouth."[329] He went on to say "Kanye West is engaging in one of the most nefarious practices yet. A black body and brain are the warehouse for the articulation and expression of anti-black sentiment."[330]

The Southern Poverty Law Center actually included the mild-mannered and meek Ben Carson on their "Extremist Watch List," citing a line in his book *America the Beautiful* where he affirmed that marriage is between a man and a woman and said Leftists are pushing the United States down the same path that led to the fall of the Roman Empire.[331]   They labeled *Ben Carson* an extremist!

---

[327] Breitbart "Utah Valley University Students Protest Candace Owens with 'End White Supremacy' Sign" by Alana Mastrangelo (March 7th 2019)

[328] Front Page Magazine "Antifa, The Real Fascists" by Matthew Vadum (August 10th 2018)

[329] Newsbusters "Dyson Slams Kanye West Speech as 'White Supremacy by Ventriloquism'" by Brad Wilmouth (October 11th 2018)

[330] Ibid.

[331] Washington Times "Slippery Slope with a Disastrous Ending, as Witnessed in the Dramatic Fall of the Roman Empire" by Jessica Chasmar (February 8th 2015)

Hollywood actress and singer Bette Midler claimed that President Trump was paying black people to come to his rallies after she kept noticing them in attendance. She said they were just props for the background.[332] Liberals don't want diversity of thought, they want everyone to be lockstep in line with the core tenants of the radical liberal agenda and many of their supporters are so dumb that they believe there are *black* white supremacists in America today, and have no clue how insane they sound.

They are afraid that if 20% of black voters leave the Democrat Party and become Republicans, that would be enough to tip the scales in favor of Republicans in elections for years to come and the Democrat Party's political power would be gravely diminished.[333]

---

[332] Los Angeles Times "Bette Midler slammed as racist for tweet about black Trump supporters" by Christie D'Zurilla (July 25th 2019)

[333] RealClearPolitics "Could Trump Win 20 Percent of the African-American Vote in 2020?" by Victor Davis Hanson (October 18th 2018)

The War on Families

Families instill moral values, carry on important cultural traditions, and provide a support network when someone goes through an emotionally or financially difficult time. And when someone is engaging in self-destructive or unscrupulous behaviors, those close to them can often see the warning signs and intervene to help get them back on track. But the Left doesn't want families to raise, teach, or protect children. They want the government to do it, along with help from the high priests of Hollywood who are held up as the moral leaders of America.

Joshua Meyrowitz, Professor of Media Studies at the University of New Hampshire, points out, "Television dilutes the innocence of childhood and the authority of adults by undermining the system of information control that supported them. Television bypasses the year-by-year slices of knowledge given to children. It presents the same general experiences to adults and to children of all ages. Children may not understand everything that they see on television, but they are exposed to many aspects of adult life from which their parents (and traditional children's books) would have once shielded them."[334]

---

[334] Questioning the Media -Mediating Communication - What Happens? by Joshua Meyrowitz page 43

He continues, "Television and its visitors take children across the globe before parents even give them permission to cross the street."[335] He said that back in 1995, when the Internet was just in its infancy, and more than a decade before social media would gain a stranglehold on an entire generation of children who access an abyss of adult content, completely unsupervised, through their own smartphones while alone in their bedrooms.

The Left's war on families is targeting the most vulnerable of our society—children. They are determined to raise the next generation to be as perverted as possible —worse than ancient Rome where it was socially acceptable for adult men to engage in sexual activity with young boys.[336] In fact we're seeing child drag queens like "Desmond is Amazing" and "Lactacia" being celebrated and featured on major television shows as if they're heroes.

NBC's *Today Show* promoted "Desmond is Amazing," the "drag kid" when he was just 10-years-old, calling him "inspiring."[337] His parents dress him up in drag and have him perform at drag queen festivals across the country.[338]

---

[335] Questioning the Media -Mediating Communication - What Happens? by Joshua Meyrowitz page 44

[336] The Independent "A Brief Cultural History of Sex" (September 23rd 2008)

[337] NBC News "Meet the 10-year-old 'drag kid' taking over social media with inspiring message" by June 18th 2018)

[338] Newsbusters "Morning Child Abuse. 'Today' Features 10-Year-Old Drag Queen" by Rachel Peterson (June 18th 2018)

He also does simulated strip teases on stage (including at gay bars) where grown men throw dollar bills at him.[339]

ABC's *Good Morning America* also promotes child drag queens, and host Michael Strahan introduced a segment saying, "Get ready for this trailblazing 11-year-old drag kid who RuPaul is calling the future, and his bravery is inspiring so many." The kid (Desmond is Amazing) then came out on stage dancing like a stripper to hoots and hollers from the audience.[340]

Good Morning America glowingly promoted Kate Hudson when reports circulated she was allegedly raising her child "genderless." Anchor George Stephanopoulos began the segment saying, "Kate Hudson is opening up about how she's trying to raise her new baby as 'genderless,' apparently that's an approach more and more Americans are trying."[341] Co-host Paula Faris went on to say the actress will be raising her 3-month-old daughter "without labels or restrictions" because "she doesn't want to assume how she'll identify herself as she's growing up."[342]

Another co-host, Lara Spencer, chimed in, saying, "That's a great conversation. It's just a great conversation," and then (lesbian) Robin Roberts

[339] The Daily Wire "11-Year-Old Boy Dressed In Drag Dances At Gay Bar, Gets Dollar Bills Thrown At Him" by Amanda Prestigiacomo (December 17th 2018)

[340] Good Morning America's YouTube channel "The 11-year-old trailblazing drag kid 'Desmond is Amazing'" (November 2nd 2018)

[341] Newsbusters "GMA: 'Genderless Babies' Is 'Healthy,' Part of 'Great Conversation'" by Gabriel Hays (January 24th 2019)

[342] Ibid.

concluded, "No judgment, no judgment. Whatever you feel is best for your child."[343]

Kate Hudson then released a statement on her Instagram saying, "Dear all my friends, fans and others who read this, recently someone asked me something along the lines of, if having and raising a girl is different from boys. My response was simple. Not really. This whole clickbait tactic of saying I'm raising my daughter to be 'genderless' is silly and frankly doesn't even make sense."[344]

Fringe lunatics had been promoting the idea of raising children "genderless" for some time, and so the media saw an opportunity to give the bizarre practice a boost by attaching a celebrity's name to it by twisting around what Kate Hudson meant. But there will come a day when major celebrities embrace the "gender neutral" agenda, and they will be hailed as heroes and held up as models for what other parents should do.

The media is increasingly glorifying "theybies," meaning children whose parents are raising them as gender neutral.[345] These child abusers call their kids "theybies" instead of babies, because they use the gender neutral pronoun "they" to refer to their kids instead of "he" or "she." *NBC News* recently recommended, "One way of shielding children from gender stereotypes: Keep their biological sex secret."[346]

---

[343] Ibid.

[344] https://www.instagram.com/p/BtL8p9FAtZF/

[345] NBC News "'Boy or girl?' Parents raising 'theybies' let kids decide" by Julie Compton (July 19th 2018)

[346] Ibid.

The radical Leftists don't want boys raised as boys, or girls as girls. They want all children to be raised as if there's no biological difference between males and females at all. They want to completely deconstruct the traditional gender roles and deny the inherent differences between the sexes. They want to invert and pervert everything that's normal including the most fundamental aspects of being human.

Every facet of the family and interpersonal relationships is under attack. CNN has even urged people to "rethink" monogamous relationships and become swingers. "Could opening your relationship to others benefit you and your partner?" they asked.[347] According to CNN, a man's wife banging other dudes "can be a healthy option for some couples and, executed thoughtfully, can inject relationships with some much-needed novelty and excitement."

The report quotes several "sex therapists" who recommend the practice, saying it "can bring back some of the initial novelty and excitement you felt at the beginning of your relationship."[348] CNN is disappointed that "non-monogamy still carries a stigma in many circles, so think about how you and your partner will address that concern."[349]

Eradicating families is a Communist tactic and as soon as they seized power in Russia in 1917 the new government started shunning families and promoting "free unions" because families raising children were said

---

347 CNN "Rethinking Monogamy Today" by Ian Kerner (April 12th 2017)

348 Ibid.

349 Ibid.

to be extensions of the old system.[350]   The Left wants everyone to be loyal first and foremost to the Party, not to their family. So they're doing everything they can to rip them apart.

In January 2018, CNN published a story advocating cuckolding as a way to "help" couple's relationships. For those who aren't familiar with "cuckolding," it's a term that originally referred to a man whose partner had been unfaithful, but has morphed into a kink fantasy that some strange couples carry out where the man watches another guy have sex with his wife or girlfriend. CNN cited a "study" by anti-Christian gay extremist Dan Savage and several others which claims that, "acting on cuckolding fantasies can be a largely positive experience for many couples."[351]

To be clear, this isn't about swinging, an open relationship, or threesomes; it's about men watching their wives have sex with another man, and CNN portrays the practice in glowing terms, and says, "Acting on adulterous fantasies may strengthen a relationship, as counterintuitive as it may sound."[352]

People are becoming so inept at how to engage in normal and healthy relationships with others that loneliness is plaguing the younger generations who rely on hook-up apps like Tinder to meet people instead of the "old fashioned way" like at school, parties, through

---

[350] The Epoch Times "The Failed Soviet Experiment With 'Free Love'" by Petr Svab (October 5th 2018)

[351] CNN "Cuckolding can be positive for some couples, study says" by Ian Kerner (January 25th 2018)

[352] Ibid.

mutual friends, or while engaging in their hobbies.[353] Their communication skills are often so poor that many don't even have the guts to break up with someone when they feel they're not compatible, so instead they engage in "ghosting" which means they just abruptly stop returning their calls or texts.[354] More than half of adults aged 18 to 34 don't have a steady romantic partner.[355]

And recently birthrates in the United States have fallen to a 32-year low.[356] For teenagers today it is now considered "normal" to be in a virtual "relationship" with someone online for months and even years and never even meet them face to face![357] Many Millennials don't even have a best friend or anyone they feel they can confide in.[358]

To fill the void created from lack of intimacy in people's lives, some are turning to unthinkably bizarre alternatives. The disturbing rise in popularity and

[353] NBC News "Despite social media, Generation Z, Millennials report feeling lonely" by Sharon Jayson and Kaiser Health News (March 8th 2019)

[354] The Independent "Millennial Dating Trends 2019: All You Need to Know, From Ghosting to Bird Boxing" by Oliva Petter and Sarah Young (February 7th 2019)

[355] SFGate "It's not just you: New data shows more than half of young people in America don't have a romantic partner" via The Washington Post by Lisa Bronos and Emily Guskin (March 21st 2019)

[356] NPR "U.S. Births Fell To A 32-Year Low In 2018; CDC Says Birthrate Is In Record Slump" by Bill Chappell (May 15th 2019)

[357] Wall Street Journal "For Teens, Romances Where the Couple Never Meets Are Now Normal" by Christopher Mims (May 18th 2019)

[358] New York Daily News "More than 20% of millennials claim to have no friends, poll finds" by Tim Balk (August 3rd 2019)

acceptance of sex bots, which are just high tech blow up dolls that people are having sex with, seems like something out of a horror movie, but it's actually happening.[359] While blow up dolls are a common gag gift brought along to bachelor parties, no normal person has ever considered actually having sex with one, but recently expensive "life-like" sex bots are being manufactured and sold to lonely losers who resort to having sex with them since their lives are so dysfunctional they can't get a date with an actual woman.[360]

The sex bot business is already a multi-million dollar a year industry and growing. Companies are even working to build models that incorporate artificial intelligence so they can have conversations with people.[361]

Google Upset About Families

In leaked documents detailing internal discussions of Google employees, one thread shows the use of the word "family" upset a bunch of them who felt it was homophobic and not inclusive enough because of its connotation as referring to a heterosexual couple with children. After one employee walked out of a company presentation over the use of the word "family," they

---

[359] The Telegraph "Sex robots on way for elderly and lonely...but pleasure-bots have a dark side, warn experts" by Sarah Knapton (July 5th 2017)

[360] Forbes "Goodbye Loneliness, Hello Sexbots! How Can Robots Transform Human Sex?" by Reenita Das (July 17th 2017)

[361] Daily Mail "March of the sexbots: They talk, they make jokes, have 'customisable' breasts - the sex robot is no longer a weird fantasy but a troubling reality" by Caroline Graham (October 29th 2017)

posted on an internal message board venting their frustration.[362]

"This is a diminishing and disrespectful way to speak. If you mean 'children,' say 'children'; we have a perfectly good word for it. 'Family friendly' used as a synonym for 'kid friendly' means, to me, 'you and yours don't count as a family unless you have children.' And while kids may often be less aware of it, there are kids without families too, you know."[363]

The complaint went on, "The use of 'family' as a synonym for 'with children' has a long-standing association with deeply homophobic organizations. This does not mean we should not use the word 'family' to refer to families, but it mean we must doggedly insist that family does not imply children...Use the word 'family' to mean a loving assemblage of people who may or may not live together and may or may not include people of any particular age. STOP using it to mean 'children.' It's offensive, inappropriate, homophobic, and wrong."[364]

It wasn't just one lone nut who got triggered because the presentation mentioned Google is trying to make "family friendly" apps and services. The documents show that about 100 other Google employees thumbed up the post, and many responses echoed the same psychotic sentiment.

"Thanks for writing this. So much yes," replied one. "Using the word 'family' in this sense bothers me too," said another. Adding, "It smacks of the 'family values'

---

[362] Daily Caller "'Disrespectful': Google Employees Melt Down Over the Word 'Family'" by Peter Hasson (January 16th 2019)

[363] Ibid.

[364] Ibid.

agenda by the right wing, which is absolutely homophobic by its very definition," and continued, "it's important that we fix our charged language when we become aware of how exclusionary it actually is. As a straight person in a relationship, I find the term 'family' offensive because it excludes me and my boyfriend, having no children of our own."[365]

The replies go on and on, all chastising Google for using the word "family." Another says, "My family consists of me and several other trans feminine folks, some of whom I'm dating. We're all supportive of each other and eventually aspire to live together. Just because we aren't a heterosexual couple with 2.5 kids, a white picket fence, and a dog doesn't mean we're not a family."[366]

Google's Vice President, Pavni Diwanji, then responded saying, "Hi everyone, I realize what we said at TGIF [the name of the event] might have caused concerns in the way we talked about families. There are families without kids too, and also we needed to be more conscientious about the fact that there is a diverse makeup of parents and families."[367]

He continued, "Please help us get to a better state. Teach us how to talk about it in inclusive way, if you feel like we are not doing it well. As a team we have very inclusive culture, and want to do right in this area. I am adding my team here so we can have open conversation."[368]

---

[365] Ibid

[366] Ibid

[367] Ibid

[368] Ibid

Celebrating Unwed Mothers

When the number of unwed mothers in America reached more than 50% in 2012, the feminist blog Jezebel celebrated the "milestone" with a headline reading, "The Increase in Single Moms Is Actually a Good Thing," because the increase in single mothers means fewer women are "relying" on men economically, and feminists view more single moms as a sign of female empowerment.

The writer was upset that experts (and ordinary people) were concerned about the growing trend since children born out of wedlock "face greater social and economic obstacles than their peers born into traditional nuclear families."[369] Liberals never want to hear about the effects of their disastrous decisions, but there's one thing they like more than single mothers, and that's women who never become mothers at all.

A report from CNBC declared, "Your friends may tell you having kids has made them happier. They're probably lying." It went on to say, "Research shows that parenthood leads to a happiness gap. Maybe that's because the pleasures of parenthood are outweighed by all the extra responsibilities, housework and, of course, the costs."[370]

The article then broke down the average costs per month of having a child and calculated how much it adds up to by the time the kid is eighteen-years-old in attempts to dissuade people from having children.

---

[369] Jezebel "The Increase in Single Moms Is Actually a Good Thing" by Hugo Schwyzer (February 22nd 2012)

[370] CNBC "You can save half a million dollars if you don't have kids" by Yoni Blumberg (August 17th 2017)

On her short-lived Netflix show, comedian Michelle Wolf (the woman who looks like Carrot Top that performed at the White House Correspondents Dinner in 2018) did a segment titled "Salute to Abortions" which included a marching band coming out on stage where she then began to rant, "It doesn't have to be a big deal, it's actually a great deal! It's about $300 dollars. That's like six movie tickets." She ended her speech saying "God bless abortions, and God bless America!"[371]

In the Hulu series *Shrill*, the lead character (Aidy Bryant) got pregnant and decided to have an abortion "before it becomes illegal," and after killing the baby she tells her roommate she's glad she "got out of a huge fucking mess" and now, "I feel very fucking powerful right now. And I just feel like I need to go out [and party]."[372]

A YouTube channel called "HiHo Kids" which features videos of young children meeting drag queens, transgender people, a gynecologist, and other individuals no child should be subjected to, even produced a video titled "Kids Meet Someone Who's Had an Abortion" where the woman tells the children about how happy she was to do it, and that it was "part of God's plan."[373]

Alabama State Representative John Rogers made a startling declaration during a debate about a proposed state law that would ban most abortions unless the fetus had a "lethal anomaly" or if the pregnancy would put the

[371] Netflix "The Break with Michelle Wolf" (June 2018)

[372] Newsbusters "Hulu Character Feels 'Really, Really Good,' 'Very F**king Powerful' After Abortion" by Rebecca Downs (March 18th 2019)

[373] KTSA "Kids Meet Someone Who's Had An Abortion" by Jack Riccardi (January 4th 2019)

mother's life at risk, saying, "Some kids are unwanted, so you kill them now or you kill them later. You bring them in the world unwanted, unloved, [and then] you send them to the electric chair. So, you kill them now or you kill them later."[374]   He wasn't being sarcastic, he supports abortion and was arguing against the bill.[375]

"Kids Cause Global Warming"

Perhaps one reason liberals are big supporters of abortion is because children are increasingly being blamed for causing global warming.   The London *Guardian* declared, "The greatest impact individuals can have in fighting climate change is to have one fewer child, according to a new study that identifies the most effective ways people can cut their carbon emissions."[376]

One of the researchers on the project said, "I don't have children, but it is a choice I am considering and discussing with my fiancé.   Because we care so much about climate change that will certainly be one factor we consider in the decision, but it won't be the only one."[377]

Other lunatics are so concerned that planet earth is doomed they're afraid to have children because they don't want to bring them into the world if it's going to soon

---

374 Real Clear Politics "Alabama State Dem Rep. Defends Abortion: 'You Kill Them Now Or You Kill Them Later'" by Ian Schwartz (May 2nd 2019)

375 CNN "Alabama lawmaker sparks backlash for 'kill them now or kill them later' comments over state abortion bill" by Veronica Stracqualursi (May 2nd 2019)

376 The Guardian "Want to fight climate change? Have fewer children" by Damian Carrington (July 12th 2017)

377 Ibid.

plunge into chaos like a science fiction movie. The *New York Times* interviewed a 32-year-old woman in a story about this madness who said, "I don't want to give birth to a kid wondering if it's going to live in some kind of 'Mad Max' dystopia."[378]

"Animals are disappearing. The oceans are full of plastic. The human population is so numerous, the planet may not be able to support it indefinitely. This doesn't paint a very pretty picture for people bringing home a brand-new baby from the hospital," said another.[379]

Others see it as a "sacrifice" they have to make to save the planet. One woman who wanted to have kids but decided not to, said "it's hard for me to justify my wants over what matters and what's important for everyone."[380] Alexandria Ocasio-Cortez even said that it's a "legitimate question" for Millennials and those in Generation Z to ask, "Is it OK to still have children?" because global warming is supposedly going to make their lives miserable.[381]

The LGBT Mafia

Every time a social media personality, actor, singer, or sports figure "comes out" as gay, liberal media outlets across the Internet all celebrate them as if they've accomplished some incredible achievement. President

---

[378] New York Times "No Children Because of Climate Change? Some People Are Considering It" by Maggie Astor (February 5th 2018)

[379] Ibid.

[380] Ibid.

[381] Fox 5 DC "Rep. Alexandria Ocasio-Cortez: 'Is it OK to still have children?'" by Fox News (February 26th 2019)

Obama made a habit of calling and "congratulating" professional athletes who decided to come out as gay.[382] When the Supreme Court ruled that gay "marriage" was legal in all fifty states, Obama had the White House lit up in rainbow colors that night to celebrate.[383]

The media is also on a mission to ruin the careers of any celebrity who dares voice opposition to gay "marriage" or gay adoption.[384] HGTV famously canceled a television show of the Benham Brothers (not to be confused with the "Property Brothers," who have a show on the network) after news reports started surfacing that the Benhams were Christians and didn't support gay "marriage."[385]

Comedian Kevin Hart was scheduled to host the 2019 Oscars until LGBT activists started spreading around one of his old bits about him not wanting his son to grow up to be gay.[386] In 2014 Mozilla CEO Brendan Eich, the creator of the popular Firefox web browser, was forced to resign after LGBT activists discovered that he had donated $1000 of his own money to support Proposition 8 in California which amended the state's constitution to define marriage as specifically between a man and a

[382] CNN "Obama congratulates Michael Sam, first openly gay player drafted by NFL" by Chelsea J. Carter and Ralph Ellis (May 11th 2014)

[383] CNN "White House shines rainbow colors to hail same-sex marriage ruling" by Allie Malloy and Karl de Vries (June 30th 2015)

[384] CNN "Benham brothers lose HGTV show after 'anti-gay' remarks" by Lisa Respers (May 9th 2014)

[385] Hollywood Reporter "Benham Brothers, Dumped by HGTV Over Anti-Gay Remarks, Could Land at 'Traditional Values' Network INSP TV" by Paul Bond (May 12th 2014)

[386] The New Yorker "Why Kevin Hart Had to Go as Oscars Host" by Michael Schulman (December 7th 2018)

woman.[387]   A gay man once filed a $70 million dollar lawsuit against a popular Bible publisher claiming that the anti-gay verses caused him "emotional distress."[388]

Kids in California, Colorado, New Jersey, and Illinois schools are now being forced to learn about "LGBT History Month" and are being taught about the "amazing contributions" LGBT people have made to the country.[389] In the UK, school children are being taught that "all genders" can have periods, not just women, and schools started adding tampon dispensers in the boys bathrooms.[390]

Since "Drag Queen Story Hour" is being held at an increasing number of public libraries across the country (where insane parents bring their small children to have drag queens read stories to them about being gay or transgender) the city council in Lafayette City-Parish, Louisiana held a meeting after many (normal) parents were outraged the event was being held in their community.

During the meeting a gay man took to the podium to support the event, saying, "I'm here to let you know that this event is something that's going to be very beautiful and for the children and the people that support it are

[387] Washington Examiner "Mozilla CEO Brendan Eich forced to resign for supporting traditional marriage laws" by Joel Gehrke (April 3rd 2017)

[388] Christian Post "Gay Man Files $70M Suit Against Bible Publishers Over 'Homosexual' Verses" by Elena Garcia (July 10th 2008)

[389] US News and World Report "These States Require Schools to Teach LGBT History" by Casey Leins (August 14th 2019)

[390] Telegraph "Boys can have periods too, children to be taught in latest victory for transgender campaigners" by Helena Horton (December 16th 2018)

going to realize that this is going to be the grooming of the next generation."[391]   Others in the meeting gasped since the term "grooming children" refers to a sexual predator attempting to persuade a child into a sexual relationship over time.[392]

One drag queen who read to children at the Houston Public Library's "Drag Queen Storytime" is a registered sex offender who had previously been convicted of aggravated sexual assault against an 8-year-old child.[393] The library failed to do background checks on the drag queens who were given access to the children and the sex offender had only been exposed after a conservative activist organization MassResistance took it upon themselves to investigate the drag queens who were reading to the kids at the events.[394]   Another drag queen reading to children at a library actually taught children how to twerk (jiggle their butts in a sexual way, as popularized by skank Miley Cyrus.)[395]

Liberals began complaining that Victoria's Secret "discriminates" against fat women and transgenders because only beautiful (and actual) women walk the runway in their fashion shows.   Online outlet "Mic"

[391] Breitbart "Watch: Drag Queen Admits He's 'Grooming Next Generation' in 'Story Hours'" by Dr. Susan Berry (November 29th 2018)

[392] "Grooming" definition in Cambridge Online Dictionary.

[393] Houston Chronicle "Houston Library apologizes after registered sex offender participated in Drag Queen Storytime" by Jasper Scherer (March 16th 2019)

[394] Newsweek "Sex Offender Busted as Drag Queen Who Read Books To Children in City Library" by Scott McDonald (March 16th 2019)

[395] LifeSiteNews "Drag queen teaches kids to 'twerk' at library story hour" by Calvin Freburger (August 7th 2019)

complained that they "normalized discrimination" and that, "It doesn't take a fashion insider to recognize that when it comes to plus-size and transgender women, as well as gender nonconforming people, Victoria's Secret would rather maintain a closed door policy. Since the brand's first runway show at the Plaza Hotel in New York City in August 1995, not a single plus-size or out transgender or gender nonconforming person has walked in the show's 23-year history."[396]

Activists then called it "hateful" when the chief marketing officer dismissed criticism, but Victoria's Secret official Twitter account soon apologized and released a statement saying, "we absolutely would love to cast a transgender model for the show."[397] Nine months later they hired their first transgender model.[398]

Just like conservative blacks are shunned and smeared by the media, so are conservative gays. *Deadspin*, a sports blog owned by Univision, published an article titled "Conservative Gays Need to Shut The Fuck Up."[399] And when Caitlyn Jenner "came out" as a Republican, liberals went nuts and completely denounced "her" as a traitor to the LGBT community despite recently having been celebrated as the most famous transgender person in the world upon announcing "her" transition.

---

[396] Mic "How Victoria's Secret normalized discrimination" by Evan Ross Katz (November 12th 2018)

[397] https://twitter.com/VictoriasSecret/status/1061106626583822338

[398] Los Angeles Times "Valentina Sampaio makes history as first transgender Victoria's Secret model" by Christi Carras (August 5th 2019)

[399] Deadspin "Conservative Gays Need to Shut The Fuck Up" by Lauren Theisen (December 12th 2018)

"She" received infinitely more hate on social media for being a Republican than "she" did for deciding to identify as a "woman," and actually said it was harder to come out as Republican than it was transgender.[400]

---

[400] CNBC "Caitlyn Jenner says it was harder to come out as Republican than transgender" by Ivan Levingston (July 20th 2016)

TV "News"

Television news is very different from newspapers and magazines which tend to cover stories in much greater detail and context than a fifteen-second sound bite, and require a reader's active attention and willingness to follow a story. Television, on the other hand, is a passive medium and relies on a quick pace, flashy graphics, and dramatic music in hopes of gaining an audience's attention and holding it long enough for the commercial break so they can get paid.

TV news only skims along the surface of issues, mentioning a few basic points, and is often just infotainment with no real substance. What the audience sees is a carefully crafted version of a story that the producers and editors want people to see, while leaving out the parts they don't want.

Famed media analyst Neil Postman noted, "Television always recreates the world to some extent in its own image by selecting parts of that world and editing those parts. So a television news show is a kind of symbolic creation and construction made by news directors and camera crews...and stranger still is the fact that commercials may appear anywhere in a news story, before, or after, or in the middle, so that all events are rendered essentially trivial; that is to say all events are treated as a source of public entertainment."[401]

---

[401] Mass Communication: Living in a Media World "Can Television Take Anything Seriously" by Ralph E. Hanson (Seventh Edition 2019)

The reason intelligent people listen to talk radio is because radio shows provide long-form interviews and in-depth discussions which explore subjects in detail during a 15 or 20 minute segment, and may even continue the discussion after the commercial break for even longer. In comparison, the average television news segment on a national evening news broadcast is just 2 minutes and 23 seconds.[402]   For local TV news it's just 41 seconds.[403] Television news is the equivalent of reading the headline of a newspaper article and the first paragraph or two.

Aside from the limitations of the television format, the days of Walter Cronkite, "the most trusted man in America" who anchored the *CBS Evening News* for 19 years, are long gone.   After his era was over we got people like Dan Rather who used fake documents in a report about George W. Bush's service record from when he was in the National Guard.[404]   And Brian Williams who fabricated a story about his plane being shot down in Iraq when he was covering the war.[405]

Most television "reporters" today aren't reporters, but are just actors.   Everyone knows Hollywood celebrities make millions of dollars a year, but most people don't think about how much money celebrity "journalists" make.   They too are performance artists not much different from a Hollywood actor reading their lines. They know when to sound somber, and when to turn up

---

[402] Pew Research Center "Video Length" by Pew Research Center: Journalism and Media Staff (July 16th 2012)

[403] Ibid.

[404] Washington Post "Dan Rather to Step Down at CBS" by Howard Kurtz (November 24th 2004)

[405] Chicago Tribune "NBC removes Brian Williams from 'Nightly News'" by Tribune Wire (June 18th 2015)

the energy and display faux outrage to the audience when the teleprompter tells them. Many of them don't believe half the things they say, they're just playing a part, and for that they get paid very well.

For example, before he was fired from the *NBC Nightly News*, anchor Brian Williams was making $10 million a year.[406] Dan Rather was making $6 million a year at CBS News.[407] At CNN Anderson Cooper makes $12 million dollars a year and has a net worth of over $100 million.[408] MSNBC morning host Joe Scarborough's divorce documents show that in 2013 he was making just under $100,000 per week![409] Matt Lauer was making $25 million a year before he was fired from NBC's *Today Show* for sexual misconduct.[410] And when Megyn Kelly was fired from NBC's morning lineup she left with a $69 million windfall, the remainder of her contract.[411]

To put these figures in perspective, Anderson Cooper's $12 million a year divided by 52 (weeks in a year) is over $230,000 a week, or over $46,000 *per show*.

---

[406] Los Angeles Times "Brian Williams' $10-million salary should buy some honesty" (February 10th 2015)

[407] CBS News "Court Tosses Dan Rather's Lawsuit Vs. CBS" (September 29th 2009)

[408] Yahoo Finance "Anderson Cooper Net Worth: His Fortune at Age 51" by Joel Anderson (June 1st 2018)

[409] TMZ "Joe Scarborough Divorce: He Earns $99,000 a Week" (October 11th 2013)

[410] Business Insider "Fired 'Today' host Matt Lauer's contract was reportedly worth $25 million a year — here's how that compares to other top TV show hosts" by Jason Guerrasio (November 29th 2017)

[411] Vanity Fair "Megyn Kelly Officially Out at NBC, $69 Million Richer" (January 12th 2019)

He makes more money *in one day* than many Americans make in *an entire year!* And for that kind of money, these television personalities will say and do almost anything.

Being a cable news contributor is also very lucrative, earning pundits an easy six-figure salary to sit around a table for an hour to give their "analysis" on various issues a few nights a week. They know what the host, producers, and network want, and that's what they deliver. They're very careful not to bite the hand that feeds them by daring to point out facts that go against the narrative the show is trying to promote.

All of the Big Three broadcast networks (NBC, ABC, and CBS) try to separate themselves from the "cable" shows, but promoting the liberal agenda remains at the core of their existence. That's not to say they don't have *some* value. The major networks are useful to learn about dangerous weather events, product recalls, health scares, etc., and they do cover some events that can't have political spin put on them and which the general public should be aware of. And it can be important to watch what they are reporting just to be aware of the latest issues they are promoting and see what their current agenda is.

They also aren't without their own major scandals that should cause viewers to remain skeptical about their integrity as "news" networks. CBS once killed a story about the tobacco industry covering up how addictive cigarettes are out of concerns that if they were sued by the tobacco companies for their report it would interfere with the pending sale of the network to Westinghouse.[412]   The incident was later made into a movie called *The Insider* (1999) starring Al Pacino and Russell Crowe.[413]

After allegedly burying a story about Nike using sweatshops to manufacture their clothes out of fears they would lose the company as a sponsor for the 1998 Winter Olympics, CBS reporters wore Nike jackets during their coverage as part of the sponsorship deal in what was widely criticized as a breach of journalistic ethics.[414]

CBS News has even digitally inserted advertisements for their own network onto fake billboards during live shots using the same technology sports broadcasts use to display banners behind home plate at baseball games. CBS inserted them onto buildings, water fountains, and even on the back of a horse-drawn carriage during "news" reports.[415]

After *ABC News* interrupted the network's broadcast for some "breaking news" about the "Russia investigation," Brian Ross falsely claimed that Michael Flynn had implicated Donald Trump in the "conspiracy," resulting in the stock market immediately dropping 350 points out of concerns that the President would now be

---

[412] Los Angeles Times "Tobacco Company Sues Source in Unbroadcast '60 Minutes' Report: Litigation: Brown & Williamson is also seeking to prevent its former employee from testifying" by Jane Hall (November 22nd 1995)

[413] New York Times "Film Drama Shines a Harsh Light on '60 Minutes' and CBS" by Peter Applebom (July 13th 1999)

[414] Los Angeles Times "CBS Woes Go Beyond the Ratings to a Swoosh" by Larry Stewart (February 15th 1998)

[415] New York Times "On CBS News, Some of what you see isn't there" by Alex Kuczynki (January 12th 2000)

impeached or arrested.[416]   General Flynn had made no such allegations and the story was completely false.

A few years earlier during their breaking news coverage of the shooting in an Aurora, Colorado movie theater by lunatic James Holmes, anchor George Stephanopoulos said that Brian Ross found something that "might be significant."   He then went on to incorrectly report that the shooter may be a member of the Tea Party because ABC found someone on Facebook with the same name who had the Tea Party listed as one of his interests.[417] It was, of course, the wrong James Holmes.

ABC News claimed that then-Attorney General Jeff Sessions delivered a speech to a "hate group" after meeting with the Christian non-profit organization Alliance Defending Freedom, one of the most powerful Christian rights legal organizations in the country.[418] Basically all Christian groups are seen as "hate groups" to the liberal Establishment, which always cites the Southern Poverty Law Center as the ultimate authority of such things.

After Oprah Winfrey accepted an award at the 2018 Golden Globes and gave an "inspiring" speech that caused many to hope she would be running for president,

---

[416] Washington Post "ABC News apologizes for 'serious error' in Trump report and suspends Brian Ross for four weeks" by Amy B Wang (December 3rd 2017)

[417] Fox News "ABC News, Brian Ross apologize for report suggesting shooting suspect tied to Tea Party" (July 20th 2012)

[418] ABC News "Jeff Sessions addresses 'anti-LGBT hate group,' but DOJ won't release his remarks" by Pete Madden and Erin Galloway (July 12th 2017)

the official NBC Twitter account tweeted out a picture of her with the caption "OUR future president."[419]

In 2015, *NBC News* launched *"NBC BLK"* (NBC Black), a new website for "black-oriented issues."[420] Apparently it just wasn't enough to cover that kind of news on their main platform, they had to dedicate an entire division to "black news." The following year they launched "NBC Out," a website featuring LGBT news, "Out" meaning "out of the closet." The site has it's own Twitter account and other social media pages dedicated to using the NBC brand to promote the LGBT agenda 24/7.

Cable News

As bad as the Big Three broadcast networks have become in recent years, cable news channels like CNN and MSNBC are much worse. They'll talk endlessly about the same story on every show, every hour, all day, to ensure maximum saturation hoping their propaganda will reach as many viewers as possible since most people just tune in for an hour or two a day.

Fox News, while still following the basic sound bite format of television news, actually does a very good job of presenting a variety of stories and perspectives, whereas CNN and MSNBC mostly have endless panel discussions with each pundit throwing in their two cents when their "research" consists of glancing over a few headlines before the show or reading the producer's notes about what the topic is for the day. Barack Obama once

---

[419] New York Post "NBC slammed for tweet endorsing Oprah as president" by Mark Moore (January 8th 2018)

[420] The Wrap "NBCBLK Editor Defends New Black Site: 'It Was Destined to Be Controversial'" by Alicia Banks (January 22nd 2015)

said that Fox viewers are living on a different planet than those who watch CNN and MSNBC.[421] Maybe he's right. Fox viewers are the ones living on planet Earth!

The Left is so fearful of Fox News that the Democratic National Committee barred them from hosting any of the twelve Democrat presidential primary debates for the 2020 election, claiming they're "state run TV" controlled by the Trump White House.[422] God forbid any of the moderators ask the candidates some real questions!

MSNBC was started in 1996 and functioned as the liberal counterpart to Fox, whereas CNN was supposedly the middle ground. CNN stands for Cable News Network and they were the first 24-hour news network in the world, started in 1980 by Ted Turner. For over 30 years they would cover news from around the globe and were once—as their trademarked slogan still (falsely) claims— one of the most trusted names in news. When something interesting was happening somewhere in the world, it was live on CNN, but in the Trump era all that changed. They rarely report on news anymore. Instead, all they do is talk about how terrible of a person Donald Trump is.

It's improv theater. The producer gives the panel a topic each night, or each segment, and like a group of actors at an improv show, the panelists pretend to be experts on the issue and put forth their opinions as if they actually know what they're talking about when in most cases they're just making it up as they go along. CNN doesn't air newscasts anymore, they air talk shows filled

---

[421] The Hill "Obama: Fox viewers 'living on a different planet' than NPR listeners" by Julia Manchester (January 13th 2018)

[422] NPR "DNC Bars Fox News From Hosting 2020 Primary Debates" by Jessica Taylor (March 6th 2019)

with endless speculation and theorizing about things they have no idea about. It's a gossip network.

CNN now covers one story—Trump. It's Trump 24/7 and virtually every minute of airtime is dedicated to complaining about him. What would once be contained in the grocery store tabloids or frivolous websites with zero editorial ethics now regularly airs on CNN. Gossip about Stormy Daniels and the "pee tape" and endless allegations from anonymous sources about how "corrupt," "incompetent," "racist," "fascist," etc., Trump is, is the only thing they talk about.

The network is desperate to prevent blue collar Democrats from supporting Trump and abandoning the Democrat Party, so after a grassroots movement called #WalkAway was started by a gay liberal named Brandon Straka encouraging people to stop voting for Democrats because the party has become insane, CNN branded the movement part of a Russian plot! They reported that despite the #WalkAway campaign being "presented as a grassroots effort by former Democrats who are critical of the party's alleged intimidation, confrontation and lack of civility and want people to walk away from the party," they said it has, "been connected to Kremlin-linked Russian bots."[423]

The #WalkAway campaign's YouTube channel and Facebook page are filled with video testimonials of average Americans from all different backgrounds who give their reasons for why they no longer support the Democrat Party and are encouraging others to "walk away" as well.[424]

---

[423] CNN "Russian bots are using #WalkAway to try to wound Dems in midterms" by David A. Love (July 17th 2018)

[424] https://www.YouTube.com/WalkAwayCampaign

CNN's poisonous anti-Trump obsession may have incited several terrorist attacks such as the man who shot up Republicans' softball practice in June 2017, severely injuring Congressman Steve Scalese, or the person who mailed white powder to Donald Trump Jr.'s apartment, causing an anthrax scare and landing his then-wife in the hospital for testing. CNN's reckless rhetoric could be the catalyst that helped push any number of mentally unstable viewers over the edge, convincing them that the Trump administration is the reincarnation of the Third Reich.

Meanwhile CNN's senior "media analyst" Brian Stelter says that Trump's base is a "hate movement" against the press. "I think what we are increasingly seeing from the president and his aides and his allies is a hate movement against the American press," Stelter whined. "When you look at the behavior around Jim Acosta and some of the other reporter at these rallies, you really do see a hate movement."[425]

Shortly after the election Stelter declared that Donald Trump becoming president was "a national emergency" and painted him as a dictator who just seized power.[426] In an interview with *New York Magazine* CNN's president Jeff Zucker admitted, "The perception of Donald Trump in capitals around the world is shaped, in many ways, by CNN," warning Trump that, "Continuing to have an adversarial relationship with that network is a mistake."[427]

---

[425] CNN "Trump leading 'hate movement' against media" (August 5th 2018)

[426] PJ Media "CNN Anchor Calls Trump's Election a 'National Emergency'" by PJ Staff (December 12th 2016)

[427] New York Magazine "CNN's Jeff Zucker on Covering Donald Trump — Past, Present, and Future" by Gabriel Sherman (January 18th 2017)

Even the *Washington Post* admitted that, "it is hard to escape the perception that Zucker issued a kind of threat."[428]

CNN was instrumental in getting Alex Jones banned from all major social media platforms after they literally lobbied the tech giants to have him removed. Before he was "unpersoned," when his YouTube channel had just one strike they gleefully reported, "InfoWars' Main YouTube Channel is Two Strikes Away From Being Banned"[429] A few days later his channel got a second strike, and outlets like *Newsweek* gloated, "InfoWars is perilously close to a permanent YouTube ban after peddling yet another debunked conspiracy theory."[430] Dozens of other outlets picked up the story about the second strike, salivating that Infowars was one strike away from permanently being banned.[431]

Even before Alex Jones' YouTube channel was deleted, CNN was organizing an advertiser boycott against all the companies whose ads were appearing before his videos played. CNN reported, "Some of the biggest brands in the U.S. had ads running on the YouTube channels for far-right website InfoWars and its founder, notorious conspiracy theorist Alex Jones, and

[428] Washington Post "CNN's president has fired a warning shot at Donald Trump" by Callum Borchers (January 19th 2017)

[429] CNN "InfoWars' main YouTube channel is two strikes away from being banned" by Paul P. Murphy (February 24th 2018)

[430] Newsweek "Florida Shooting Conspiracy Theories and Alex Jones, Infowars In Hot Water with YouTube" by Gillian Edevane (February 27th 2018)

[431] The Hill "Infowars one strike away from YouTube ban" by Julia Manchester (February 27th 2018)

they say they had no idea YouTube was allowing their advertising to appear there."[432]

Well, how did they learn their ads were running on Alex's channel? Because CNN made of list of which ads were running, and then contacted the advertisers to pressure the companies into pulling them! Their story goes on, "CNN has discovered ads on InfoWars' channels from companies and organizations such as Nike, Acer, 20th Century Fox, Paramount Network, the Mormon Church, Moen, Expedia, Alibaba, HomeAway, the NRA, Honey, Wix and ClassPass." At the end of their story they admitted, "Many of the brands — including Nike, Moen, Expedia, Acer, ClassPass, Honey, Alibaba and OneFamily — have suspended ads on InfoWars' channels after being contacted by CNN for comment."[433]

MSNBC is usually not quite as insane as CNN but it's still almost always off the rails. Donny Deutsch, who is a regular contributor on the *Morning Joe* show, has challenged President Trump to a fight on air,[434] and their other regular panelists say things like Trump's name is the "modern day swastika."[435] They also regularly compared him to a dictator and call him a white supremacist.[436]

---

[432] CNN "Advertisers flee InfoWars founder Alex Jones' YouTube channel" by Paul P. Murphy and Gianluca Mezzofiore (March 3rd 2018)

[433] Ibid.

[434] Washington Times "Donny Deutsch issues Trump 'serious' fight challenge: 'I'll meet you in the schoolyard, brother'" by Douglas Ernst (June 30th 2017)

[435] Daily Caller "MSNBC Guest: Trump Name Is The 'Modern Day Swastika' [VIDEO]" by Amber Athey (August 7th 2017)

[436] Newsbusters "MSNBC: 'Everyone' Agrees Trump's a White Supremacist; Prove You're Not Racist by Voting Democrat" by Kritine Marsh (August 1st 2019)

When President Trump announced that he would be meeting face to face with Kim Jong Un, MSNBC claimed it was to "distract" the media from talking about his alleged affair with Stormy Daniels.[437]

The network's darling is lesbian Rachel Maddow whose monologues are convoluted streams of consciousness rattling off all kinds of social justice warrior buzzwords without ever really making a point. Her show is so fanatical and hyper-partisan that the *New York Times* banned their reporters from even appearing on it out of concern it will tarnish their credibility.[438]

The Intercept's Glenn Greenwald admitted, "I used to be really good friends with Rachel Maddow [but] I've seen her devolution from this really interesting, really smart, independent thinker into this utterly scripted, intellectually dishonest, partisan hack."[439]

MSNBC's research department is so awful they took seriously a parody Twitter account that listed its location as a city in Russia and tweeted satire about a variety of issues (calling itself Boston Antifa). MSNBC reported that it was more "evidence" that Russian bots were active on Twitter.[440] They also fell for a tweet posted by the

---

[437] Business Insider "Joe Scarborough and Mika Brzezinski say Trump's North Korea surprise is a 'painfully obvious' distraction from porn star sex scandal" by Eliza Relman (March 9th 2018)

[438] The Hill "New York Times reinforces policy prohibiting reporters from appearing on cable shows like Maddow" by Joe Concha (May 31st 2019)

[439] The Wrap "Glenn Greenwald Blasts Rachel Maddow: 'Intellectually Dishonest, Partisan Hack'" by Jon Levine (January 22nd 2018)

[440] Skeptic Review "Boston Antifa Explains Parody: Vladivostok, Russia, Geo-Tagging & More" by Gretchin Mullen (November 17th 2017)

popular parody account for North Korea, the "DPRK News Service" which MSNBC cited in a report attacking President Trump.[441]

Immediately after Robert Mueller wrapped up his two-year long investigation into the Trump campaign's alleged "collusion" with the Russians and found none, CNN and MSNBC's ratings dropped like a stone over night. After stringing along their viewers for two years giving the impression that any day now Mueller would announce he found "proof" Trump was a Russian agent and that his impeachment and imprisonment was imminent, hundreds of thousands of disappointed viewers finally quit tuning in.

Following the Mueller nothing burger, Rachel Maddow's viewership dropped by almost 20%.[442] Anderson Cooper's prime time show on CNN got only 835,000 viewers, and for weeks couldn't break a million.[443] Meanwhile Fox News continued to dominate, getting more viewers than MSNBC and CNN combined.[444]

Even *Newsweek* magazine, which is part of the anti-Trump smear machine, reported, "MSNBC's Rachel Maddow Found Huge Ratings Success Covering Trump

---

[441] Mediaite "MSNBC Falls for Parody North Korean Twitter Account Attacking Fox News" by Alex Griswold (August 10th 2015)

[442] Associated Press "Maddow, other MSNBC hosts see ratings drop, Fox up" by David Bauder (March 27th 2019)

[443] BigLeaguePolitics "Tucker Gets More Viewers Than All of CNN Combined, Fox Early News Beats MSNBC Prime Time" by Tom Pappert (April 4th 2019)

[444] Fox News "Fox News dominates CNN, MSNBC in Wednesday primetime ratings, topping both networks' combined viewership" (March 28th 2019)

and Russia — So What Now?"[445]   Election years are always huge ratings boosters for cable news, and the regular viewers who suffered through two years of endless speculation and listened to countless conspiracy theories about Trump and the Russians obviously aren't the sharpest tools in the shed.   Most have already forgotten all about the massive deception they were victims of and due to their short attention spans and lack of intellectual capacity, these cable news companies will continue on as if they did nothing wrong, and hundreds of thousands of people will still tune in.

Normal Americans wonder how anyone could watch them again after the massive fraud the "news" networks had engaged in, but it's easy to underestimate how many stupid people there are out there.   After all, the *Jerry Springer Show* aired for 27 years and was able to keep audiences coming back every day to watch another group of trailer trash fight with each other about who cheated on who and who the father is of some poor child; and despite how mindless and repetitive the show was, enough people kept tuning in every day for it to stay on air for almost three decades.

[445] Newsweek "MSNBC's Rachel Maddow Found Huge Ratings Success Covering Trump and Russia — So What Now?" by Tim Marcin (March 25th 2019)

Internet "News" Sites

Just like the Internet sparked the creation of countless different kinds of businesses selling everything from books to airline tickets, it also gave birth to new "news" companies as well. While the brand name newspapers and television networks eventually began migrating their content online, unknown entrepreneurs threw their hat in the news business as well, creating digital-only magazines and "news" sites like the Huffington Post, BuzzFeed, the Daily Beast, Politico, Axios, Vox, Slate, Vice News, and many others.

Since the barriers to entry are so low, and these companies didn't need to invest in gigantic printing presses or develop supply chains to deliver their product to readers' homes every morning, many of them saw the incredible opportunities the Internet opened up. But while most newspapers and magazines require people to buy them, the vast majority of Internet news sites are free to read.

All they had to do was get people to click on their articles and the advertisements on the website would fund their operation, so instead of focusing on producing quality content that people would be willing to pay for, they began flooding the Internet with sensational clickbait, throwing all journalistic standards out the window with one goal in mind—drive traffic to the articles, no matter what.

The *Huffington Post* was one of the first "successful" online "news" outlets. It was started in 2005 specializing in clickbait trash and other pop culture nonsense, but due to spamming the Internet with countless articles on anything and everything, they generated a lot of traffic and made a name for themselves as one of the most viewed online "news" outlets.[446]   In 2011 they were purchased by AOL for $315 million.[447]

When Conan O'Brien was the comedian at the 2013 White House Correspondents Dinner he mocked the Huffington Post for being invited, saying, "All the Washington news media here tonight including the stars of online journalism.   I see the Huffington Post has a table, which has me wondering if you're here, who's covering Miley Cyrus's latest nip slip? Who's assembling today's top 25 yogurt related tweets?   [Or] 7 mistakes you're making with bacon?   That's a real one, and you should be ashamed of yourselves!"[448]

The Huffington Post (later rebranded as HuffPost) being welcomed as part of the Washington press corps marked the beginning of the end of journalism.

BuzzFeed

BuzzFeed is another online abomination which took advantage of the new clickbait business model. The site was created in 2006, and began churning out ridiculously

---

[446] eBizMBA "Top 15 Most Popular Political Websites - January 2019"

[447] Reuters "AOL to buy The Huffington Post for $315 million" by Anthony Boadle and Jennifer Saba (February 6th 2011)

[448] Archive.org "CSPAN April 27th 2013 White House Correspondents Dinner"

dumb quizzes about pop culture and recycling the same handful of topics over and over again to litter Google's search results with their spam, often in the form of listicles like: "37 Things White People Need to Stop Ruining in 2018;" "21 Things That Almost All White People Are Guilty Of Saying;" and "33 Things That Almost All White People Are Guilty Of Doing."

They seem to hate white people so much that after the White House announced the National Day for the Victims of Communism a BuzzFeed reporter declared that the phrase "victims of Communism" was a "white nationalist talking point."[449] Aside from their distain for white people, BuzzFeed also can't stand heterosexual people (known as normal people to those not infected with the liberal pathogen.) When *Star Wars: The Last Jedi* was released, despite Disney turning the movie into a feminist propaganda piece, BuzzFeed still wasn't happy because there were no LGBT characters and suggested that Finn (John Boyega) and Poe Dameron (Oscar Issac) should have had a "romance" as part of the plot.[450]

BuzzFeed is perhaps the worst clickbait bottom feeder online and makes the *National Enquirer* look like a Pulitzer Prize winning publication. Outside of the community of morons who actively visit their website, BuzzFeed is best-known for publishing the fake news story about Donald Trump allegedly being caught on tape with hookers peeing on him in a Russian hotel.

The story about the now-infamous "dossier" had been circling internally at most of the major news outlets but

---

[449] The Wrap "BuzzFeed Reporter Apologizes for 'Very Dumb' Remarks About Communism" by Jon Levine (November 8th 2017)

[450] BuzzFeed "Why LGBT Representation Didn't Make It Into 'The Last Jedi'" by Adam B. Vary (December 18th 2017)

nobody had reported on it because it was so ridiculous and there wasn't a shred of evidence to back it up, but BuzzFeed decided they would get the "scoop" and ran with it.

Then the allegations were all over social media and "Golden Showers" was trending on Twitter which provided cover for other "news" outlets to repeat the story. BuzzFeed often does the dirty work for Democrats by publishing salacious allegations and hyping them up enough to then get amplified by mainstream outlets which hide under the cover of qualifiers like "BuzzFeed reports" and "according to BuzzFeed." This way, they can give the impression that *they're* not making the claims, it's someone else and they're just passing it along because "if true" it would be a big story.

Vice News

Vice News is another popular online outlet which regularly celebrates the most bizarre sexual perversions and promotes degenerates as modern day heroes. Some of their headlines are literally: "We Interviewed the Zoophilia Advocate Who Had Sex with a Dolphin;" "Ever Fantasized About Ingesting an Animal Through Your Anus?" "How to Make Breakfast With Your Vagina;" "Why Can't I Consent to Sex with My Brother?" "Dear Straight Guys, It's Time to Start Putting Things In Your Butt;" "Was Jesus Gay?" "Getting Cocaine Blown Up Your Butt;" and "Should Every Man Be Penetrated At Least Once In His Life?" It should be no surprise that

Vice News is also on the forefront of celebrating child drag queens and sexualizing children.[451]

Vice's founder Shane Smith became a billionaire from peddling this kind of cancer.[452]   In the early 2010s they regularly made viral videos on interesting topics that other news outlets wouldn't cover, like traveling to Columbia to investigate scopolamine (also known as the Devil's Breath) which allegedly puts people into a chemically induced hypnotic trance where they will do anything they're told,[453] and visiting Kim Dotcom's estate in New Zealand and letting him give his side of the story regarding the massive copyright infringement case he's facing for running the file-sharing site Megaupload.[454] But Vice quickly devolved into the most perverted of online outlets.

Like all the other large Leftist web-based media outlets, Vice seems to be obsessed with criticizing white people and sees "white supremacists" around every corner.   They literally reported that, "Racist and white supremacist ideas have become more visible among the Chinese Canadian right."[455]   So Chinese people living in Canada are white supremacists now?   There's no point in trying to make sense of their insanity.   It's best to just stay

---

[451] Twitchy "What was that about exploitation? Now VICE Canada is celebrating the next generation of drag queens" by Brett T. (June 6th 2019)

[452] Forbes "Vice Media's Shane Smith Is Now A Billionaire" by Natalie Robehmed (June 20th 2017)

[453] Vice "World's Scariest Drug (Documentary Exclusive)" on YouTube (May 11th 2012)

[454] Vice "Kim Dotcom: The Man Behind Megaupload" on YouTube (January 5th 2014)

[455] https://twitter.com/vicecanada/status/1042156417577365505

away from them so their poisonous propaganda doesn't enter your view because it will only make you upset.

In 2015, Disney invested over $400 million into Vice, but four years later had lost all of their money and wrote it off on their taxes.[456] George Soros came to the rescue in mid-2019 and "invested" another $250 million dollars into the failing media company so they could continue to operate.[457] The "investment" from Soros was really just a donation to help them cover their operating expenses for the next few years so they could keep pumping out their liberal propaganda regardless of how much money it cost them to produce or whether they earned any revenue from it.

Vox

Vox is another well-funded online outlet that sees white supremacist boogeymen around every corner, and paints anyone to the right of Karl Marx as an alt-right Nazi. Vox largely functions as an activist organization working to destroy the careers of conservatives by painting targets on their back and smearing them with labels that are difficult to shake. In 2015 they were given $200 million dollars by NBC to do their dirty work without tarnishing the NBC name.[458]

---

456 The Hollywood Reporter "Disney Discloses New $353 Million Write-Down on Vice Media Investment" by Natalie Jarvey (May 8th 2019)

457 Variety "Vice Media Gets $250 Million in Debt Funding From George Soros, Other Investors" by Todd Spangler (May 3rd 2019)

458 New York Times "NBCUniversal Invests $200 Million in Vox Media" by Emily Steel (August 12th 2015)

For years Vox has been obsessed with PewDiePie, who held the title of YouTube's most subscribed channel for six years, and thinks that he is putting out secret white supremacist messages to his viewers.[459]   Of course they labeled me one of YouTube's "most extreme" creators in a video they produced crying about how conservatives were making viral anti-feminist and anti-illegal immigration videos on YouTube.[460]

Vox came to most people's attention in June 2019 when one of their activists (who calls himself a "journalist") named Carlos Maza tried to get Steven Crowder completely banned from YouTube for calling him a "lispy queer" and an "anchor baby."   Just as gay pride month kicked off, Carlos Maza rallied his fans to pressure YouTube to ban Crowder for "bullying" him and for using "hate speech," despite Maza often referring to himself as a "queer" and the Q in LGBTQ stands for just that.

The little sissy spent an entire weekend ranting on Twitter about how miserable his life was and kept harassing YouTube to ban Crowder for his "homophobic attacks."   YouTube then demonetized Crowder's entire channel, along with many others the company claimed were posting "offensive" content.   More on that in the chapter on YouTube.

In case there is any doubt as to whether or not Vox hates the First Amendment, for the 4th of July they published an op-ed titled "3 Reasons the American Revolution Was a Mistake," which starts off saying, "This

---

[459] Vox "YouTube's most popular user amplified anti-Semitic rhetoric. Again" by Aja Romano (December 13th 2018)

[460] Vox "YouTube's messy fight with its most extreme creators" (October 19th 2017)

155

July 4, let's not mince words: American independence in 1776 was a monumental mistake. We should be mourning the fact that we left the United Kingdom, not cheering it."[461]

It goes on to wish we would have remained a British colony because slavery would have supposedly been abolished sooner, fewer Native Americans would have been oppressed, and we would have a parliamentary system of government instead of a separation of powers (the three-branch system, which we currently have).

The writer also added his belief that we would have passed a carbon tax, since that's what happened in Britain, whereas such a proposal has (thankfully) so far failed to get enough support in the United States. The article concluded that, "The main benefit of the revolution to colonists was that it gave more political power to America's white male minority."[462] Of course! It's always the white man's fault!

The Daily Beast

The *Daily Beast* is another unscrupulous online outlet that often functions as a political activist organization instead of a "news" website and regularly depicts Trump supporters as a bunch of bigots. They like to publish stories that smear rising conservative social media personalities as "far-right" to brand them as "extremists" in attempts to derail their careers before a major network hires them as contributors. It's their way of trying to kill

---

461 Vox "3 Reasons the American Revolution Was a Mistake" by Dylan Matthews (July 3rd 2019)

462 Ibid.

off the next generation of conservative voices before they become household names.

The "far-right" label is often associated with neo-Nazism and by muddying up the search results for peoples' names with a bunch of salacious articles about them it can cause real damage for current and future employment. Headlines like "Meet Candace Owens, Kanye West's Toxic Far-Right Consigliere,"[463] and "Mike Cernovich and Jack Posobiec, the Far Right's Twin Trolls, Taste Their Own Bitter Medicine,"[464] and "Pro-Gun Parkland Teen Kyle Kashuv Apologizes for 'Inflammatory' Racial Comments" are commonly deployed to digitally tar and feather conservatives.[465]

The *Daily Beast* calls YouTube a "radicalization factory" for the "far-right" and says that it's "pulling YouTubers down the rabbit hole of extremism."[466] Like others of their ilk, they often push for more censorship of right-wing content under the smokescreen of fighting "racism" and "extremism." Defame, demonetize, and deplatform is their M.O.

After a joke video depicting Nancy Pelosi as drunk and slurring her words went viral on Facebook, the *Daily Beast* doxed the person who allegedly made it, revealing his name, the city he lives in, and what he does for a

---

[463] Daily Beast "Meet Candace Owens, Kanye West's Toxic Far-Right Consigliere" by Amy Zimmerman (May 9th 2018)

[464] Daily Beast "Mike Cernovich and Jack Posobiec, the Far Right's Twin Trolls, Taste Their Own Bitter Medicine" by Lloyd Grove (July 23rd 2018)

[465] Daily Beast "Pro-Gun Parkland Teen Kyle Kashuv Apologizes for 'Inflammatory' Racial Comments" by Will Sommer (May 23rd 2019)

[466] Daily Beast "Inside YouTube's Far-Right Radicalization Factory" by KellyWeill (September 18th 2018)

living. The "reporter" (activist) who cyber-stalked the meme maker had apparently messaged his Facebook friends, including his ex-girlfriend, fishing for information about him.[467]

Don't Fall for Their Tricks

If you use social media, the best thing you can do is block these Leftist clickbait accounts, and don't share their links no matter how outrageous their articles are because these sites often rely on hate-clicks, which means they know people will share the links on their social media accounts with the intention of showing their friends how insane the articles are. Unfortunately trying to "expose" them this way just drives more traffic to their website which is what they want. They don't care if the people clicking the articles like them or hate them, as long as they get the traffic and thus the ad revenue from it.

Oftentimes articles are purposefully inflammatory and designed to get attention because of how outlandish they are, even though the people writing them may not even believe a word of it, but are simply publishing outrageous things in hopes that people will spread them around so they can get a bunch of hate-clicks from it.

So instead of posting links to these outlets, take a screenshot of their headline and post that, along with a summary of the article and your commentary so you're not driving any more traffic to their websites. Starve them of traffic! Or post an article from a conservative website that is covering what the Leftist sites are reporting instead of giving them any more page views

---

[467] Fox News "Daily Beast accused of 'doxxing' alleged creator of 'Drunk Pelosi' video" by Frank Miles (June 2nd 2019)

directly. It may be best to just ignore them altogether sometimes and not even mention them so that you don't inadvertently inspire anyone to visit them out of curiosity.

And be sure to bookmark and follow conservative sites like Fox News, Breitbart, the Drudge Report, Daily Caller, the Washington Times, Townhall, The Federalist, Washington Examiner, Newsbusters, PJ Media, Red State, One America News, WorldNetDaily, and National Review.

The End of Print Journalism?

In early 2018 the *New York Times* CEO predicted their print edition may only last another ten years before it becomes economically unsustainable to keep it going.[468] Newspaper circulation has been on a steady decline since the Internet revolution, and many magazines are struggling as well. *PC Magazine* ceased printing a physical edition in 2009 and is now just a website. *Computerworld* followed suit in 2014. *Teen Vogue* magazine and *Self* did the same thing in 2017.

Newsweek, once considered to be one of the staples of the news magazine industry ever since its creation in 1933, even quit issuing a print edition at the end of 2012 due to financial problems.[469] About a year later after it had been bought by another media organization (IBT Media) they re-launched the print edition, but continue to struggle.

---

[468] CNBC "New York Times CEO: Print journalism has maybe another 10 years" by Kellie Ell (February 12th 2018)

[469] Wall Street Journal "Newsweek Quits Print: After 79 Years, the Title Will Be Digital Only" by Keach Hagey (October 19th 2012)

Despite having over 3 million Twitter followers, most of *Newsweek's* tweets barely get a dozen interactions, leading many people to think they bought millions of fake followers in order to appear popular.[470]   In 2018 *Newsweek* was accused of fraudulently inflating the traffic to their website in order to present advertisers with false numbers, causing numerous online ad vendors to pull their ads.[471]   So buying fake Twitter followers surely seems right up their alley.

CNN's president Jeff Zucker complained at an industry conference that his network was having a difficult time monetizing their content online since so many videos are spread through social media with CNN clips being posted to YouTube, Twitter, and Facebook. "In a Google and Facebook world, monetization of digital and mobile continues to be more difficult than we would have expected or liked," he said.[472]

What he means is, there is just too much competition from other websites and YouTube channels, and since there are so many different links being shared on social media, CNN's web traffic has dramatically dropped and with fewer people actually watching them on cable they're not getting the revenue from the long blocks of commercials.

Because a lot of people use ad blocker plug-ins on their browsers which automatically hide banner ads from websites, the *Washington Post* recently began blocking

---

[470] https://twitter.com/DonaldJTrumpJr/status/1116426290817638400

[471] The Wall Street Journal "Ad-Tech Firms Blacklist Newsweek Sites, Alleging Website-Traffic Manipulation" by Lara O'Reilly and Lukas I. Alpert (March 7th 2018)

[472] New York Post "Jeff Zucker joins fight to monetize mobile journalism" by Richard Morgan (February 26th 2018)

people from being able to see their articles if their browser is using an ad blocker, requiring people to turn it off or white list (allow ads on) their site in order to even see what's on the website at all.[473]

The New York Times began limiting people's ability to read free articles on their website to ten per month by either tracking their IP address or placing cookies on their computer, and later reduced it to just five articles a month.[474] When that number is exceeded, the articles are blacked out and a notice pops up saying you have exceeded the allowed free articles limit and it encourages you to become a digital subscriber for $4 per month (for the first year) which then automatically changes to $15 a month from then on. The business model of displaying digital ads next to articles on their website just isn't working anymore because there is too much competition now with countless websites all using the same ad servers.

Mainstream Asking for Donations

Things are getting so dire for the major online "news" businesses that some are now asking for donations. At the bottom of every *Guardian* article now there is a notice that reads, "Since you're here...we have a small favor to ask. More people are reading the *Guardian* than ever but advertising revenues across the media are failing fast. And unlike many news organizations, we haven't put up a paywall — we want to keep our journalism as open as we

---

[473] Business Insider "The Washington Post is blocking people with ad blockers from reading its articles" by Max Slater-Robins (September 10th 2015)

[474] The Verge "The New York Times cuts free articles limit from 10 to five per month" by Natt Garun (December 1st 2017)

can. So you can see why we need to ask for your help. The *Guardian's* independent, investigative journalism takes a lot of time, money, and hard work to produce. But we do it because we believe our perspective matters — because it might well be your perspective too. If everyone who reads our reporting, who likes it, helps fund it, our future would be much more secure. For as little as $1, you can support the *Guardian* – and it only takes a minute. Thank you."[475]

In August 2017, BuzzFeed "News" started asking for donations at the bottom of all their articles too. There's a banner that reads "Play a bigger role in our journalism" encouraging people to donate $5 dollars a month to them which readers get zero benefits for other than being added to a BuzzFeed email list. People who donate $100 get an "exclusive BuzzFeed News tote bag."[476] Soon we may see major media outlets join Patreon!

---

[475] https://contribute.theguardian.com/components/epic/inline-payment

[476] The Wall Street Journal "BuzzFeed News Asks Readers to Chip In With Donations" by Benjamin Mullin (August 27th 2018)

Wikipedia

Encyclopedia Britannica is the world's oldest encyclopedia, first published in the late 1700s. For many generations they were the standard in school libraries and some homes if parents decided to spend the $1000 plus dollars for the 32-volume set. But in 2012 the company announced they were no longer going to print the books (after 244 years), and instead Encyclopedia Britannica became an online only edition available for a small yearly subscription fee.[477] Unfortunately in the Internet age where everyone wants everything for free, Encyclopedia Britannica has been largely forgotten and Wikipedia has become the new standard "encyclopedia," which is both sad and disturbing.

Wikipedia is one of the top search results, if not *the* top search result, for almost anything you Google, and gets 33 *billion* page views a month.[478] And you probably know that literally anyone can edit almost any article on the site, anonymously, without even registering as an editor. In theory, other editors will watch over new updates and remove or correct them if someone posts incorrect information, but this often results in "edit wars" where people go back and forth posting something and then others change it, and then others change it back, and

---

[477] The Guardian "Encyclopedia Britannica halts print publication after 244 years" by Tom McCarthy (March 13th 2012

[478] Pew Research Center "Wikipedia at 15: Millions of readers in scores of languages" by Monica Anderson, Paul Hitlin, and Michelle Atkinson (January 14th 2016)

on and on. So depending on when you read an article on Wikipedia, information could be completely different or even missing entirely.

For benign pages about things like plants and animals there may be little controversy about what is said about them, but for pages that are biographies of people, particularly political figures (and even for some products and corporations which have entries on the site) they are usually a battleground between different editors fighting to have the final word in terms of what is (and is not) said about the topic.

Wikipedia is a major part of the *Liberal Media Industrial Complex* smear machine because it solidifies the liberal consensus about individuals by using careless and defamatory online articles as the "sources" for labeling someone a racist, sexist, homophobe, etc. Once outlets like the HuffPost, Daily Beast, Vox, etc., publish an article making baseless claims about a person, then the Wikipedia editors update that person's page to paint them in a false light and cite the salacious hit pieces as the source in the footnotes, cementing the allegations in the target's Wikipedia page.

Because public figures have to prove "actual malice" in a defamation case, unlike private citizens, its difficult to win a judgment against "news" outlets for libel because they can easily claim they "thought" what they were writing was accurate, or it's their opinion that someone is "far-right," "racist," "Islamophobic," etc. Often they'll sneakily add a weak qualifier about someone they're smearing by saying they are an individual "who some people call far-right." *Who* calls them that? A few random trolls on Twitter, so technically "some people" have called them that and it's a devious way many of these outlets try to get labels to stick.

They also know that suing them can easily cost a plaintiff a million dollars in legal fees, and even if they win a judgment for the defamation, that person will still be on the hook for their own legal costs, which may be much more than the actual judgement awarded to them for the defamation in the first place.

For months Wikipedia had a section on Tomi Lahren's page saying she was considered "White Power Barbie," because an article in the London *Guardian* labeled her that simply because she's a beautiful blonde woman who has had a few viral videos criticizing Black Lives Matter.[479] Wikipedia is such a pit of disinformation and slander that Ron Paul was included on their white supremacist list for three weeks before editors finally fixed it.[480] Wikipedia even listed the California Republican Party's ideology as "Nazism" for a period of time.[481]

There is even an entire Wikipedia page titled "Racial Views of Donald Trump" which paints him as a huge racist, detailing how he is a "birther" for questioning Barack Obama's heritage; taking his comments about "fine people" on "both sides" of the Confederate statue controversy out of context, and including a whole long list of supposed "evidence" that he's a racist because he

---

[479] The Guardian "The rise of Tomi Lahren, the media star lampooned as 'white power Barbie'" by Jason Wilson (September 23rd 2016)

[480] Zero Hedge "Wikipedia Listed Ron Paul On 'White Supremacists' List For 3 Weeks Before Removing Him" by Tyler Durden (July 26th 2018)

[481] CBS News "Google blames Wikipedia for 'Nazism' tag on California GOP" (June 1st 2018)

referred to El Salvador, Haiti and parts of Africa as "shit hole countries" and makes fun of Elizabeth Warren, calling her Pocahontas.

In September 2018 a Democrat congressional staffer doxed several Republican Senators including Lindsey Graham by posting their home addresses and phone numbers right on their Wikipedia pages.[482] The perpetrator was later arrested and sentenced to 4 years in prison for computer fraud and sharing restricted private information, showing the seriousness of his crime and that the lack of oversight and editorial control makes Wikipedia the Internet's equivalent of a wall in a gas station bathroom.

Wikipedia editors fiercely protect the Antifa page, and (at the time of this writing) have successfully prevented any references to their violent and terrorist activities. The subsections of the article are "History," "Ideology and Activities," and "Notable Activism;" but nothing about their violence at all.[483] These are the scum who wear black masks and look like members of ISIS that show up at events to harass, intimidate, and assault Trump supporters with sticks, bricks, and mace. This is the same group that went to Tucker Carlson's house, banged on his door, and shouted threats through a megaphone.[484]

---

[482] Washington Post "Former Democratic aide pleads guilty to 'doxing' GOP senators, threatening employee" by Spencer S. Hsu (April 6th 2019)

[483] As of the time of this writing in July 2019 although that could change. But since Antifa has been engaged in repeated violent acts for years, that's something that should have been included on their Wikipedia page long ago.

[484] Mediaite "Mob Gathers Outside Tucker Carlson's Home: 'We Know Where You Sleep at Night!'" by Joseph A. Wulfsohn (November 7th 2018)

After Antifa members assaulted Quillette journalist Andy Ngo at an event in Portland, Oregon in June 2019, punching him in the face and throwing milkshakes on him (causing him to be hospitalized for a brain hemorrhage) word of the incident made national news.[485]   President Trump even mentioned the attack but Wikipedia editors decided that it wasn't "significant" enough to warrant being included on the Antifa page.[486]

Wikipedia is also preventing any mention of the terrorist attack on an Immigrations and Customs Enforcement [ICE] facility in Tacoma, Washington, where an Antifa member approached the property armed with a rifle and firebombed the building, resulting in him being shot and killed by police. He had also posted a manifesto online before his attack using language from Alexandria Ocasio-Cortez, claiming the United States was keeping illegal immigrants in "concentration camps."   His manifesto began declaring "I am Antifa."[487]

Congresswomen Alexandria Ocasio-Cortez and Ilhan Omar refused to condemn the attack when specifically asked about it.[488]   Others, like Black Lives Matter activist Shaun King, appeared to celebrate it and encouraged people to "liberate" the "concentration camps" by any

---

[485] The Washington Times "Journalist Andy Ngo beaten up by Antifa activists at Portland protest" by Valerie Richardson (June 29th 2019)

[486] Breitbart "Wikipedia Protecting Antifa: Wikipedia Editors Protect Antifa by Censoring Andy Ngo Assault, ICE Attack" by T.D. Adler (July 18th 2019)

[487] Fox News "Washington ICE detention center attacker Willem Van Spronsen wrote 'I am Antifa' manifesto before assault" by Travis Fedschun (July 15th 2019)

[488] NewsBusters.org "The 'Squad' Won't Condemn Antifa Terrorism....WHERE Are The Media?" by Tim Graham (July 17th 2019)

means necessary because illegal aliens are being "tortured" inside.[489]

The FBI reported that Antifa has been engaging in terrorist activities, and members of the Senate, including Ted Cruz of Texas and Bill Cassidy of Louisiana introduced an official resolution deeming them a terrorist organization.[490] But not a word of any of this is included on the Wikipedia page about Antifa.[491]

Meanwhile the Wikipedia page for disgraced former FBI agent Peter Strzok says the text messages he and his mistress Lisa Page exchanged speaking of having an "insurance policy" to derail the Trump administration is just a "conspiracy theory" saying, "The revelation of the text messages led Republican congressmen and right wing media to start pushing conspiracy theories to the effect that Strzok was involved in a secret plot to undermine the Trump presidency."[492]

There have been controversies surrounding certain Wikipedia editors being paid to protect pages of political figures as well as big names in tech and the media.[493] Others, like myself, have no hope of ever having a fair or accurate representation on Wikipedia. Right now my

---

[489] https://twitter.com/shaunking/status/1144944444992450560

[490] TownHall "Republicans Craft Resolution Condemning Antifa As A 'Domestic Terrorist Organization'" by Timothy Meads (July 19th 2019)

[491] As of July 2019. Increased pressure could change this, but the fact remains, for months (or perhaps years) Wikipedia editors have vigorously protected the page, scrubbing any references to Antifa's violence.

[492] https://en.wikipedia.org/wiki/Peter_Strzok (Accessed May 2nd 2019)

[493] Breitbart "Wikipedia Editors Paid to Protect Political, Tech, and Media Figures" by T.D. Adler (March 26th 2019)

page says that I'm best known for being a "conspiracy theorist" because I wrote a few books about the Illuminati when I was younger with the subtitle of "Facts & Fiction" separating the facts from the fiction, because they *are* a historical group that became a pop culture phenomena in the early 2010s.   It's an interesting subject I was fascinated with for a period of time, but the Wikipedia editors forever want me branded as a "conspiracy theorist" for daring to look into the topic.

And while I have had a sizable YouTube audience steadily growing ever since 2006, at the end of the 2016 presidential election my channel exploded. But for years after that (and currently at the time I'm writing this) the editor overlords at Wikipedia won't allow ANY mention of my YouTube stats on my page, which is standard for professional YouTubers.

Several liberal YouTubers whose channels that are much smaller than mine, like that of Kyle Kulinski who runs the Secular Talk channel, and David Pakman have their Wikipedia pages loaded with details about their subscriber counts and viewership and all the news sites which have mentioned them; but not mine. My YouTube subscriber count isn't allowed to be mentioned at all.[494] Wikipedia gives the impression that my career ended in 2015, when in reality it took off in 2016, and I was the

---

[494] As of August 2019, although this could change if I happen to get some favorable media coverage highlighting my subscriber count, but it hasn't been allowed on my page which has been up since 2007.

first conservative YouTube channel to reach 1 million subscribers.[495]

Despite my 2017 book, *The True Story of Fake News,* reaching the #15 best seller spot (of all books) on Amazon (and #1 in its category for weeks) the Wikipedia editors say it's not "significant" enough to mention on my page! My book which came out the following year, *Liberalism: Find a Cure,* also hit #15 on Amazon best seller's list (of all books, not just a certain category) but they still refuse to even mention it! One of the editors who fiercely guards my page wrote on the Talk Page discussion about the edits that, "The books were removed via consensus at some point because there were no reliable sources that mentioned them as being significant."[496]

Another editor writing about why my YouTube subscriber count is not allowed on the page says, "I think there is enough evidence that subscriber counts have been manipulated in the recent past that we should not be including this information in this article."[497]

They also removed (and are preventing any mention of) all the television shows I've appeared in, including *Secret Societies of Hollywood* on the E! channel, *America Declassified* on the Travel Channel, *America's Book of Secrets* on the History Channel, *Conspiracy Theory with Jesse Ventura* on TruTV, as well as shows on the

---

[495] SocialBlade.com lists the historical YouTube statistics for all channels. Under "Detailed Statistics" it shows my channel reached 1 million subscribers in May 2017, and Paul Joseph Watson followed in August 2017, then PragerU in September 2017, Stephen Crowder in November 2017, and Ben Shapiro's Daily Wire in October 2018, and Next News Network in February 2019

[496] TonyBallioni 23:23, 2 February 2019 (UTC)

[497] Barkeep49 17:19, 30 January 2019 (UTC)

Sundance Channel and interviews on Fox News. These appearances are all listed on IMDB and other media outlets, but the Wikipedia editors have decided that mentioning them would make me look too popular, so they dumped them down the memory hole and are preventing anyone from adding them back to the page.

Larry Sanger, the co-founder of Wikipedia (who is no longer with the organization), chimed in on Twitter when I was complaining about this, saying, "If these idiots don't like you, then they will ignore their own f'n rules. You're far from being the first this has happened to. It pisses me off. Arrogant little SOBs."[498]

He now calls Wikipedia "a broken system" and says "Wikipedia has long since decided to turn the other cheek when influential editors make articles speak with one point of view, when they dismiss unpopular views, or when they utterly fail to do justice to alternative approaches to a topic."[499]

The *Washington Times* did an article about my "battle" with Wikipedia after I made a YouTube video about it, but instead of fixing the page the editors scrubbed any mention of my education credentials, deleting the fact that I have a bachelor's degree in Communication. They then added a few lines that I once made "numerous homophobic statements" about a Korean boy band after they played at the American Music Awards. I had simply tweeted a picture of them with the caption, "Meet the Korean lesbian pop group BTS featured at the American Music Awards #AMAs last night."

---

[498] https://twitter.com/lsanger/status/1096227555466596352

[499] 150Sec.com "'Wikipedia is a broken system,' says co-founder Larry Sanger" by Sophie Foggin (May 22nd 2019)

It was clearly a joke because the band members looked very feminine and had blue hair like a stereotypical lesbian. *Teen Vogue* magazine wrote an article about my tweet because the group's teeny bopper fans got upset and started a petition on Change.org urging the band to sue me, and *that* is the "reliable" source Wikipedia used to add a section to my page branding me "homophobic."

They also added a line about how I had been temporarily suspended from Twitter for making "transphobic" comments (in reality saying there are only two genders.) They're trying to paint me in the most negative light possible, citing random articles from little-known or garbage websites that happened to mention jokes I've made on Twitter, while at the same time preventing any real information about my career, my credentials, and my success from being mentioned at all.

Wikipedia founder Jimmy Wales (who now lives in England) got so triggered when President Trump visited the UK in June 2019, he tweeted that he was leaving the country until Trump returned to the United States.[500] He was widely mocked in the replies, including by me, causing him to block me. (He later unblocked me after people continued to ridicule him over the block.)

Google has donated millions of dollars to Wikipedia to help cover their operating expenses,[501] and guess who else has given them millions as well—George Soros.[502]

---

[500] https://twitter.com/jimmy_wales/status/1135456897899945984

[501] Tech Crunch "Google.org donates $2 million to Wikipedia's parent org" by Megan Rose Dickey (January 22nd 2019)

[502] Wikimedia Foundation "George Soros, founder of Open Society Foundations, invests in the future of free and open knowledge" by Kaitlin Thaney (October 18th 2018)

You'd think with all their money they could have just funded the Encyclopedia Britannica and made *that* free to the world instead of giving it to such a garbage website filled with inaccuracies and biased information, but then the Left's army of online trolls wouldn't be able to edit entries about people and political policies they want to control the perception of.

Author's Note: If you haven't already, please take a moment to rate and review this book on Amazon.com, Kindle, Google Play, iBooks, or wherever you bought it from, to let other potential readers know how valuable this information is.

Almost all of the one-star reviews on Amazon for my last two books "The True Story of Fake News" and "Liberalism: Find a Cure" are from NON-verified purchases which shows the "reviewers" probably didn't even read them and just hate me.

So if you could help me offset their fake one-star reviews by leaving a real one yourself since you actually read the book, that would help a lot!

Thank you!

Google

Google is the most-visited website in the world, and is so popular that "Google" has become a verb meaning to look something up. They dominate not just the search engine industry, but others as well, since a large number of the most popular mobile apps are also owned by Google (like G-mail, Google Maps, Chrome, Google Play, Google Drive, Google News, etc.).

Most people assume Google knows the answers to everything, and think the top search results for what they're looking for is the correct answer. Studies have shown that over 90% of the time people click on what is served up on page one and rarely even look at page two or beyond.[503] The ranking of search results gives Google an enormous amount of power since each page shows just ten different results out of hundreds of thousands, or millions of possible webpages. They can easily prevent people from finding articles or websites by just dropping them down to page two or three in the results.

Google's ability to surface certain information they want to promote while suppressing what they don't like by manipulating their algorithm gives them enormous power to artificially boost certain companies, products, or political candidates and causes over others.

Speaking of the 2016 election, one Google engineer wrote in internal emails, "This was an election of false

---

[503] Search Engine Watch "No. 1 Position in Google Gets 33% of Search Traffic [Study]" by Jessica Lee (June 20th 2013)

equivalencies, and Google, sadly, had a hand in it."[504] They then suggested manipulating the search results to bury articles from Breitbart and the Daily Caller, saying, "How many times did you see the Election now card with items from opinion blogs (Breitbart, Daily Caller) elevated next to legitimate news organizations? That's something that can and should be fixed."[505]

"I think we have a responsibility to expose the quality and truthfulness of sources—because not doing so hides real information under loud noises...Beyond that, let's concentrate on teaching critical thinking. A little bit of that would go a long way. Let's make sure that we reverse things in four years—demographics will be on our side."[506]

Google insiders also discussed manipulating the search results to counter President Trump's proposed "Travel Ban" in January 2017 which would have prevented people living in countries with high rates of terrorist activity from entering the United States for a period of time. *The Wall Street Journal* reported, "Google Workers Discussed Tweaking Search Function to Counter Travel Ban,"[507] and detailed, "Days after the Trump administration instituted a controversial travel ban in January 2017, Google employees discussed ways they might be able to tweak the company's search-related

---

[504] The Daily Caller "Exclusive: Google Employees Debated Burying Conservative Media In Search" by Peter Hasson (November 29th 2018)

[505] Ibid.

[506] Ibid.

[507] The Wall Street Journal "Google Workers Discussed Tweaking Search Function to Counter Travel Ban" by John D. McKinnon and Douglas MacMilan (September 20th 2018)

functions to show users how to contribute to pro-immigration organizations and contact lawmakers and government agencies, according to internal company emails."[508]

Those emails showed that, "employees proposed ways to 'leverage' search functions and take steps to counter what they considered to be 'Islamophobia.'"[509] After they were leaked, Google issued a statement denying that they had actually done it, and said the plan was just a "brainstorm of ideas."[510]

A Google employee who has been leaking information to Breitbart told them, "I know there are efforts to demote anything non-PC, anti-Communist and anti-Islamic terror from search results. To what extent that has been successful, I don't know."[511] PJ Media did an examination of the search results for the word "Trump" in the Google News tab and calculated that 96% of the results were from liberal media outlets.[512] Similar informal tests have been done by searching for various other topics, such as when Fox News founder Roger Ailes died people noticed that most search results painted him as a monster, with articles from Rolling Stone declaring

---

[508] Ibid.

[509] Ibid.

[510] Fox Business "Google employee discussions on altering search function after travel ban raise bias concerns" by Thomas Barrabi (September 21st 2018)

[511] Breitbart "Former Google Employee: 'There Are Efforts to Demote Anything Non-PC from Search Results'" by Allum Bokhari (August 8th 2017)

[512] PJ Media "96 Percent of Google Search Results for 'Trump' News Are from Liberal Media Outlets" by Paula Bolyard (August 25th 2018)

he was "one of the worst Americans ever" surfacing at the top, along with others like one from NBC News claiming he "built a kingdom on exploited bias," and the London *Guardian* saying he helped "create this nightmare world."[513]   A study at Northwestern University's Computational Journalism Lab also found that the majority of search results on Google News were from left-leaning outlets.[514]

If you search for the same key words on Google and Bing, or Duck Duck Go, you'll often notice dramatically different results.   On numerous occasions when doing research for this book I have Googled various topics trying to find articles that I had seen in the past so I could use them as the citations and had a difficult time finding many of them on Google, but when I looked on other search engines they were in the top results.   Sometimes when I was even searching for an article's exact title after having copied and pasted it into my notes when I first saw it posted on social media, it wouldn't show up on the first page of search results on Google.

Google even rolled out a new "fact check" widget as part of their supposed fight against "fake news" but after a report from the *Daily Caller* showed the feature was targeting mostly conservative news sites in attempts to paint their overall reporting as inaccurate or misleading, (while ignoring false stories published by BuzzFeed, the Huffington Post, Vox, Salon, and others) Google shut

---

[513] World Net Daily "Does Google have a liberal bias? Search Results for Roger Ailes Speak Volumes" via Heat Street (May 21st 2017)

[514] Washington Times "Handful of 'left leaning sources' dominate Google's 'top stories' study finds" by Gabriella Munoz (May 12th 2019)

down the feature saying they "encountered challenges" and admitted they were "unable to deliver the quality" they hoped to provide their users.[515]

Google deleted Dr. Patrick Moore from the list of Greenpeace founders after he made headlines for insulting Alexandria Ocasio-Cortez over her ridiculous Green New Deal and praised President Trump.[516] Google often displays what are called "knowledge panels" as the top search results for certain topics, which are small boxes highlighting a few main points about the subject. And prior to his headline-making comments about the moronic Congresswoman, Dr. Patrick Moore was included in the knowledge panel when someone searched for "Greenpeace founders," but immediately after insulting her royal highness, Google mysteriously scrubbed him from it.[517]

The knowledge panel for the popular pro-life movie *Unplanned* (2019) listed the genre as "propaganda" when it first came out, instead of "drama," "action," or "science fiction" like all other movies are labeled. As usual, after word went viral on social media of this "mistake" Google fixed it.[518]

A group at the American Institute for Behavioral Research and Technology concluded a study in April 2018

---

[515] The Daily Caller "Google Suspends Fact Check Project, Rediting The DNCF Investigation with Decision" by Eric Lieberman (January 19th 2018)

[516] Daily Caller "Tech Tyranny!' Greenpeace Co-Founder Claims Google Scrubbed Him From List of Founders" by Virginia Kruta (March 17th 2019)

[517] World Net Daily "Google makes Greenpeace co-founder 'vanish'" by Art Moore (March 18th 2019)

[518] Daily Caller "Google Backs Down After Labeling Pro-Life Movie 'Propaganda'" by Mary Margaret Olohan (April 12th 2019)

after looking into how much Google's search results could influence undecided voters by surfacing negative or positive results about certain issues and candidates and reported that such manipulation could shift the preference of those voters between 20 and 80 percent.[519] The same research team led by search engine expert Dr. Robert Epstein concluded that during the 2018 midterm election, Google had been able to flip three key congressional seats from Republican to Democrat due to the prevalence of pro-Democrat bias in the search results.[520]

A former Google employee who worked as a "design ethicist" where he studied the ethics of using technology to persuade people, later warned in a TED talk, "A handful of people, working at a handful of technology companies, through their choices will steer what a billion people are thinking today."[521]

Even Google News has recently changed to prevent people from finding exactly what they are looking for. The "News" tab is used to retrieve only search results from mainstream and brand name news sources, not just any random website like the main Google search page. You used to be able to select specific topics you're interested in and Google News would show recent stories about those topics all on one page, but in 2017 they changed the layout making it much more difficult to customize your Google News feed, and now you have to

---

[519] Breitbart "EXCLUSIVE — Research: Google Search Manipulation Can Swing Nearly 80 Percent of Undecided Voters" by Allum Bokhari (April 24th 2018)

[520] Breitbart "Research: Google Search Bias Flipped Seats for Democrats in Midterms" by Allum Bokhari (March 22nd 2019)

[521] TED "How a handful of tech companies control billions of minds every day" (July 26th 2017)

click on each individual topic you're interested in, making it tedious and cumbersome, thus encouraging users to rely on the Google News home page which contains stories curated by their editors instead of creating a custom feed to see only the topics *you* want to read about.

Then in March 2018 Google announced their "News Initiative" plan promising to give $300 million dollars to various "news" organizations over the next three years, as well as offer them various tools and services in order to help them expand their online presence.[522] They have so much money they're just giving it away, probably to garbage websites like Vox, the Daily Beast, and HuffPost.

The Internet created an even playing field allowing someone on a laptop in their kitchen to create a website (or YouTube channel) which gave them access to the same number of potential readers (or viewers) as brand name newspapers and TV networks, and completely changed the power dynamics in media, since ordinary people could bypass the traditional gatekeepers of editors and producers who decide what gets published on their platforms.

But this power shift has caused a massive backlash and we're seeing the very tech companies which created the infrastructure that empowered the individual now quietly working to tip the scale back in favor of the massive corporations their technology once disrupted.

Champions of "Diversity"

Google's corporate culture is liberal to the core, and one brave conservative employee leaked a video of an

---

[522] Fortune "Google Has Announced a $300 Million Initiative to Support News Organizations" by Eli Meixler (March 21st 2018)

internal meeting held just after the 2016 election showing all the senior executives sitting around talking about how disgusted they were with Donald Trump's victory and that they're "sure" most people in the company agree.[523]

Google is such a "champion" for "diversity" and "social justice" that there are reportedly tampon dispensers in men's bathrooms because "some men menstruate."[524]   In August 2017 Google fired engineer James Damore after he wrote and circulated a memo internally titled "Google's Ideological Echo Chamber" which was critical of the company's corporate culture and their diversity policies which were aiming to hire more women.

Damore pointed out that because of the biological differences between men and women, most women tend to be more interested in social activities than engineering (people rather than things).   Google soon fired him for "sexism" for daring to point out well-established facts about the differences between men and women. Various psychologists including Geoffrey Miller, a professor at the University of New Mexico; Jordan Peterson, professor of Psychology at the University of Toronto; Lee Jussim, social psychology professor at Rutgers University; and others publicly defended Damore's memo as being scientifically sound.

Damore then filed a class action lawsuit against Google and is suing them for discrimination against conservatives and white men since their diversity policies

---

[523] CNET "Google's Sergey Brin calls 2016 election 'offensive' in leaked video" by Richard Vieva (September 12th 2018)

[524] Breitbart "Rebels of Google: Tampons Kept in Men's Restrooms Because 'Some Men Menstruate'" by Lucas Nolan (August 17th 2017)

are inherently discriminatory because they openly favor women and people of color in the hiring process instead of choosing applicants who are best qualified for the job, regardless of their race or gender.[525]

Has Google Committed Treason?

Billionaire tech investor and PayPal co-founder Peter Thiel says the FBI and CIA should investigate Google for possibly committing treason because of their "decision to work with the Chinese military and not with the US military."[526]   Google had been secretly working on a special search engine for China that was compatible with their strict censorship rules and would have linked people's phone numbers to their searches so the Communist government could monitor what everyone was looking up.[527]

The project was only revealed after someone leaked documents to *The Intercept* in August 2018. Google had already been working with the Communist Chinese government since 2006 on their "Google.cn" (Google China) which allowed officials to blacklist certain search terms, but Dragonfly, the codename of the newer system they were working on, was going to be fully compatible

---

[525] Tech Crunch "James Damore just filed a class action lawsuit against Google, saying it discriminates against white male conservatives" by Connie Loizos (January 8th 2018)

[526] CNET "Trump backs billionaire supporter Peter Thiel's calls for Google investigation" by Dhara Singh and Sean Keane (July 17th 2019)

[527] The Guardian "Google's prototype Chinese search engine links searches to phone numbers" by Noah Smith (September 18th 2018)

with China's "social credit score" system which tracks and rates citizens based on their personal activities.[528]

Senator Josh Hawley called Google "the most dishonest company to appear before Congress" after one of their executives testified before a Senate Intelligence Committee and was evasive in many of his answers.[529]

Creepy Google

There are also serious privacy issues with Google for those who use it in the U.S. and other countries around the world. Most people don't think about it too often, but they're telling Google more than they tell their spouse or their best friend since people sometimes search for answers about relationship or health problems they are keeping to themselves.

Google knows exactly who you are and keeps a log of everything you've searched for and what links you've clicked on. All of this information is then analyzed and sorted to create detailed profiles of people, their personalities, interests, income, and other data points about them.

When asked about the privacy concerns surrounding Google, then-CEO Eric Schmidt responded, "There is what I call the creepy line. The Google policy on a lot of things is to get right up to the creepy line and not cross it."[530] They are, however, so creepy, that in the future

---

[528] Forbes "Project Dragonfly And Google's Threat To Anti-Democratic Processes" by Julian Vigo (October 18th 2018)

[529] https://twitter.com/HawleyMO/status/1151287368382656519

[530] Washington Post "Eric Schmidt: Google's Policy Is To 'Get Right Up To The Creepy Line And Not Cross It'" by Nick Saint (October 1st 2010)

they want to wire the Internet directly into people's brains.[531]

Google engineer Ray Kurzweil is one of the leading proponents of Transhumanism and hopes to one day upload his brain into the Internet so he can become a god-like "immortal" being.[532] Such megalomaniacal goals seem like science fiction and have been the plot of various films like *The Lawnmower Man* (1992) and *Transcendence* (2014), but Kurzweil is serious and has the backing of one of the world's wealthiest tech companies.

Google is also a lead developer of artificial intelligence which an increasing number of tech leaders and scientists worry may quickly get out of control and end up exterminating or enslaving the human race.[533] Other companies, including Elon Musk's Neuralink, are developing brain-computer interfaces in hopes of enabling humans to merge with AI by turning us all into cyborgs.[534] But these are topics for a whole other book.

Google's former motto was "Don't be evil," a phrase that was also included in their official code of conduct, but in April 2018 they quietly removed all references of it, and sadly it seems more every day that is exactly what they are becoming.

---

[531] CNET "Google boss predicts Google implant will put the Web in your head by 2020" by Richard Trenhold (November 10th 2010)

[532] PBS News Hour "Inventor Ray Kurzweil sees immortality in our future" (March 24th 2016)

[533] Time "5 Very Smart People Who Think Artificial Intelligence Could Bring the Apocalypse" by Victor Luckerson (December 2nd 2014)

[534] Business Insider "Elon Musk believes AI could turn humans into an endangered species like the mountain gorilla" by Isobel Asher Hamilton (November 26th 2018)

Rise of Social Media

From the creation of the printing press in 1439 to the telegraph in 1837, to radio in 1895 and television in 1927, each new form of media revolutionized society, but the development of the Internet far surpassed all previous communication technologies, especially since it's now fully mobile and in our pocket wherever we go. It's changed almost everything from how we interact with our friends to how we get our news and entertainment, and people gauge what topics and events are the "most popular" because they're "trending" on social media.

As futurist George Gilder noted, "Computer networks give every hacker the creative potential of a factory tycoon of the industrial era and the communications power of a TV magnate of the broadcasting era."[535] That's the capability of what's been dubbed Internet 2.0, or the two-way communication networks the Internet now enables, instead of just static websites.

Comedian Dane Cook was one of the first comics to use social media to promote himself in the early 2000s through MySpace, and many of his early critics called him a better marketer than a comic because they didn't see his humor as all that funny but couldn't deny his popularity. "I remember getting ready to play Madison

---

[535] Media/Impact: An Introduction to Mass Media (12th Edition) by Shirley Biagi page 176

Square Garden," he recalled to the *Hollywood Reporter*. "I posted once on MySpace and without spending a dime on any promotion or advertising, we sold out."[536]

Similarly, Tila Tequila became the most popular person on MySpace in 2006 from posting racy photos of herself, taking advantage of the new medium and getting floods of friend requests from lonely losers online who hoped to connect with her.[537] Her popularity on My Space opened the door for her (bisexual) dating show *A Shot at Love with Tila Tequila* on MTV in 2007, which began her 15 minutes of fame.

In the early years of social media most people just saw the technology as something to use for fun, and a way to entertain themselves or reconnect with old friends, but as time went on the true power and ability to influence large numbers of people through it became apparent.

One member of the Obama administration called journalists on social media "force multipliers" (a fancy term for propagandists) and admitted, "We have our compadres, I [would] reach out to a couple people, and you know I wouldn't want to name them." These people were "prominent Washington reporters and columnists who [would] often tweet in sync with [Obama's] messaging."[538]

Obama's former campaign "mastermind" David Axelrod admitted, "over the last couple of years, there's been an investment in alternative means of

---

[536] Hollywood Reporter "Bring On the Haters: Dane Cook Is Plotting a Comedy Comeback" by Ryan Parker February 13th 2019)

[537] Slate "Tila Tequila for President" by Jonah Weiner (April 11th 2006)

[538] New York Times "The Aspiring Novelist Who Became Obama's Foreign-Policy Guru" by David Samuels (May 5th 2016)

communication: using digital more effectively, going to nontraditional sources, understanding where on each issue your constituencies are going to be found. I think they've approached these major foreign-policy challenges as campaign challenges, and they've run [social media] campaigns, and those campaigns have been very sophisticated."[539]

Amateur video caught Hillary Clinton collapsing at the 9/11 memorial after her campaign and the mainstream media kept dismissing growing concerns that there was something wrong with her health in the final stretch of the 2016 presidential election.[540] The video first went viral through social media before finally getting covered in the mainstream press because so many people were talking about it. The Washington Post, which had been calling questions about her health "conspiracy theories," then finally admitted, "Hillary Clinton's health just became a real issue in the presidential campaign."[541]

A bartender working at a fundraiser held by Mitt Romney in 2012 captured the then-presidential candidate on video talking about how 47% of the country wouldn't vote for him because they'll support Obama no matter what since they want free hand outs so he wasn't going to pay much attention to them.[542] Liberals pretended to be outraged and accused Mitt of not caring about half of the

---

[539] Ibid.

[540] The Washington Post "Hillary Clinton's health just became a real issue in the presidential campaign" by Chris Cillizza (September 11th 2016)

[541] Ibid.

[542] ABC News "The Lesson of Mitt Romney's 47-Percent Video: Be Nice to the Wait Staff?" by Chris Good (March 14th 2013)

country, particularly lower income folks, and the video proved to be quit damaging to his campaign.

Bloggers were the ones who first debunked the fake documents *CBS News* anchor Dan Rather claimed were the service records of George W. Bush from his time in the National Guard.[543]   Matt Drudge's *Drudge Report* website first broke the Monica Lewinsky scandal when other outlets were sitting on the story and refused to cover it.[544]   Facebook and Google now account for 25% of all advertising spending, both online and off.[545]   Social media has swallowed up the news business, and the power-shift has been revolutionary.

Getting "News" on Social Media

We all know kids love their devices, and virtually live their lives on them. An entire generation of children have been raised on them, and get babysat by smartphones since parents use them to keep kids occupied while seated in the shopping cart at the grocery store and even at the dinner table.   It's how they communicate with their friends, listen to music, watch movies, and so it only makes sense that's where they get their news.

A study conducted by Internet security company Anchor Free for the Jack Meyers Knowledge Exchange reported, "When asked to identify their two primary

---

[543] The Los Angeles Times "No Disputing It: Blogs Are Major Players" by Peter Wallsten (September 12th 2004)

[544] Washington Post "Twenty years ago, the Drudge Report broke the Clinton-Lewinsky scandal" by Annys Shin (January 11th 2018)

[545] Business Insider "Google and Facebook dominate digital advertising — and they now account for 25% of all ad sales, online or off" by Caroline Cakebread (December 7th 2017)

sources of news, the majority of this cohort name Instagram (29 percent), You Tube (22 percent), and Facebook (15 percent) as the media where they are most likely to read/see the news. Fewer than a quarter of young people depend on newspaper or television news, with 8 percent reading national newspapers such as the New York Times, Washington Post, and USA Today, 10 percent watching broadcast and cable network news, and 6 percent exposed regularly to local television news or newspapers...By comparison, a stunning 82 percent of Gen Z and younger millennials include among their primary news sources Reddit, Twitter, Facebook, YouTube, BuzzFeed, Instagram, Snapchat and their desktop newsfeed."[546]

Media advisor Jack Myers warned, "Without the traditional filters of trusted news organizations and journalists, this new generation of potential voters may be highly susceptible to fake and biased news and may find it difficult to discern fact from fiction. Compounding this reality, Instagram — the #1 source of news for young people — is dependent almost exclusively on visual images, and none of the major social media channels invest meaningfully in original news reporting, nor do they provide user-tools for deeper investigative analysis of their content."[547]

Of course it's not just kids who are increasingly relying on social media for their news, it's everyone.

---

[546] The Ripon Forum "How Generation Z Gets their News" by Jack Myers (Volume 52, No1 February 2018)

[547] Ibid.

THE LIBERAL MEDIA INDUSTRIAL COMPLEX

Homeland Security Studying Influencers

Because so many people are now getting their news from social media and there are millions of ways stories can be planted online and go viral governments around the world are very interested in tracking and studying the flow of information through these new channels of distribution. In 2018 the Department of Homeland Security revealed they were developing systems to monitor the social media feeds of various journalists, bloggers, and social media influencers in order to "identify any and all media coverage related to the Department of Homeland Security or a particular event."[548]

In other words there are very serious national security concerns, as well as issues and events local law enforcement need to monitor on social media because they can easily cause real-world consequences.

A report in the *Chicago Sun Times* notes, they were building a database "to monitor the public activities of media members and influencers" so the government would have the ability "to create unlimited data tracking, statistical breakdown, and graphical analyses on ad-hoc basis."[549] They reportedly are tracking 300,000 different accounts to create a realtime information matrix of topics that are being talked about and how they spread.

Shortly after the 2016 election I myself was contacted by the United States Special Operations Command which integrates various branches of the U.S. Armed Forces

[548] Chicago Sun Times "Homeland Security to compile database of journalists and 'media influencers'" by Sun-Times Staff (April 7th 2018

[549] Ibid.

192

because they wanted to interview me and even send a team of researchers to observe me working so they could learn how my YouTube channel had become so popular in the final stretch of the 2016 election. I declined their request.

Operation Earnest Voice

Around 2011 the U.S. government launched a program called Operation Earnest Voice which uses specialized software that allows military personnel to create and manage fake social media profiles of various "people" in order to use them for propaganda purposes.[550]

The government claims they're only doing this on websites outside the United States because technically (until President Obama amended it in 2012) it was a violation of the Smith-Mundt Modernization Act for the military to target our own citizens with propaganda, but it's hard to believe that such technology isn't being used by U.S. government agencies in black ops on the major social media platforms to influence the American people.

Obviously all countries engage in cyber warfare, and in the 21st century that means flooding social media with bots and trolls to push certain agendas or to disrupt various discussions. The London *Guardian* surprisingly admitted in 2015 that, "Israel Defense Forces have pioneered state military engagement with social media, with dedicated teams operating since Operation Cast Lead, its war in Gaza in 2008-9. The IDF is active on 30

---

[550] The Guardian "Revealed: US spy operation that manipulates social media" by Nick Fielding and Ian Cobain (March 17th 2011)

platforms – including Twitter, Facebook, YouTube and Instagram – in six languages."[551]

The Chinese government was caught using Twitter trolls and posting propaganda videos on YouTube designed to demonize protesters in Hong Kong in the Summer of 2019 when pro-democracy demonstrations broke out.[552]

And everyone knows Russia used social media to cause disruption during the 2016 election by promoting both pro-Trump and anti-Trump content, however its effect has been greatly exaggerated by Democrats, causing a modern day moral panic. It's rarely reported that the biggest Black Lives Matter page on Facebook, which had over 700,000 followers, was found to be run by a white guy in Australia who was using it to scam people into donating money to him.[553]

Another huge Black Lives Matter Facebook page called "Blactivist" (meaning black activist) which had over 360,000 followers was found to be part of Russia's disinformation campaign against the United States and used the page to incite division and fan the flames of racism.[554]

Michael Moore even promoted and attended a protest outside of Trump Tower in New York City that had been

---

[551] The Guardian "British army creates team of Facebook warriors" by Ewan MacAskill (January 31st 2015)

[552] Engadget "YouTube pulls hundreds of channels tied to Hong Kong influence campaign" by Richard Lawler (August 23rd 2019)

[553] Washington Post "Facebook's most popular Black Lives Matter page was a scam run by a white Australian, report says" by Amy B Wang (April 10th 2018)

[554] CNN "Exclusive: Fake black activist accounts linked to Russian government" by Donie O'Sullivan and Dylan Byers (September 28th 2017)

organized by the Russians.[555]   So to say that Russian meddling in American social media circles was just to support Donald Trump over Hillary Clinton is just plain false.

Social Media Causing Mental Health Problems

While social media is a powerful tool, it is hard to control. And it seems with every benefit it brings comes the equivalent of an equal sized detriment. The younger generations are getting lost in a world of isolation and have few real-world friendships or interactions. Social media is being increasingly linked to mental disorders amongst teens since it has become a fixture in their lives.[556]   Feeling the need to share how "great" and "perfect" one's life is through carefully choreographed Instagram photos or Facebook posts appears to be increasing people's anxiety and depression.[557]

Many people have become literally addicted to their phones, not to mention that social media blew the door wide open for kids to be cyber-bullied 24-hours-a-day by their fellow classmates who are now able to harass them when they're not even at school, and can reach them when they're supposedly in the safety of their own homes. Teen suicide rates have skyrocketed due to cyber bullying because now kids can never get away from their bullies

[555] Fox News "Michael Moore participated in anti-Trump rally allegedly organized by Russians" by Gregg Re (February 20th 2018)

[556] NBC "Social media linked to rise in mental health disorders in teens survey finds" by Shamard Charles (March 14th 2019)

[557] Time "Why Instagram Is the Worst Social Media for Mental Health" by Amanda Macmillan (May 25th 2017)

no matter where they go.[558]   One study even found that close to 6% of kids aged 12 through 17 have set up fake social media accounts and cyber bullied *themselves* so they could get attention for being a "victim."[559]

Many people are also developing "mean world syndrome," which is a term coined by professor George Gerbner who was the dean of the communication department at the University of Pennsylvania. He was a leading researcher in the effects of mass media and concluded that the more time someone spends consuming mass media, the more distorted their view of how the world actually gets, ultimately leading them to think society is a much more dangerous and "mean" place than it actually is since their perceptions are shaped through the warped representations of the world by the media, which amplifies atrocities, arguments, and divisions.

Gerbner's "mean world syndrome" phenomenon was coined in the age of television, and now that most people are glued to their phones and are consuming an almost nonstop diet of media, one can see how the syndrome has only gotten worse. Spending too much time on social media and being bombarded by the never-ending political conflicts and fear-mongering about things like global warming, mass shootings, and racism is wreaking havoc on the mental health of millions.

Many people are getting so depraved that when they witness a tragedy like a car accident or an assault, instead of helping the victims or calling for help, their first

---

[558] New York Post "Rise in teen suicide connected to social media popularity: study" via Associated Press (November 14th 2017)

[559] USA Today "Cyberbullying's chilling trend: Teens anonymously target themselves online, study finds" by N'dea Yancey-Bragg (November 8th 2017)

thought is to take pictures so they can post them on social media.[560]

No Customer Service

Despite the Big Tech companies being an integral part of most people's lives; unlike almost every other company that offers products or services to the public, there are no customer service phone numbers at Facebook, Twitter, YouTube, or Google. You can't get anyone on the phone there to talk with them about problems you've experienced or the grievances you have with their companies. Despite names like Mark Zuckerberg and Jack Dorsey attached to them, they remain faceless corporations you can't get in touch with.

There's no local branch you can visit where you can ask to speak with a manager, and instead users are relegated to sending tweets or submitting a "help ticket" from within the apps' dashboard, and those attempts to get answers often only result in automated responses thanking you for contacting them and saying they'll try to look into it. The social media giants are actually strangely anti-social.

For those of you who read my previous book, *The True Story of Fake News: How Mainstream Media Manipulates Millions*, you know I dedicated different chapters to Facebook, Twitter, Google, and YouTube, where I detailed their Orwellian manipulation and censorship, but since their underhanded activities have only continued, it is necessary to dedicate chapters to each

---

[560] New York Post "Man fatally stabbed on subway while onlookers post on social media" by Tamar Lapin (January 17th 2018)

of them again in this book to discuss their more recent activities.

I'll keep the overlapping information to a minimum and mostly cover what they've been doing since the publication of my previous book because you need to know how far they're going to regain control of the genie they let out of the bottle.

Facebook

For countless millions of people Facebook became the family photo album, their contact list, and even their diary of sorts. First started in 2004 as a social network for college kids, it quickly expanded to become the most popular one in the world used by 2.2 *billion* monthly active users.[561] Its dominance made founder Mark Zuckerberg the youngest billionaire in history at the age of twenty-three.[562]

For those naive enough to fill in all the entry boxes when they first signed up for Facebook, the company knows not only who you're friends with, who you're dating or married to (as well as when you break up or get a divorce), but also which TV shows, movies, and music you like, which restaurants and businesses you visit, what cities you travel to, where you work, your birthdate, your personal interests, hobbies, and more.

It's free because *you* are the product and your personal data is what you are trading in exchange for using Facebook. NSA whistleblower Edward Snowden noted, "Businesses that make money by collecting and selling detailed records of private lives were once plainly described as 'surveillance companies.' Their rebranding as 'social media' is the most successful deception since

---

[561] NBC News "Facebook hits 2.27 billion monthly active users as earnings stabilize" by Jason Abbruzzes (October 30th 2018)

[562] Business Insider "How old 15 self-made billionaires were when they earned their first billion" by Kathleen Elkins (February 17th 2016)

the Department of War became the Department of Defense."[563]

Many millennials and Generation Z kids either quit Facebook or never signed up, and prefer Instagram (which is owned by Facebook) and SnapChat because they don't want be on the same social network as their parents. Despite the endless scandals about abusing users' personal information, Facebook hasn't gone the way of MySpace (at least not yet) and remains one of the world's top social networks.

While people use Facebook for various reasons—like keeping in touch with friends and family, many use it to share news stories and videos about political issues, but it wasn't until after the 2016 presidential election that Facebook saw this as a problem. As you know, the Democrats largely blamed Facebook for Hillary's loss, citing the spread of supposed "fake news" about her they claimed had caused people to see her in a negative light and not vote for her.

Hillary was supposed to pound the final nails in the coffin of the United States of America, and usher in the New World Order for her globalist puppet masters, but Donald Trump canceled those plans. The war mongering neocons in the Bush administration, followed by the charismatic socialist Barack Obama had set the stage, knocking out most of the legs from under our once-great Republic.

But the election of Donald Trump changed everything, and he began to right the ship. The scheming globalists were furious. The very tools that Facebook had proudly created so people could share information with others were now seen as a problem because they disrupted the

---

[563] https://twitter.com/Snowden/status/975147858096742405

traditional channels of distribution that were controlled by major media companies. If anyone posted a message, link, photo, or video, that post could be seen by as many people who read the *New York Times* or watch the *NBC Nightly News* from other Facebook users simply clicking the "share" button. But all that had to change because the "Russians" had posted "fake news" about Hillary Clinton.

Rob Goldman, Vice President of Ads at Facebook, admitted, "The majority of the Russian ad spend happened AFTER the election. We shared that fact, but very few outlets have covered it because it doesn't align with the main media narrative of Trump and the election."[564] He was reprimanded for revealing the truth, but Facebook would go on to completely change the way their platform functioned under the guise of stopping "fake news."

Before Facebook, people used to "bookmark" their favorite websites on their Internet browser, and would use that list to navigate to their news sources, but Facebook (and Twitter) have largely replaced browser bookmarks, and by weaseling their way in between news websites and their potential audience, it is Facebook, not the users, who are now in control of what articles people see.

Manipulating Users' Feeds

Most people used to assume—and many probably still do—that if they follow certain accounts on Facebook they're going to get posts from those pages in their news feeds, but the algorithms detect keywords in posts and identify the source of links and Facebook's proprietary

---

[564] https://twitter.com/robjective/status/964680123885613056

technology throttles the reach of content they don't want people to see and often limits the reach so posts only show up in a few people's news feeds.

For example, when Wikileaks first released a batch of hacked DNC emails, Facebook blocked links to them claiming they were "malicious" or "spam." Only after Wikileaks tweeted about their links being blocked and people began clamoring about it did Facebook fix it.[565]

There were even reports that when people tried to share certain links to articles exposing Jussie Smollett's hate crime hoax they were blocked from posting and a pop-up notified them that, "This post goes against our Community Standards, so no one else can see it."[566]

Facebook even patented technology to shadow ban people so they could prevent certain posts from being seen by others without giving any indication to the person who posted it that such censorship was occurring. The Abstract on their patent explains the process, "[T]he social networking system may receive a list of proscribed content and block comments containing the proscribed content by reducing the distribution of those comments to other viewing users. However, the social networking system may display the blocked content to the commenting user such that the commenting user is not made aware that his or her comment was blocked, thereby providing fewer incentives to the commenting user to

---

[565] New York Post "Facebook Admits to blocking Wikileaks links in DNC email hack" by Bruce Golding (July 24th 2016)

[566] PJ Media "Censored: Facebook Bans Conservative Articles on Jussie Smollett Hate Hoax" by Tyler O'Neil (February 18th 2019)

spam the page or attempt to circumvent the social networking system filters."[567]

Facebook has admitted conducting several experiments on users to test how well they could manipulate people by making changes to what they see in their news feeds.[568] In 2010 they toyed with 60 million people's newsfeeds to see if they could increase voter turnout in the midterm election that year and concluded they were able to get an extra 340,000 people to the polls.[569]

On their own website they bragged about a case study which found that, "Facebook as a market research tool and as a platform for ad saturation can be used to change public opinion in any political campaign."[570] They cited the study as an attempt to court advertisers and to show just how powerful their platform is, hoping to get them to run targeted ads.

Hopefully it's common knowledge now that Facebook was caught suppressing conservative news from appearing in the trending section in 2016 and artificially injecting other topics into the list to give the false impression that certain stories were organically viral from so many people talking about them.[571]

---

[567] Gizmodo "Facebook Patents Shadow Banning" by Bryan Menegus (July 16th 2019)

[568] The Guardian "Facebook sorry – almost – for secret psychological experiment on users" by Dominic Rushe (October 2nd 2014)

[569] UC San Diego News Center "Facebook Boosts Voter Turnout" by Inga Kiderra (September 12th 2012)

[570] Facebook.com "Case Study: Reaching Voters with Facebook Ads (Vote No on 8)" (August 16th 2011)

[571] Gizmodo "Former Facebook Workers: We Routinely Suppressed Conservative News" by Michael Nunez (May 9th 2016)

After Facebook announced they were changing the algorithm to favor posts from people's friends over the businesses, brands, and media pages they were following, Donald Trump's engagement dropped 45%.[572]   The Western Journal did a survey and analyzed the engagement of 50 different news pages ranging from the Washington Post to the Daily Caller and found that after these algorithm changes, conservative outlets averaged a 14% drop in traffic, while liberal media accounts increased by 2%.[573]

In June 2019, Tomi Lahren had the "Boosting" feature disabled on her account, which is a way for public figures and brand pages to get their posts to actually show up in the news feeds of the people who follow them by paying Facebook different dollar amounts to allow what they post to be seen by people following the page.[574]

For anyone running a professional Facebook page (like mine), whatever we post is severely suppressed and only a small fraction of the people who follow the page will see it unless we "Boost" the post, which is a huge revenue generator for Facebook.   Tomi Lahren became famous because her videos went viral on Facebook, but once the Boost feature was disabled she couldn't even pay

---

[572] Breitbart "EXCLUSIVE: Trump's Facebook Engagement Declined By 45 Percent Following Algorithm Change" by Allum Bokhari (February 28th 2018)

[573] Western Journal "Confirmed: Facebook's Recent Algorithm Change Is Crushing Conservative Sites, Boosting Liberals" by George Upper and Shaun Hair (March 13th 2018)

[574] https://twitter.com/TomiLahren/status/1141129134359269376

Facebook to distribute them in the news feeds of people following her page.[575]

A slide from a presentation given to Facebook moderators to teach them what kind of content is inappropriate details what the company says is "destructive behavior" by "trolls" and lists doxing and harassment alongside "toxic meme creation," and "red-pilling normies to convert them to their worldview," and also includes an "example video" of Lauren Chen (formerly known as Roaming Millennial), a moderate conservative YouTuber who now works for The Blaze.[576]

A "normie" is a slang term meaning a normal person, or in the context of certain Internet subcultures means someone who is not part of the group in question. But Facebook considers that word to be an indicator that the person posting it might be a right-wing "troll."

Things have changed so much since the early days of Facebook that it's a completely different platform than it was when it first rose to popularity in the late 2000s. They have been getting increasingly less tolerant of different views and their algorithms can easily hide people's posts or automatically suspend accounts for posting what they deem to be "hate speech," which you know is just a code word for something that hurts liberals' feelings or facts they won't want people to know about.

In August of 2018, a senior manager at Facebook posted on their internal message board a thread titled "We

---

[575] After filing several complaints with Facebook and publicly calling attention to the feature being disabled, they later restored it and said it was just another "error."

[576] Project Veritas "Facebook Insider Leaks Docs; Explains 'Deboosting,' 'Troll Report,' & Political Targeting in Video Interview" (February 27th 2019)

Have a Problem With Political Diversity" that explained, "We are a political monoculture that's intolerant of different views." It went on to say, "We claim to welcome all perspectives, but are quick to attack — often in mobs — anyone who presents a view that appears to be in opposition to left-leaning ideology."[577] That person has probably been fired by now but they were brave enough to point out what is obviously wrong with the corporate culture there.

PayPal co-founder and Facebook board member Peter Thiel left Silicon Valley and moved to Los Angeles because he was sick of the Leftist culture that permeates the tech industry in Northern California.[578] Thiel reportedly considered resigning from Facebook's board over disagreements with Mark Zuckerberg and sold three-quarters of his Facebook stock before leaving Silicon Valley.[579]

Helping Mainstream News

In July 2018 Facebook announced they were partnering with CNN, ABC, Univision, and other mainstream networks and began paying them to do

---

[577] The New York Times "Dozens at Facebook Unite to Challenge Its 'Intolerant' Liberal Culture" by Kate Conger and Sheera Frenkel (August 28th 2018)

[578] Fortune "Why Peter Thiel Is Leaving Silicon Valley for L.A." by Chris Morris (February 15th 2018)

[579] Reuters "Peter Thiel sells most of remaining Facebook stake" (November 22nd 2017)

special livestreams Monday through Friday.[580] Their goal was to, "create a curated news hub of content that would be seen as more credible than many of the random posts cycling through the News Feed."[581] Anderson Cooper's Facebook show, called "Full Circle" usually averaged around 1,500 live viewers and lasted a year.[582] CNN now claims they're going to try streaming the show on their app, CNNgo, instead of Facebook.

Six months after launching the new livestreams Facebook announced they would soon be investing $300 million into various news organizations to help them "boost" their online presence.[583] People like me have to pay Facebook to "Boost" our posts so they actually show up in the news feeds of fans following our pages, while at the same time Facebook is paying hundreds of millions of dollars to mainstream media channels to help them get out their messages!

The liberal bias is obvious but goes deeper than most people think. Sheryl Sandberg, Facebook's Chief Operating Officer, wrote to Hillary Clinton's campaign manager on June 6th 2015, saying "I still want HRC to win badly. I am still here to help as I can."[584] Facebook

---

[580] Variety "Facebook Paying for News Shows From ABC News, CNN, Fox News, Univision, Others" by Todd Spangler (June 6th 2018)

[581] Advertising Age "Facebook Gets CNN to Bring Anderson Cooper To It's New Media Venture" by Garett Soan (June 6th 2018)

[582] Variety "CNN Is Pulling Anderson Cooper's Show Off Facebook, Will Launch 'Go There' on Social Platform This Summer" by Todd Spangler (June 12th 2019)

[583] NBC News "Facebook investing $300 million in local news initiatives" (January 15th 2019)

[584] Zero Hedge "Facebook COO Sandberg To John Podesta: 'I Want Hillary To Win Badly'" by Tyler Durden (March 20th 2018)

openly plays favorites, for example they have a real name policy, except for transgender people, who can open an account in any name they want.[585] The company even put up a huge Black Lives Matter banner on their campus.[586] They also give out employee bonuses based on how much they're doing for "social justice."[587]

Facebook Censoring People

In October 2018, Facebook deleted over 800 accounts for publishing what they called "political spam" and "sensational political content."[588] One of the pages belonged to Brian Kolfage, a disabled veteran who lost both his legs and one arm in the Iraq War. After retiring from the military due to his injuries he took over management of a Facebook page called "Right Wing News" and helped it build up a following of over three million people.[589] But Facebook banned the page, destroying Brian Kolfage's thriving online business, while leaving content farms like BuzzFeed and Vox to continue littering Facebook with their political spam.

---

[585] BBC "Facebook amends 'real name' policy after protests" by Dave Lee (December 15th 2015)

[586] Fortune "Facebook's Employee Bonuses Now Hinge on 'Social' Progress" by Michael Lev-Ram (February 6th 2019)

[587] CNET "Facebook ties employee bonuses to progress on social issues" by Steven Musil and Queenie Wong (February 5th 2019)

[588] The Hill "Facebook removes over 800 accounts, pages for political spam" by Ali Breland (October 11th 2018)

[589] Breitbart "Facebook Deletes Disabled Veteran's Page Without Warning — After Taking $300,000 for Ads" by Lucas Nolan (October 16th 2018)

The day after British activist Tommy Robinson released a documentary on YouTube showing his undercover investigation into the BBC as they were planning to air a hit piece on him, he was banned from Facebook and Instagram (which is owned by Facebook).[590] Because he's been a vocal opponent of the Islamization of England, he has been branded an "Islamophobe." After Facebook banned him, activists and "journalists" smelled blood and started pressuring YouTube to ban him too.

"His YouTube channel has hundreds of thousands of followers and includes films viewed by millions of people," complained Damian Collins, a Member of Parliament.[591] He continued, "Far-right groups are exploiting social media to spread their messages of hate, and the YouTube [Up Next] feature helps them by directing viewers to even more of this content once they start to engage with it." He concluded, "I believe YouTube should also ban Tommy Robinson from their platform."[592] More on this in the chapter on YouTube.

The official Facebook page for Britain First, an anti-immigration organization working to stop the flood of Muslims from the Middle East into the UK was also banned for "Islamophobia." Their page had over 2 million followers, showing it isn't just a fringe group, but they have a large number of supporters in the UK.[593]

---

[590] The Guardian "Tommy Robinson banned from Facebook and Instagram" by Alex Hern and Jim Waterson (February 26th 2019)

[591] The Independent "Tommy Robinson: YouTube under pressure to join Facebook and Instagram in banning far-right activist" by Tim Wyatt (February 27th 2019)

[592] Ibid.

[593] BBC "Facebook bans Britain First pages" by Rory Cellan-Jones

In April 2019 Facebook (and Instagram) banned Faith Goldy, a conservative Canadian journalist who has been smeared as a white supremacist because she too is critical of the massive influx of non-assimilating Muslims into Europe.[594] The *Huffington Post* gleefully took credit for persuading Facebook to ban her, posting a story titled, "Facebook Bans Faith Goldy After HuffPost Report On White Nationalism Content."[595] Facebook said, "Individuals and organizations who spread hate, attack, or call for the exclusion of others on the basis of who they are have no place on our services."[596]

After Comedy Central's Jim Jeffries recorded an interview with a Jewish political commentator from Australia named Avi Yemini, who is critical of Muslim immigration into Western countries, he was permanently banned from Facebook for "hate speech."[597] The ban came not necessarily because of his interview on Comedy Central, but because he had secretly recorded the interview himself, and exposed how deceptively edited it was when they aired it.[598] The truth of what Comedy Central had done to him couldn't be seen, so they banned him.

---

[594] CNET "Facebook, Instagram ban Faith Goldy as they purge white nationalist groups" by Queenie Wong (April 8th 2019)

[595] Huffington Post "Facebook Bans Faith Goldy After HuffPost Report On White Nationalism Content" by Andy Campbell (April 9th 2019)

[596] Ibid.

[597] Breitbart "Facebook Bans Jewish Veteran After Exposé of Jim Jefferies' Deceptive Editing" by Lucas Nolan (March 26th 2019)

[598] RedState "YouTuber Who Outwitted Comedy Central Drops More Hidden Footage Exposing Their Lies" by Brandon Morse (April 10th 2019)

Facebook's moderators despise any criticism of mass immigration and the effects non-assimilating newcomers have on the countries they come to occupy. After a German historian posted a short essay about Islam's historic impact on Germany, he was banned for 30 days for "hate speech."[599] Facebook even deletes accounts of Palestinians at the direction of the Israeli government if they deem the people to be engaging in "incitement" due to their complaints about how the Palestinian people are treated.[600]

Facebook took down an event page for an anti-caravan protest that was scheduled to happen when hundreds of migrants from Central America were to make it to the U.S.-Mexico border.[601] It may not be much longer before they consider the term "illegal alien" to be a "racist slur" and a violation of their terms of service in the same way posting the n-word is (if you're white).

Like all the other major social networks, conservatives are at risk of having their pages shut down for "hate speech" for being "non-inclusive." But it's not just supposed "extremists" like Tommy Robinson and Faith Goldy. In December 2018, Franklin Graham, son of evangelist Billy Graham, was suspended by Facebook for a post he made almost two years earlier criticizing singer Bruce Springsteen for canceling a concert in North Carolina to protest a proposed bill that would have

---

[599] PJ Media "Facebook Bans German Historian for Saying 'Islam Is Not Part of German History'" by Tyler O'Neil (April 9th 2018)

[600] The Intercept "Facebook Says It Is Deleting Accounts at the Direction of the U.S. and Israeli Government" by Glenn Greenwald (December 30th 2017)

[601] Breitbart "Facebook Takes Down Event Page for Anti-Caravan Protest" by Allum Bokhari (April 28th 2018)

required people to use the bathroom that corresponds to their biological sex.

Graham's post said in part, "Mr. Springsteen, a nation embracing sin and bowing at the feet of godless secularism and political correctness is not progress," and urged the state's legislators to "put the safety of our women and children first!" But a Facebook moderator decided that calling liberals "godless" was a violation of their policy forbidding "dehumanizing language," so they suspended him.[602]

After the incident started making headlines Facebook lifted the ban and said the moderator had made a "mistake" in their decision. Facebook even censored the Declaration of Independence after it was posted by a small newspaper's page (*The Vindicator*), claiming it was "hate speech" because it includes the phrase "merciless Indian Savages."[603] The paper had posted it a few days before the Fourth of July to celebrate Independence Day.

I was suspended in April 2017 for criticizing a Dove Soap commercial that featured "real moms" and their babies because it included a transgender "woman" who is the biological father of "her" child but identifies as the baby's "mom."[604] Facebook considers it "hate speech" to denounce such insanity. Then in January 2019, I was suspended for one week after making a comment about

---

[602] The Washington Post "Evangelist Franklin Graham claims Facebook 'is censoring free speech' after it blocked him" by Michael Brice-Saddle (December 30th 2018)

[603] Washington Post "Facebook censored a post for 'hate speech.' It was the Declaration of Independence." by Eli Rosenberg (July 5th 2018)

[604] Breitbart "Facebook Suspends YouTuber for Disliking 'Transgender Mother' Commercial" (April 14th 2017)

there being a lot of crime in black communities. I appealed it, and it was denied.

Residents know the local news begins every night in Chicago, Milwaukee, Detroit, Baltimore, etc, with shootings, stabbings, and robberies which occurred in black ghettos, but those stories are just fifteen-second sound bites on the local news and are then forgotten about by everyone except those directly affected—like the victims' family and friends.

But when a black person is killed by a white man, or the suspect is a white man, then the keyboard warriors amplify the story to the national level as if there's an epidemic of white men assassinating random black people in America. They denounce "evil" "racist" white people and make ridiculous and hateful generalizations about the entire white race, but that's allowed on Facebook. You just can't post certain facts and statistics about black crime in America.

The truth is, black men make up only about 7% of the U.S. population, but are responsible for 50% of the total murders.[605] It's a distressing statistic no one in the mainstream media dares to point out, and if you simply mention this on Facebook, your post may likely be removed and you'll get issued a suspension for "hate speech."

Black conservative commentator Candace Owens was suspended because of a post saying liberalism is a greater threat to black people in America than white supremacy, and for including some statistics about fatherless homes in

---

[605] U.S. Department of Justice "Homicide Trends in the United States, 1980-2008" by Alexia Cooper and Erica L. Smith (November 2011)

the black community.[606]   It's "hate speech" even when black people mention certain uncomfortable facts about their communities. Leaked documents later revealed that Facebook had labeled her a "hate agent" and was offering employees "extra credit" if they could dig up dirt on her and find any previous statements she's made or groups she has endorsed that they consider to be objectionable.[607]

Facebook sensations Diamond and Silk, two black sisters who support Donald Trump by doing a hilarious routine where one of them rants while the other acts as a "hype girl" by adding cleverly timed one or two word comments to emphasize what the other is saying, have also been censored by Facebook. Their videos became so popular that they were invited to Trump rallies during his 2016 campaign and then later to the White House once he won.

Their content is 100% family friendly but Facebook deemed them "unsafe" and suppressed the reach of their page, which at the time had 1.2 million followers.[608] As usual, after the issue started making headlines, Facebook lifted the restrictions on their page and said it was just another "enforcement error."[609]

Facebook also reportedly removed posts and memes by people who were (correctly) referring to the man who

[606] Fox News "Facebook temporarily suspends Candace Owens over post about 'liberal supremacy'" by Christopher Howard (May 17th 2019)

[607] Breitbart "EXCLUSIVE: Facebook Includes Candace Owens On 'Hate Agents' List" by Allum Bokhari (May 17th 2019)

[608] The Hill "Diamond and Silk slam Facebook after company deems their rhetoric 'unsafe to the community'" by Joe Concha (April 9th 2018)

[609] NPR "Facebook Admits 'Enforcement Error' In How It Handled Content From Pro-Trump Duo" by Tim Mak (April 15th 2018)

shot and killed a police officer in California as an "illegal alien" and a "murderer."[610] Criticizing illegal aliens, even if they're murderers, is "hate speech."

A writer for the *Gateway Pundit* named Lucian Wintrich, who is a gay, referred to himself as a "fag" in a post, and seven months later their AI system detected it and banned him for 30-days for "hate speech" just for using the word.[611]

Facebook even blocked President Trump's social media director Dan Scavino from replying to people in the comments, claiming his posts were "spam." Shortly after the President tweeted about the restriction, Facebook "fixed" it and said it was just another "error."[612]

Banning "Dangerous Individuals"

In May 2019, Facebook (and Instagram) permanently banned Paul Joseph Watson, Milo Yiannopoulos, Laura Loomer, and Nation of Islam leader Louis Farrakhan; labeling them all "dangerous individuals" and "extremists."[613] What's especially interesting is that news reports were published about their ban a full hour before they were actually banned, because Facebook had been

---

[610] The Western Journal "Facebook Suspends Account for Calling Alleged Cop Killer an 'Illegal Immigrant'" by Kara Pendleton (December 30th 2018)

[611] https://twitter.com/lucianwintrich/status/937391808363016192

[612] Fox News "Facebook apologizes to Trump's social media director for temporarily restricting his account" by Chris Ciaccia (March 19th 2019)

[613] CNN "Facebook bans Louis Farrakhan, Milo Yiannopoulos, InfoWars and others from its platforms as 'dangerous'" by Oliver Darcy (May 3rd 2019)

secretly coordinating with CNN and other outlets but botched the timing of the big announcement.[614]

Loomer, Milo, and Watson were banned because they are critical of the Islamization of Europe, so they have all been branded "Islamophobes," and Facebook decided to throw Louis Farrakhan in the mix as a cover to give the appearance that they weren't just removing vocal opponents of Islam.

The *Atlantic* initially reported, "Any account that shares Infowars content will see it removed, unless the post is explicitly condemning Infowars [or Alex Jones]. Facebook and Instagram will remove any content containing Infowars videos, radio segments, or articles (again, unless the post is explicitly condemning the content) and Facebook will also remove any groups set up to share Infowars content and events promoting any of the banned extremist figures, according to a company spokesperson."[615] They later "updated" their article and removed the part about people having to explicitly condemn Alex Jones if they are to post anything about him.

At this rate it won't be long before Facebook bans people who say abortion is murder, citing their policy against "hate speech." Or if you dare say you don't believe in gay "marriage," or call it "marriage" in quotes (because a marriage is between a man and a woman.) That's "hateful."

If Facebook was around in the 1960s, they would have banned Martin Luther King because what he was saying

---

[614] Wired "Facebook Bans Alex Jones, Other Extremists—but Not as Planned" by Paris Martineau (May 2nd 2019)

[615] The Atlantic "Instagram and Facebook Ban Far-Right Extremists" by Taylor Lorenz (May 2nd 2019)

was "dangerous" to the social order. The FBI at the time, led by J. Edgar Hoover, considered King to be an enemy of the State and the bureau engaged in all kinds of nefarious activities trying to derail his message.[616]

Meanwhile the Palestinian terrorist organization Hamas has an official Facebook page (and Twitter account).[617] So does the Muslim Brotherhood, which is listed as a terrorist organization in multiple countries.[618] They can have Facebook pages, but Alex Jones, Paul Joseph Watson, Tommy Robinson, Milo Yiannopoulos, and Laura Loomer can't.

Instagram

Unlike Facebook and Twitter, Instagram (which is owned by Facebook) is more about photography than news, but people do share political memes and news-related posts there, and in recent years they have enabled users to upload videos, so it too has become a place for vlogs.

For years just about the only thing that would get removed by Instagram's moderators for violations of their terms of service were pictures that included nudity or gory and gratuitous violence, but once the Orwellian era began and the Thought Police are now cracking down on free speech online, censorship on Instagram became common.

---

[616] New York Times "Ex-Officials Say F.B.I. Harassed Dr. King to Stop His Criticism" by Nicholas M. Horrock (March 9th 1975)

[617] https://twitter.com/HamasInfoEn

[618] https://twitter.com/Ikhwanweb

They have censored a few different memes that I had posted, one of them showed a picture of actor Tobey Maguire from a scene in *Spiderman* looking at a picture of President Trump giving a speech to the Boy Scouts Jamboree, and then below it showed Tobey wearing "CNN glasses" which caused him to see Adolf Hitler talking with a group of Hitler Youth. The message is clear —anything President Trump does when seen through the lens of CNN is sinister, but that meme violated Instagram's terms of service.

They also censored a meme I had posted showing a happy white couple with two young children that was captioned, "White people — the only race you can legally discriminate against." As you know, there is a war on white people being waged by the Left in America today and whites are being blamed for everyone else's problems, but just pointing out the Left's open discrimination (and hatred) of white people is a violation of Instagram's terms of service.

As the Jussie Smollett hate crime hoax was unraveling, Instagram took down a Scooby-Doo meme from my account which showed the characters surrounding a "ghost" they had captured after unmasking it to reveal who it really was, and the "ghost" had Jussie's face photoshopped onto it. Instagram said that was "harassment" and "bullying." They also took down one of Donald Trump Jr.'s posts about Jussie Smollett's hoax as well.[619]

After conservative commentator Kayleigh McEnany posted a picture on her Instagram of Elizabeth Warren's

---

[619] Daily Caller "Don Trump Jr. Slams Instagram After Smollett Post Deleted: 'Why Don't You Want The Truth Out There?'" by Amber Athey and Katie Jerkovich (February 18th 2019)

newly discovered Texas Bar Registration card showing she listed "American Indian" as her race, that post was removed and Kayleigh was given a notification she had violated Instagram's terms of service by "bullying" Warren.[620]

Instagram has also begun testing new technology to fact-check memes by adding pop-ups that appear next to certain posts they deem "false" and even hiding them so they don't show up when people are searching for particular hashtags.[621]

The Thought Police don't just patrol social media for what people post, they also keep a lookout for things that people "like." During the 2018 season of *The Bachelorette*, one of the frontrunners (who got the "first impression rose") made headlines after people were combing through his social media accounts and found that he had "liked" several "inflammatory" memes that made fun of illegal aliens, transgender people, and radical feminists.[622] He literally just clicked the "like" button on a few funny memes making fun of social justice warriors and he was smeared in the press as a xenophobic, transphobic, sexist, and forced to apologize.

[620] Washington Times "Instagram deletes Kayleigh McEnany post on Elizabeth Warren, issues 'bullying' warning" by Victor Morton (February 6th 2019)

[621] The Verge "Facebook is turning its fact-checking partners loose on Instagram" by Jon Porter (May 7th 2019)

[622] Hollywood Reporter "'Bachelorette' Frontrunner Under Fire for Liking Controversial Social Media Posts" by Jackie Strause (May 29th 2018)

What It's Doing To Our Brains

Steve Jobs wouldn't allow his kids to even use an iPad when they were little, admitting in 2012 (two years after it was released), "Actually we don't allow the iPad in the home," in response to an interviewer saying his kids must love it.[623] He knew how addictive they could be and how people, especially children, were vulnerable to being completely consumed by them. Apple CEO Tim Cook doesn't have kids but says he has placed restrictions on what his nephew can do with technology, and he doesn't want him using social media.[624]

Bill Gates also limited the amount of screen time he allowed his kids to engage in and wouldn't let them have cellphones until they were 14-years-old, despite them complaining that other kids in their class were able to have one.[625] But using tablets or smartphones to surf the web or watch videos is one thing. Social media apps opened up a whole new world to waste people's time and warp their minds.

The former president of Facebook, Sean Parker, later admitted the site creates an artificial social-validation feedback loop that is, "exploiting a vulnerability in human psychology" and "literally changes your relationship with society, [and] each other. It probably interferes with

---

[623] Business Insider "Here's why Steve Jobs never let his kids use an iPad" by Eames Yates (March 4th 2017)

[624] Business Insider "Apple CEO Tim Cook: I don't want my nephew on a social network" by Rob Price (January 19th 2018)

[625] SF Gate "Bill Gates didn't allow his kids to have cell phones until age 14" by Amy Graff (April 21st 2017)

productivity in weird ways. God only knows what it's doing to our children's brains."[626]

Former Facebook executive Chamath Palihapitiya warned, "The short-term, dopamine-driven feedback loops we've created are destroying how society works," referring to the validation people get from likes, hearts, and thumbs up on their posts.[627] He also pointed out how "social media" is making people anti-social, saying it's harming civil discourse and spreading misinformation and hoaxes that have real world consequences.

He mentioned how a hoax about a kidnaping spread through WhatsApp (which is owned by Facebook) in India and led to the lynching of seven innocent men who were killed by a local mob. "That's what we're dealing with. And imagine taking that to the extreme, where bad actors can now manipulate large swathes of people to do anything you want. It's just a really, really bad state of affairs." He also said his children "aren't allowed to use that shit."[628]

A Google engineer posted a lengthy thread on his Twitter account about the dangers of Facebook, starting off saying, "The problem with Facebook is not *just* the loss of your privacy and the fact that it can be used as a totalitarian panopticon. The more worrying issue, in my opinion, is its use of digital information consumption as a psychological control vector."[629]

---

[626] The Guardian "Ex-Facebook president Sean Parker: site made to exploit human 'vulnerability'" by Olivia Solon (November 9th 2017)

[627] The Verge "Former Facebook exec says social media is ripping apart society" by James Vincent (December 11th 2017)

[628] Ibid.

[629] https://twitter.com/fchollet/status/976563870322999296

He went on to tweet, "The world is being shaped in large part by two long-time trends: first, our lives are increasingly dematerialized, consisting of consuming and generating information online, both at work and at home. Second, AI is getting ever smarter."[630]

"These two trends overlap at the level of the algorithms that shape our digital content consumption. Opaque social media algorithms get to decide, to an ever-increasing extent, which articles we read, who we keep in touch with, whose opinions we read, whose feedback we get."[631]

"If Facebook gets to decide, over the span of many years, which news you will see (real or fake), whose political status updates you'll see, and who will see yours, then Facebook is in effect in control of your political beliefs and your worldview."[632]

"This is not quite news, as Facebook has been known to run since at least 2013 a series of experiments in which they were able to successfully control the moods and decisions of unwitting users by tuning their newsfeeds' contents, as well as prediction user's future decisions."[633]

"In short, Facebook can simultaneously measure everything about us, and control the information we consume. When you have access to both perception and action, you're looking at an AI problem. You can start establishing an optimization loop for human behavior. A RL loop."[634]

---

[630] https://twitter.com/fchollet/status/976564096605679616

[631] https://twitter.com/fchollet/status/976564511858597888

[632] https://twitter.com/fchollet/status/976565324622344192

[633] https://twitter.com/fchollet/status/976565553761476608

[634] https://twitter.com/fchollet/status/976565723597176832

"A loop in which you observe the current state of your targets and keep tuning what information you feed them, until you start observing the opinions and behaviors you wanted to see."[635]

"The human mind is a static, vulnerable system that will come increasingly under attack from ever-smarter AI algorithms that will simultaneously have a complete view of everything we do and believe, and complete control of the information we consume."[636]

"Importantly, mass population control — in particular political control — arising from placing AI algorithms in charge of our information diet does not necessarily require very advanced AI. You don't need self-aware, super-intelligent AI for this to be a dire threat."[637]

"We're looking at a powerful entity that builds fine-grained psychological profiles of over two billion humans, that runs large-scale behavior manipulation experiments, and that aims at developing the best AI technology the world has ever seen. Personally, it really scares me," he concludes.[638]

Even one of Facebook's co-founders says the company is now "un-American" and is calling on the government to break it up. "The most problematic aspect of Facebook's power is Mark [Zuckerberg's] unilateral control over speech," he said in a *New York Times* op-ed. "There is no precedent for his ability to monitor, organize

---

[635] https://twitter.com/fchollet/status/976567526023872513

[636] https://twitter.com/fchollet/status/976568469679357952

[637] https://twitter.com/fchollet/status/976568588378152960

[638] https://twitter.com/fchollet/status/976569442728525824

and even censor the conversations of two billion people."[639]

---

[639] New York Times "It's Time to Break Up Facebook" by Chris Hughes (May 9th 2019)

Twitter

Fake news and idiotic ideas spread faster on Twitter than perhaps any other social media platform.[640] Unlike Facebook status updates which can be rather lengthy, Twitter is designed for short and quick messages (limited to 280 characters) and with the click of the retweet button, a tweet posted from anyone can soon be in front of the eyes of millions of people.

It's a place where people share first and think later, and it's often a sea of angry people arguing with each other and jumping to conclusions based on out of context statements, photos, or video clips; and quickly spread the falsehoods even further without a second thought.[641] By the time the facts come out, the misinformation has already gone viral and shown up on the trending list—poisoning the opinions of countless others.

Few people delete their tweets which fueled fake news fires, and fewer still issue retractions when learning of their mistake. Even in those rare occasions the retractions receive little attention compared to the initial tweets, since they aren't retweeted thousands of times, not to mention most of the damage has already been done.

When there's a tragic event like a mass shooting, the wannabe sleuths online often end up naming and doxing

---

[640] Science Magazine "Fake news spreads faster than true news on Twitter—thanks to people, not bots" by Katie Langin (March 8th 2018)

[641] Engaget "Twitter's fake news problem is getting worse" by Nicole Lee (February 17th 2018)

the wrong suspect, and take someone's photo from a social media account with the same name as the suspect and spread it around claiming they're the killer.[642]

Who knows what will happen when deepfake videos become more popular and carefully crafted hoax clips are spread through Twitter. The effects could be devastating beyond measure and it's something I'll cover in detail later in the chapter titled "The Future of Fake News."

Spreading misinformation through Twitter isn't just something that random idiots do online. Many mainstream media journalists regularly engage in the practice, or amplify fake news through retweets. Dave Weigel of the *Washington Post* tweeted a photo of the audience at a Trump event in Florida that went viral, claiming the event had a ton of empty seats, disputing the President's statement that people had to be turned away because the stadium was over capacity. People starting calling the President a liar because the "prestigious" Washington Post said otherwise, but Weigel's photo was taken hours before the event had actually started which is why there were rows of empty seats.[643]

Just hours after President Trump was inaugurated, a *Time* magazine reporter claimed that he removed the bust of Martin Luther King Jr. from the Oval Office, posting a photo of the table where it sat, claiming it was gone, insinuating Trump is such a racist he couldn't stand to see the face of MLK in his new office and got rid of it on his first day as president. It turns out that someone was just

---

[642] New York Magazine "All the Mistakenly Identified 'Suspects' in the Boston Bombing Investigation" by Joe Coscarelli (April 19th 2013)

[643] The Hill "Washington Post reporter apologizes for tweet on crowd size at Trump rally" by Julia Manchester (December 9th 2017)

standing in front of it, blocking it from view, and the bust was still there.[644] But countless liberals tweeted their disgust after being duped by an "authoritative" *Time* magazine reporter who made the claim.

There are countless vipers who live online, glued to their phones, and derive a sense of power from the amount of likes and retweets they get. And many function as a volunteer army, ready to attack any target on demand. It's where liberals harass companies that advertise on Fox News, and where they flood the mentions of anyone who dares speak out against garbage like corporations pandering to gays and transgenders during "Pride" month.

Twitter can suck you in, wasting hours of your time while you argue with idiots about anything and everything since your mentions can easily turn into an endless flow of responses from more and more people as those triggered by your tweets keep sharing them with their followers, rallying others to join in on the dogpile.

Twitter is often a dangerous and mind-bending place. As a *New York Times* columnist wrote after the Covington Catholic debacle, it is, "the epicenter of a nonstop information war, an almost comically undermanaged gladiatorial arena where activists and disinformation artists and politicians and marketers gather to target and influence the wider media world."[645]

An article in *The Week* went even further, warning that Twitter actually poses a threat to our democracy, saying,

[644] Daily Caller "Trump Calls Out Time Magazine For Fake News Story About Removing MLK Bust From Oval Office" by Saagar Enjeti (January 21st 2017)

[645] New York Times "Never Tweet" by Farhad Manjoo (January 23rd 2019)

"Extreme partisan polarization is combining with the technology of social media, and especially Twitter, to provoke a form of recurrent political madness among members of the country's cultural and intellectual elite."[646]

It continued, "But too little attention has been paid to what may be the most potent facet of the social media platform: its ability to feed the vanity of its users. There's always an element of egoism to intellectual and political debate. But Twitter puts every tweeter on a massive stage, with the nastiest put-downs, insults, and provocations often receiving the most applause. That's a huge psychological incentive to escalate the denunciation of political enemies. The more one expresses outrage at the evils of others, the more one gets to enjoy the adulation of the virtual mob."[647]

The piece concluded (accurately) that, "more and more the venom has been bleeding into the real world, with boycotts, doxings, firings, death threats, and groveling apologies offered to placate mobs wielding digital pitchforks. It increasingly feels like it's just a matter of time before real-world violence breaks out in response to an online conflagration."[648]

After a Black Lives Matter supporter ambushed a group of police officers during one of the movement's marches in Dallas, Texas in 2016, a surviving officer sued Twitter and Facebook for allowing the social media

---

[646] The Week "How Twitter could be the death of liberal democracy" by Damon Linker (January 22nd 2019)

[647] Ibid.

[648] Ibid.

networks to radicalize the gunman, saying they were used "as a tool for spreading extremist propaganda."[649]

The shooter's Facebook profile pic was him making a black power salute and he followed various black supremacist pages.[650] While the tech companies are determined to ban anyone posting support for "white supremacy," they turn a blind eye to radical black power groups and those who promote their extremist ideologies and anti-white hatred. Twitter is a known safe haven for Antifa, with countless Antifa accounts active, many of which regularly promote violence against conservatives.[651]

The launch of Twitter was a carefully crafted campaign involving various celebrities like Oprah Winfrey, Ashton Kutcher, and even CNN, which promoted Twitter's "Million Followers Contest" in 2009 when the site first appeared on the public's radar. Now practically every television show and political cause has a hashtag and everyone wants you to "follow" them on Twitter.

It's interesting to note that the CIA actually created "Cuban Twitter" so they could monitor everyone's online activity in the country and manage the spread of information in order to undermine the government

[649] CBS DFW "DART Officer Sues Social Media Giants Over 2016 Downtown Police Ambush" by Andrea Lucia (February 14th 2019)

[650] The New York Times "Suspect in Dallas Attack Had Interest in Black Power Groups" by Jonathan Mahler and Julie Turkewitz (July 8th 2016)

[651] NewsBusters.org "Twitter Bans Doxxing, But Why Are Antifa Accounts Still Active?" by Corinne Weaver (October 4th 2018)

there.[652] It's not unreasonable to think that the CIA has the same interest and control over Twitter in America (and all other major social media sites) as well.

It certainly is odd that Twitter awarded the coveted blue verified checkmark to a supposed eight-year-old Syrian refugee, despite the minimum age to be allowed on Twitter is thirteen.   Starting in 2016 "Bana al-Abed" began posting photos of the civil war-torn country, urging people around the world (in English) to help. Her tweets soon began making headlines, gaining her over 322,000 followers, and she was even invited to the 2018 Academy Awards and brought on stage for a performance by Andra Day and Common for their song "Stand Up for Something."[653]

President Trump had wanted to stop intervening in foreign affairs that didn't directly affect the United States, and what better way to undermine his efforts than showcase an eight-year-old Syrian girl using social media to beg for help?

You should never believe what you see on Twitter. In 2013 the Associated Press account was hacked and tweeted that the White House had been bombed and President Obama was injured. The tweet was also said to have caused the stock market to fall until it was discovered that it was a hoax.[654] A rogue employee even took it upon himself to delete President Trump's entire

[652] Guardian "US secretly created 'Cuban Twitter' to stir unrest and undermine government" via Associated Press (April 3rd 2014)

[653] Washington Post "Syrian refugee girl gets star treatment at the Oscars" by Christina Barron (March 5th 2018)

[654] Washington Post "Market quavers after fake AP tweet says Obama was hurt in White House explosions" by Dina ElBoghdady (April 13th 2013)

account in November 2017. If one low level employee has the administrative control to delete the President's account, what would stop someone from hijacking the account and posting tweets as the President himself? Even if the false tweets were deleted and exposed within a few minutes, the damage they would inflict on international relations or the economy could be enormous.

While Democrats cry about "Russian bots and trolls" manipulating Twitter by tweeting out certain hashtags hoping to boost them into the trending module or mass-"liking" certain tweets to give the appearance that the message is resonating with more people than it actually is; the effect they have is often minimal. One of Twitter's executives, Nick Pickles, testified at a Congressional hearing that just 49 Russian Twitter accounts were involved in trying to artificially boost support for Brexit [the proposal for England to leave the European Union] and those collective tweets had only been liked 637 times and retweeted just 461 times.[655]

While troll farms run by foreign governments or domestic political activist organizations should be a concern, Twitter and the other major tech companies have safeguards in place to detect and prevent most of this inauthentic activity from disrupting the platforms. The biggest threat in this modern information war comes from the tech companies themselves, since they hold the power over what billions of people see and hear, and with small changes to their algorithms can hide or amplify certain issues or events in order to further their own political agendas.

---

[655] Engaget "Twitter says 49 Russian accounts tried to sway Brexit voters" by Mallory Locklear (February 8th 2018)

Massive Liberal Bias

After years of avoiding the issue, Twitter's CEO finally admitted "It's no secret that we are largely left leaning, and we all have biases. That includes me, our board, and our company."[656] They are so liberal in fact, that Jack Dorsey actually apologized for eating at Chick-Fil-A after he tweeted that he just used Square's Cash App to buy lunch there, which triggered a flood of angry responses from many of his followers because Chick-Fil-A's CEO doesn't support gay "marriage."[657]

Jack Dorsey has been photographed hanging out with Black Lives Matter activist Deray McKesson and the two even did a joint interview together in 2016 at the popular Recode Code Conference.[658] Twitter also hired a woman named Dr. Patricia Rossini to examine "civil discourse" on the platform because everyone knows Twitter has become a nasty place, but an examination of Dr. Rossini's past tweets reveal that she believes the basic tenets of the Republican Party are hate, racism, and homophobia.[659]

The leader of Twitter's new "task force" on "uncivil discourse," Rebekah Tromble, thinks that President Trump is a Nazi and has "quintupled down on his

[656] The Washington Post "Inside Facebook and Twitter's secret meetings with Trump aides and conservative leaders who say tech is biased" by Tony Romm (June 27th 2018)

[657] Business Insider "Twitter CEO Jack Dorsey forced to apologize for eating Chick-fil-A during Pride Month" by Hayley Peterson (June 11th 2018)

[658] Recode "Full video: Twitter CEO Jack Dorsey and #BlackLivesMatter activist DeRay McKesson at Code 2016" by Recode Staff (June 8th 2016)

[659] https://twitter.com/patyrossini/status/756329790907490304

commitment to white nationalists."[660]   Democrat Congressman Ted Lieu from California tweeted out a photo of himself and the party's new social media star Alexandria Ocasio-Cortez at what he described as a "training session" on Twitter, noting representatives from the company were in attendance helping Democrats learn to be more social media savvy.[661]

Twitter also allows people to post pornography, and is an easy place for children to access it.[662] Most porn stars have Twitter accounts which contain a steady stream of hard core pornographic videos and pictures with no effective safeguards to prevent kids from following such accounts and seeing their explicit posts.

What's Trending

Twitter's "Trending" list is supposed to be the top ten list of the most tweeted about topics or hashtags of the moment, but most users are unaware of the manual curation that is often involved.   Topics are regularly artificially boosted to give the appearance that they are "popular" while others are suppressed to prevent people from looking into them further.

Oftentimes if something trends on Twitter, it then starts making national headlines.   Whether it's a local issue in a small town that, for whatever reason, goes viral

---

[660] https://twitter.com/RebekahKTromble/status/897792260821090304

[661] https://twitter.com/tedlieu/status/1085901851927687168

[662] The Sun "TWISTED TWITTER: Channel 4 doc shows kids get unlimited access to porn on social media sites" by Rod McPhee (July 2nd 2019)

and starts trending, or something stupid that a celebrity said or did—if it trends, it then makes headlines.

For over six consecutive months starting in the Spring of 2019 every single Sunday pro-LGBT hashtags like #LGBTangels, #LGBTQsquad, #unitedLGBT, #rainbowLGBT, LGBTQoftwitter, etc. would be on the top ten trending list.[663]   The hashtag campaigns are organized by liberal groups likely in coordination with Twitter which then inserts them into the trending list to regularly expose people to selfies of teenagers "coming out" online, in attempt to normalize homosexuality and gender bending.

In his testimony to the Senate Subcommittee on Crime and Terrorism, Twitter's lawyer admitted the company had censored almost half of all tweets using the hashtag #DNCLeak when Wikileaks first published the hacked emails from the Democratic National Committee, despite their systems only linking 2% of the tweets to supposed Russian troll farms.[664]

When you click on the Search tab (the magnifying glass icon) on a mobile device, which you need to do in order to get see the Trending list, first you are taken to a page that contains a featured story (they call a "Moment") which is always chosen by Twitter that supposedly has something to do with what's trending, but always attempts to frame the issue in a certain light. In an interview with *Rolling Stone,* Jack Dorsey admitted, "We can amplify the

---

[663] It started as early as March 3rd 2019, and occurred every Sunday through at least September 1st 2019 when I was finalizing this manuscript to be sent off to the proofreader.

[664] LawAndCrime.com "Twitter's Lawyer Admits Hiding Tweets With '#DNCLeak' And '#PodestaEmails' Hashtags" by Colin Kalmbacher (November 2nd 2017)

counter-narrative [to what Trump is saying]. We do have a curation team that looks to find balance. A lot of times when our president tweets, a "Moment" occurs, and we show completely different perspectives."[665]

Shadow Banning

In July 2018 conservative Twitter users started noticing that when they looked up top Republican members of Congress in the Twitter Search bar that many of their names were mysteriously missing. Devin Nunes, Matt Gaetz, Jim Jordan, Mark Meadows, John Ratcliffe, Republican Party chair Ronna McDaniel, and many others (including myself) were all shadow banned from the Search box to make it more difficult for people looking us up to find our accounts.

Surprisingly the very liberal Vice News did an investigation into the shadow banning "allegations" and admitted, "Twitter is limiting the visibility of prominent Republicans in search results — a technique known as 'shadow banning' — in what it says is a side effect of its attempts to improve the quality of discourse on the platform."[666]

The article went on to detail that prominent Republican members of Congress "no longer appear in the auto-populated drop-down search box on Twitter" and that, "It's a shift that diminishes their reach on the

---

[665] Rolling Stone "Twitter CEO Jack Dorsey: The Rolling Stone Interview" by Brian Hiatt (January 23rd 2019)

[666] Vice News "Twitter appears to have fixed 'shadow ban' of prominent Republicans like the RNC chair and Trump Jr.'s spokesman" by Alex Thompson (July 25th 2018)

platform — and it's the same one being deployed against prominent racists to limit their visibility."[667]

Vice also pointed out that the shadow banning was not implemented on any Democrats they looked up, noting "Democrats are not being 'shadow banned' in the same way, according to a VICE News review.   [Ronna] McDaniel's counterpart, Democratic Party chair Tom Perez, and liberal members of Congress — including Reps. Maxine Waters, Joe Kennedy III, Keith Ellison, and Mark Pocan — all continue to appear in drop-down search results.   Not a single member of the 78-person Progressive Caucus faces the same situation in Twitter's search."[668]

Many conservatives began noticing this anomaly but it wasn't until Florida Congressman Matt Gaetz called out the shadow banning that it began making headlines.[669] Then President Trump tweeted about it and the issue couldn't be ignored.[670] A reporter for Axios then tweeted that he, "Must admit that when some [Republican] sources have complained about this to me I mocked them to their face as conspiracy theorists.   This Vice article makes me rethink that, and response from Twitter is inadequate."[671]

Twitter then released a statement, saying, "We do not shadow ban," but then in the very next sentence admitted,

[667] Ibid.

[668] Ibid.

[669] The Hill "Republican feels 'victimized' by Twitter 'shadow banning'" by Juliegrace Brufke (July 25th 2018)

[670] https://twitter.com/realDonaldTrump/status/1022447980408983552

[671] https://twitter.com/jonathanvswan/status/1022175120373309441

"You are always able to see the tweets from accounts you follow (although you may have to do more work to find them, like go directly to their profile)."[672] They played with the definition of shadow banning too, defining it as, "deliberately making someone's content undiscoverable to everyone except the person who posted it." That's why it's more appropriate to label it shadow *suppressing* or *throttling* than to call it a "ban."

Earlier that year an undercover journalist at Project Veritas had spoken with various former and current employees of Twitter including a Content Review Agent who admitted that there were a lot of "unwritten rules" about shadow banning and that "It was never written, it was more said."[673] A Policy Manager for Twitter's Trust and Safety council named Olinda Hassan said the company was working on down-ranking "shitty people" so their tweets don't show up.[674]

A former software engineer at Twitter told the undercover journalist, "One strategy is to shadow ban so you have ultimate control. The idea of a shadow ban is that you ban someone but they don't know they've been banned, because they keep posting and no one sees their content. So they just think that no one is engaging with their content, when in reality, no one is seeing it."[675]

---

[672] Twitter official blog "Setting the record straight on shadow banning" by Vijaya Gadde and Kayvon Beykpour (July 26th 2018)

[673] Project Veritas "UNDERCOVER VIDEO: Twitter Engineers To 'Ban a Way of Talking' Through 'Shadow Banning,' Algorithms to Censor Opposing Political Opinions" (January 11th 2018)

[674] Ibid.

[675] RealClear Politics "'Project Veritas' Hidden Camera: Twitter And Reddit Use 'Shadow Ban' Algorithms to Censor Political Opinions" by Tim Haines (January 12th 2018)

Twitter most likely uses shadow *throttling* (instead of a full shadow ban) to limit the reach of certain users, so some people are able to see and interact with their tweets, but far less than if no such filter was activated on the accounts. Facebook admits they limit the distribution of posts unless users pay to "Boost" the post, so it's foolish to think Twitter isn't shadow throttling accounts as well using a filter to limit the reach of people the company has deemed politically problematic.

When Twitter CEO Jack Dorsey sat down for a rare interview with CNN in August 2018 he said that the company is considering removing the "like" button from all tweets, and hiding people's follower counts.[676] A few months later he repeated the same thing, indicating they may get rid of the "like" button "soon."[677]

Hiding the number of "likes" and retweets people's posts get would make shadow banning certain individuals or tweets about specific topics almost impossible to detect, because without being able to see how many people are clicking "like" on a post, users wouldn't know if their followers were actually seeing the post at all.

People who use Twitter get a feel for how many "likes" an average tweet gets, and if all of a sudden their engagement dropped 95% and went from getting twenty likes per tweet to only one or two, they would notice something was wrong and suspect that people weren't seeing their tweets. Some have pointed out that certain tweets they have posted appear to them when they're logged in, but when looking at their feed from a different

---

[676] CNN - Interview with Jack Dorsey (August 19th 2018)

[677] The Telegraph "This, he said, is to promote more 'healthy' conversations" by Margi Murphy (October 29th 2018)

browser (not logged in) they don't show up, adding to the concerns that Twitter is shadow banning certain tweets.[678]

Censoring Accounts by Suspending Users

Twitter CEO Jack Dorsey once said his goal was to have Twitter function as a basic utility, like water.[679] And in their early years, Twitter executives used to call their company the "free speech wing of the free speech party," but as the culture changed, and the social justice warriors clamored for more censorship, Jack Dorsey said their once unofficial motto about being the free speech wing of the free speech party was actually just "a joke."[680]

While he may have been idealistic when starting the company, he later succumbed to pressure to "reign in" the wild, wild west nature of Twitter and rolled out increasingly strict policies resulting in a number of high profile people being permanently banned for saying things that are commonplace on Twitter.

Milo Yiannopoulos got banned permanently in July 2016 for trolling "comedian" and actress Leslie Jones about how horrible the all-female *Ghostbusters* remake was.[681] Political operative and unofficial Trump advisor Roger Stone got banned in October 2017 after going off about several CNN hosts including Don Lemon, Jake

---

[678] Daily Caller "Twitter Censors 'The Federalist' Co-Founder Over Lisa Page Tweet" by Amber Athey (March 18th 2019)

[679] SearchEnginLand "Twitter as utility, like running water? That's the goal, says CEO" by Pamela Parker (February 14th 2011)

[680] Breitbart "Twitter CEO Jack Dorsey: Our Free Speech Motto Was a 'Joke'" by Charlie Nash (October 18th 2018)

[681] The Guardian "Milo Yiannopoulos, rightwing writer, permanently banned from Twitter" by Elle Hunt (July 20th 2016)

Tapper, and Ana Navarro for "using an expletive" to describe them and saying they should be "mocked" and "punished" for constantly lying about the President.[682]

Tommy Robinson was permanently banned from Twitter for posting facts about crimes committed by Muslims in the UK.[683] Twitter has suspended other people's accounts for posting facts about black crime statistics in America as well.[684]

Jayda Fransen, another vocal critic of Muslim immigration to the UK and founder of "Britain First," was banned less than one month after President Trump retweeted a few of her videos showing violent Muslim mobs attacking people, which put her on the radar of activist groups who wanted to take her down for spreading "Islamophobia."[685]

Blogger Chuck Johnson was banned for saying he was going to "take out" Black Lives Matter troll DeRay McKesson, meaning expose him and take him out of the game, but Twitter claimed it was a threat of violence.[686] Johnson responded on his blog saying "Twitter doesn't seem to have a problem with people using their service to coordinate riots [referring to the recent spree of Black

[682] New York Times "Roger Stone Suspended From Twitter After Expletive-Laden Tweets" by Jacey Fortin (October 29th 2017)

[683] BBC "Tommy Robinson banned from Twitter" (March 28th 2018)

[684] Breitbart "Twitter Is Banning Conservatives for Posting Facts" by Allum Bokhari (May 9th 2018)

[685] The Wrap "Twitter Drops 'Britain First' Leader and Other Alt-Right Accounts" by Sean Burch (December 18th 2017)

[686] Politico "Troll Charles Johnson banned from Twitter" by Dylan Byers (May 26th 2015)

Lives Matter riots that had been occurring]. But they do have a problem with the kind of journalism I do."[687]

Supposed "white supremacist" Jared Taylor was also banned, along with the account for his American Renaissance organization as a part of a crack down on "abusive content," but Taylor doesn't use slurs or heated rhetoric and seems like a mild-mannered senior citizen who is just pushing back against anti-white racism, and celebrating European culture and achievements. Despite being called a "white supremacist" he actually says that Jews and Asians on average have higher IQs than white Europeans.[688]

Gavin McInnes, founder of the Proud Boys [conservative men's fraternity], was banned after he was falsely labeled the leader of a "hate group." He then sued the Southern Poverty Law Center for defamation.[689] Comedian Owen Benjamin was banned after going on a rant about anti-gun activist David Hogg where he said "Don't you think it's weird that you are telling grown men how to live when you barely have pubes?"[690]

Comedian Anthony Cumia, who was once co-host of the Opie and Anthony show, was banned in June 2017 for "harassing" a writer for The A.V. Club after he called her a "fat old trans looking twat."[691] YouTuber Sargon of

---

[687] Ibid.

[688] CNN Special "State of Hate" (2019) hosted by Fareed Zakaria which includes an interview with Jared Taylor where he says this.

[689] NBC News "Proud Boys founder Gavin McInnes sues Southern Poverty Law Center over hate group label" via Associated Press (February 4th 2019)

[690] https://twitter.com/kenklippenstein/status/981359404875505669

[691] The Laugh Button "Anthony Cumia's Twitter account suspended, allegedly following a fight with an A.V. Club writer" (July 12th 2017)

Akkad was banned in August 2017 for posting sarcastic comments that included "racial slurs."[692]

Free speech activist Lindsay Shepherd was banned in July 2019 for "misgendering" a transgender "woman" who sexually harassed her. The "woman" attacked Shepherd, who had just had a baby, saying "At least my pussy is tight and not loose after pushing out a 10 pound baby."[693] This same "woman," who goes by the name Jessica Yaniv, has been filing discrimination claims against waxing salons for refusing to do a Brazilian wax on "her" penis.[694]

Lindsay Shepherd responded, "This is how men who don't have functional romantic relationships speak. But…I guess that's kinda what you are!" At least I have a uterus, you fat ugly man."[695] Twitter then banned Lindsay Shepherd for calling "Jessica" a man, and not the transgender "woman" who clearly violated Twitter's policy against sexual harassment.

Street artist Sabo, who is like an American version of Banksy, was banned in April 2018 for the generic reason of "abusive behavior."[696] It's likely they considered him posting pictures of his street art, which is technically

---

[692] JRE Clips Channel on YouTube "Twitter Exec Reviews Sargon of Akkad's Ban | JRE Twitter Special" Trust and Safety leader Vijaya Gadde talk with Joe Rogan and Tim Pool about Sargon's ban (March 5th 2019)

[693] Ibid.

[694] The Daily Wire "Woman Forced To Close Business After Refusing To Wax Male Genitals Of Transgender Person" by Amanda Prestigiacomo (July 21st 2019)

[695] Breitbart "Free Speech Activist Lindsay Shepherd Banned from Twitter for 'Misgendering'" by Alana Mastrangelo (July 17th 2019)

[696] The Wrap "Right-Wing LA Street Artist Sabo Banned From Twitter" by Sean Burch (April 14 2018)

vandalism, to be a violation of the rules. Many other lesser known conservatives have also been banned but don't get any media attention because they aren't public figures with an active fanbase who can alert others about what happened.

CNN's Brian Stelter once tattled to Twitter asking them if President Trump violated their terms of service by "threatening North Korea" in a tweet saying he has a "nuclear button" that is much bigger and more powerful than Jim Jong-Un's when the two were having a heated war of words about North Korea testing missiles and threatening Japan.[697]

The @MAGAphobia account, which documented acts of violence and harassment against Trump supporters, was banned in May 2019 for a reason that was never given.[698] Perhaps it was for "showing graphic violence" since the account posted pictures of victims and videos of them being assaulted. Only mainstream media accounts are allowed to post graphic content so they can carefully choose how to frame certain issues, while ignoring others. Even a parody account called the "Alexandria Ocasio-Cortez Press" was banned, even though it was clearly a parody, and labeled a parody in the account's bio in accordance with Twitter's terms of service.[699]

Meanwhile, Twitter refused to shut down an account that organized a harassment campaign against senator Jeff

---

[697] CNS News "CNN: 'Dangerous' 'Fascist' Trump 'Threatening' Our Lives With His WWE Tweet" (July 2nd 2017)

[698] Washington Times "Twitter suspends Jack Posobiec's @MAGAphobia account for tracking violence against Trump supporters" by Douglas Ernst (May 78th 2019)

[699] Fox News "Twitter permanently suspends AOC parody account for being misleading" by Sam Dorman (May 7th 2019)

Flake after he voted in favor of confirming Brett Kavanaugh to the Supreme Court. The person said, "I am starting a National @DemSocialists working group to follow Jeff Flake around to every restaurant, cafe, store, etc he goes to for the rest of his life and yell at him."[700] Inciting harassment is supposed to be against Twitter's terms of service, but moderators usually look the other way when liberals do it.

Comedian Kathy Griffin's account wasn't penalized after she called for the doxing of the Covington Catholic kids who went viral for wearing MAGA hats during their trip to the nation's Capital.[701] When the account @HouseShoes, the verified account of a DJ and hip hop producer tweeted out to his supporters that "I want you to fire on any of these red hat bitches when you see them. On sight," and "IF WE COULD WIPE THESE FAMILIES OUT WE WOULD BE IN A MUCH BETTER PLACE," and his account wasn't suspended.[702] Actor Peter Fonda tweeted rape threats to President Trump's young son Barron and Twitter let him keep his account.[703]

An investigation by Breitbart found dozens of pedophiles using Twitter to openly promote pedophilia. Some of them refer to themselves as MAPs (Minor-Attracted Persons) and others call themselves "anti-

[700] https://twitter.com/anastasiakeeley/status/1047930583777779714

[701] Fox News "Kathy Griffin calls for doxing student's identities after viral video at Native American march: 'Shame them'" by Tyler McCarthy (January 21st 2019)

[702] Newsbusters "Twitter Deletes Some Covington Threats, Ignores Others" by Alexander Hall (January 22nd 2019)

[703] Politico "White House reports Peter Fonda tweet on Barron Trump to Secret Service" by Christopher Cadelago (June 20th 2018)

contact pedophiles" meaning they're attracted to children but claim to not act on their desires.[704] One of them tweeted, "MAPs have every right to talk (including, yes, on public blogs) about their fantasies, sexual and romantic, as long as sexually explicit material is hidden from children. It's not bad or disrespectful to talk about people you think are cute."[705]

Other news outlets have covered the issue of admitted pedophiles being allowed on Twitter as well, and Members of Parliament in England have denounced Twitter for allowing the accounts to remain active, some of them having been operating for years.[706]

While Twitter doesn't seem to have much of a problem with pedophiles openly fantasizing about molesting children, Laura Loomer got permanently banned for criticizing Ilhan Omar, the Muslim congresswoman from Minnesota, after Loomer said she was anti-Semitic and is a member of a religion in which "homosexuals are oppressed" and "women are abused."[707]

Not long after Laura Loomer was banned, the Congresswoman made headlines and was denounced by members of her own party, including Nancy Pelosi, for comments she made about AIPAC [The American Israel Public Affairs Committee], the largest Israeli lobbying

---

[704] Breitbart "Twitter Allows Self-Proclaimed Pedophiles to Spread Their Message on Its Platform" by Charlie Nash (December 4th 2018)

[705] http://archive.is/T9EUe

[706] Daily Mail "Twitter under fire from MPs and child safety campaigners for failing to block accounts used by paedophiles to discuss their sick cravings" by Abe Hawken (December 11th 2017)

[707] NBC News "Laura Loomer banned from Twitter after criticizing Ilhan Omar" by Linda Givetash (November 22nd 2018)

organization, after many deemed her criticism anti-Semitic.[708] So Loomer was right about Ilhan Omar, but got banned for being "Islamophobic" and posting "hate speech" about Muslims. Later a video clip surfaced of Ilhan Omar appearing to mock Americans who were fearful of Al-Qaeda in the aftermath of the 9/11 terrorist attacks.[709]

A writer named Meghan Murphy, who refuses to accept transgender "women" as real women, was banned for simply referring to a transgender "woman" as a "he" (a violation called "misgendering" someone).[710] A world-renowned expert in gender dysphoria, Dr. Ray Blanchard, was suspended for tweeting that transgenderism was a mental disorder.[711] He didn't say it to be mean, he said it as part of a thread about the condition, (which up until May 2019 was classified as a mental disorder by the World Health Organization — and still is by many psychiatrists around the world, including the American Psychiatric Association's DSM-5) but some facts are considered hate speech now.[712]

---

[708] Politico "Ilhan Omar apologizes after Pelosi denounces tweet as anti-Semitic" by Melanie Zanona and Heather Caygle (February 11th 2019)

[709] The Daily Caller "Ilhan Omar Blows Off Al-Qaeda, Mocks Americans For Fearing Them in Recently Surfaced Video" by Virginia Kruta (April 12th 2019)

[710] National Review "Journalist Sues Twitter for Banning Her over 'Women Aren't Men' Tweets" by Mairead Mcardle (February 11th 2019)

[711] Breitbart "Twitter Blacklists Famed Gender Dysphoria Researcher Ray Blanchard" by Neil Munro (May 13th 2019)

[712] Psychiatry.org "What Is Gender Dysphoria?" by the American Psychiatric Association

After I tweeted that there are only two genders and insinuated the rest of the 50+ "gender identities" liberals have come up with were mental disorders, I was suspended for that too. My account was also disabled from uploading videos longer than 2 minutes and 20 seconds because they said I had posted "Inappropriate Content," and I have been banned from running ads on Twitter too.

I have also been suspended for calling Kevin Spacey a "Satanic scumbag" and telling him to "burn in Hell" after an actor came forward and claimed Spacey made aggressive sexual advances on him when he was just 14-years-old.[713] My tweet was considered to be "hateful" because he's a gay man who is above reproach.

Actor James Woods' account was suspended for posting a satirical meme making fun of Democrats, showing three soy boys with the caption, "We're making a woman's vote worth more by staying home," and included the hashtag #LetWomenDecide and #NoMenMidterm. Twitter claimed it was in violation of their policy forbidding posting content that "has the potential to be misleading in a way that could impact an election."[714]

Twitter suspended the account of Austin Petersen who was running for Senate in Missouri in 2018 just one week before the primary.[715] Twitter even banned Republican

---

[713] USA Today "Who is Anthony Rapp, the actor who accused Kevin Spacey of sexual harassment?" by Jayme Deerwester (October 30th 2017)

[714] Associated Press "Actor James Woods bashes Twitter after getting locked out" by Amy Forliti (September 2018)

[715] Daily Caller "Twitter Issued GOP Candidate Temporary Ban Week Before Election" by Kyle Perisic (July 31st 2018)

Senate candidate Marsha Blackburn from running pro-life ads during her campaign because they were deemed "inflammatory"[716]   The official account for the anti-abortion movie *UnPlanned* was briefly suspended by Twitter during the film's opening weekend in March 2019.[717]   As usual, the suspension caused a wave a backlash and Twitter later restored it saying it was another "mistake."

Twitter also suspended a user for calling Maxine Waters a "crazy old lying lunatic in a bad wig."[718]   A recent change to Twitter's terms of service says they will ban anyone who is "amplifying hate groups" by posting articles about them, or even retweeting other tweets about them.   (That only applies to right-wing "hate groups" though. Supporting Antifa, black power groups, and other far-left movements is fine).

After a bunch of *Huffington Post* and BuzzFeed employees got laid off in February 2019, a lot of people mocked them by responding with "Learn to Code" after they posted Dear Diary-style tweets crying about being let go, and so Twitter began suspending accounts for using that phrase or hashtag, claiming it was "abusive behavior."[719]

---

[716] Politico "Twitter pulls Blackburn Senate ad deemed 'inflammatory'" by Kevin Robillard (October 9th 2018)

[717] Hollywood Reporter "Anti-Abortion Movie's Twitter Account Briefly Suspended" by Paul Bond and Katie Kilkenny (March 30th 2019)

[718] The American Mirror "Twitter suspends user for calling Maxine Waters 'crazy old lying lunatic in a bad wig'" by Kyle Olson (March 3rd 2018)

[719] Daily Caller "Daily Caller editor in chief locked out of account for tweeting 'learn to code'" by Amber Athey (February 6th 2019)

The saying "Learn to Code" is a reference to news outlets publishing stories encouraging coal miners who are getting laid off as clean energy companies replace their jobs to do just that. Expecting a fifty-year-old coal miner to become a software engineer is insane and shows how out of touch the journalists were who recommended they do just that, so people threw "Learn to Code" back in their faces, but that's "harassment."

When CEO Jack Dorsey appeared on Joe Rogan's podcast in February 2019, Joe brought up Alex Jones being banned and pointed out that Twitter was the last major platform to do so after (briefly) allowing him to keep his account in the wake of YouTube, Facebook, iTunes, etc, banning him. When Joe asked, "What did he do on your platform, that you all were in agreement that this is enough?" Jack responded, "Ah, I'm not — I'm not sure what the, what the actual like, ya know, violations were."[720] (That's an exact quote.)

Alex was banned for telling off CNN's Oliver Darcy outside of the Jack Dorsey congressional hearing in September 2018, where Jones denounced Oliver for pressuring all the social media companies to get him banned. The confrontation was broadcast live on Twitter via Periscope and so Twitter quickly banned Jones for "harassing" a supposed "journalist."[721]

It's important to point out that Oliver Darcy was working in the capacity of a journalist at the time, on public property, while he was covering an event about social media; thus confirming everything Alex Jones was saying about the censorship of conservatives. Oliver

---

[720] Joe Rogan Experience #1236 - Jack Dorsey (February 1st 2019)

[721] NPR "Twitter Bans Alex Jones And InfoWars; Cites Abusive Behavior" by Avie Schneider (September 6th 2018)

Darcy later admitted that CNN had "presented Twitter with examples of [violations of Twitter's terms of service] available on both the InfoWars and Jones account."[722]

In August 2019 a group of Leftists gathered outside Senator Mitch McConnell's house after sunset to harass him and some of them made threatening statements saying he should be killed, and when he posted a short video on his Twitter account showing the angry mob and what they were saying, *he* was suspended and the video removed for allegedly violating their terms of service prohibiting making threats, even though he had just posted evidence of what people were doing to him![723] His staff appealed the suspension but the appeal was denied.[724]

Only after growing outrage and media coverage did Twitter lift his suspension and restore the video.[725] Mitch McConnell is the Senate Majority Leader, the most powerful Senator in the country, yet was censored when he tried to show his fellow Americans that Leftists had surrounded his home to intimidate and threaten him.

---

[722] CNN "Twitter says InfoWars hasn't 'violated our rules.' It looks like that's not the case" by Oliver Darcy (August 9th 2018)

[723] CNBC "Twitter locks Mitch McConnell's campaign account for tweet violating threats policy" by Marc Rod (August 8th 2019)

[724] CBS News "Twitter suspends Mitch McConnell's campaign account after posting video of protesters threatening him" by Christopher Brito (August 8th 2019)

[725] The Wrap "Twitter Reverses Mitch McConnell Suspension, Says Protest Video 'Will Be Visible'" by Sean Burch and Lindsey Ellefson (August 9th 2019)

Twitter Verification

The "verified" checkmark on someone's social media account is a confirmation that the account actually belongs to that person, and isn't being run by someone else pretending to be them. Public figures like celebrities and journalists usually get them to prevent imposter accounts from impersonating them, and having a verified account is often seen as a sign that someone is "important" and so every wannabe rapper and blogger wishes to get one, but you have to apply, and Twitter won't just verify anyone's account.

They have, however, verified numerous Black Lives Matter activists' accounts whose credentials are basically that they're anti-police trolls who spend their entire lives on Twitter spewing hatred of police and white people. Virulent racist troll Tariq Nasheed, who accuses almost every white person in America of being a "suspected white supremacist," has been verified. Other Black Lives Matter trolls like Shaun King and Deray McKesson have also been rewarded with verified accounts.

Twitter also verified Sarah Jeong, a new editorial board member at the *New York Times*, despite a series of racist tweets about "dumbass fucking white people" and saying she gets "joy" out of being "cruel to old white men."[726] Twitter also verified loads of fringe LGBT social media personalities, and plenty of pro-feminist and pro-abortion trolls in order to give them more clout online.

Meanwhile, popular conservatives like James O'Keefe, Carpe Donktum, Gary Franchi, David Harris Jr.,

---

[726] Breitbart "Twitter Verifies Sarah Jeong Without Making Her Delete Racist Posts" by Charlie Nash (August 16th 2018)

Brandon Tatum, David Horowitz, and others have been denied verification for years.[727]   Before they were permanently banned, Tommy Robinson, Laura Loomer, and Milo Yiannopoulos had been *unverified*.

Twitter released a statement saying "Reasons for removal [of verification checkmark] may reflect behaviors on and off Twitter that include: Promoting hate and/or violence against, or directly attacking or threatening other people on the basis of race, ethnicity, national origin, sexual orientation, gender, gender identity, religious affiliation, age, disability, or disease" and even, "Supporting organizations or individuals that promote the above."[728]

Twitter verified the "Parkland kids," a small group of anti-gun activists who became social media stars over night after a lunatic shot up their high school on Valentine's Day 2018 in Parkland, Florida. One of them, David Hogg, went on to sic his nearly 500,000 followers onto the advertisers of various Fox News shows, harassing them to pull their ads from the network.[729] Twitter even hosted the Parkland kids for a live Q&A to help them promote their "March For Our Lives" event where they demanded more gun control laws.[730]

---

[727] Project Veritas "Why James O'Keefe Isn't Verified On Twitter" by Laura Loomer (September 1st 2016)

[728] Twitter.com "Verified account FAQs

[729] SF Gate "Here Are the 27 Advertisers David Hogg Convinced to Dump Laura Ingraham" by Brian Welk (April 13th 2018)

[730] The Blaze "Twitter only invites anti-gun Parkland students to Q&A panel. Pro-gun student has perfect response" by Chris Enloe (March 18th 2018)

Never Tweet

There's a meme that looks like the sign-up page for Twitter but reads "Get fired from your job in ten years" just above the link to open an account, and it's not that far from the truth. What you say in a tweet can be perfectly fine if it was just said amongst a group of friends, but often our enemies are lurking quietly on Twitter, watching and waiting for one little slip up, and even complete strangers who happen to come across your tweet may feel compelled to enact "revenge" because you said something on the Internet that offended them.

People often like to go digging through old tweets of their enemies, hoping to find years or decade-old tweets saying "racist," "homophobic," or "sexist" things so they can derail their career. Twitter's search function allows people to search anyone's Twitter feed for any keyword or phrase, making this tactic extremely simple. (I advise, if you use Twitter, to consider a "tweet delete" app which allows you to easily search for and delete old tweets which contain certain words or phrases. Or regularly delete your tweets that are older than six months in order to avoid past tweets posted years ago from coming back to haunt you.)

Oftentimes when someone becomes famous, people will go nosing around their old tweets typing in keywords like "nigger" and "faggot" into the search to see if they've ever tweeted anything with those words in the past so they can retweet them, trying to get the person in trouble. This is exactly what happened right after Kyler Murray won the 2018 Heisman Trophy. A reporter for *USA Today* took it upon himself to search through his past tweets and found some "homophobic" ones from when he was fifteen-years-old.[731]

When Milwaukee Brewers pitcher Josh Hader was chosen to pitch in the 2018 All-Star Game, people dug up some of his old tweets from when he was in high school and it made headlines because he used the "n-word" in a few tweets.[732] He then apologized and deleted his entire account. The same thing has happened to "Mr. Beast," a popular YouTuber, and singer Shawn Mendes.[733]

The best example of what can happen when you tweet is the disaster that occurred to a woman named Justine Sacco in 2013 who had just 170 followers. When boarding a flight to South Africa she tweeted, "Going to Africa. Hope I don't get AIDS. Just kidding. I'm white!" and then got on the plane without thinking anything of it. She didn't say it as a racist insult about the AIDS epidemic there, but meant it as a sarcastic jab at Americans who she said lived in "a bit of a bubble when it comes to what's going on in the third world," since she herself was born in South Africa and returning there to visit family.[734]

But somebody following her got offended and retweeted it, and then their followers saw it and got triggered and retweeted it, and then she soon began

---

[731] USA Today "Kyler Murray apologizes for homophobic tweets that resurfaced after he won Heisman Trophy" by Scott Gleeson (December 9th 2018)

[732] USA Today "Josh Hader apologizes for racist tweets, claims they 'don't reflect any of my beliefs now'" by Gabe Lacques (July 18th 2018)

[733] NBC New York "Shawn Mendes Apologizes for Past 'Racially Insensitive Comments'" by Corinne Heller (August 24th 2019)

[734] New York Times Magazine "How One Stupid Tweet Blew Up Justine Sacco's Life" by Jon Ronson (February 12th 2015)

trending from so many people being upset about her tweet even though she was just some random person on Twitter. She and her tweet then became a national news story and she ultimately ended up getting fired from her job.[735]

Twitter is often fueled by anger with people venting their political frustrations through tweets like irate sports fans yelling at the TV. For others it's a narcissistic circus where they derive their self-worth by getting likes and retweets since the immediate engagement can become addicting because their notifications release dopamine similar to getting a small payout from a slot machine at the casino.

The instant gratification of getting feedback becomes a deeply engrained habit that's hard for people to break. Perhaps the only good thing about Twitter is President Trump's tweets. Previously, to hear what a President had to say, he would have to hold a press conference or give an interview, but now with Twitter he can fire off his thoughts on anything at any time, day or night, and then the media reports on it—often over-reacting to the point of having a meltdown.

There have been calls to ban him, and groups have even started petitions and presented them to Twitter with the foolish hope they would shut down his account, but he's still there. Twitter's co-founder Evan Williams even said he was sorry for his creation helping Donald Trump get out his message during his campaign in 2016 after Trump told the *Financial Times* that without it, he didn't

---

[735] ABC News "Justine Sacco, Fired After Tweet on AIDS in Africa, Issues Apology" by Kami Dimitrova, Shahriar Rahmanzadeh and Jane Lipman (December 22nd 2013)

think he would have won.[736] "If it's true that he wouldn't be president if it weren't for Twitter, then yeah, I'm sorry," Williams said.[737]

Trump knows and loves the power of Twitter, but the big question is—will he still tweet after he's left office? Barack Obama broke the unwritten rule of not criticizing his successor, and it's been the tradition of former presidents to not inject themselves into matters involving the next administration, but both Barack Obama and George W. Bush have been openly criticizing the Trump administration, so after he leaves office he may not sit by silently, and could regularly criticize the next administration as well, and it will be hard for people to ignore what he's saying since his Twitter feed has become such a newsmaker.

There may be only one way for the *Liberal Media Industrial Complex* to silence Donald Trump, which is why they are constantly painting him as the reincarnation of Adolf Hitler, and incessantly calling him a fascist dictator, because they are hoping to incite some unhinged lunatic who believes what they say to assassinate him.

---

[736] Financial Times "Donald Trump: Without Twitter, I would not be here — FT interview" by Lionel Barber, Demetri Sevastopulo and Gillian Tett (April 2nd 2017)

[737] New York Times "'The Internet is Broken' @ev Is Trying to Salvage It" by David Streitfeld (May 20th 2017)

YouTube

Most people don't realize this but YouTube is the second largest search engine in the world, after Google of course, and it's also part of the same conglomerate since Google bought YouTube in 2006 for 1.6 billion dollars. Later corporate restructuring put both of them under the new umbrella company Alphabet Inc. When referring to YouTube many people consider it a part of Google, but it should be considered its own separate entity, which it technically is, with its own CEO — Susan Wojcicki.

For the better part of a decade after YouTube was launched, it was largely seen as just a website for user generated entertainment. It was the place for people to upload funny cat videos and show themselves doing stupid "Internet challenges," but a small group of people (myself included) knew from YouTube's beginning that it was a powerful tool that could be used to share news and analysis about current events and other important issues that weren't being properly addressed by mainstream outlets. It was like having our own public access cable channel where we could do anything we wanted with the potential to reach an audience of millions, and for some of us, that started happening on a regular basis.

For over a year after the 2016 election, the mainstream media's war on "fake news" (in reality a war on independent news and ordinary people using social media to get out their message) focused almost exclusively on Facebook and Twitter since the news giants saw them as being responsible for completely losing their power to control the national narrative surrounding major issues and events.

The mainstream media could no longer prevent certain information from becoming widely known and millions of people were spending their time scrolling through Facebook, and Twitter, and watching YouTube videos instead of engaging with the traditional news outlets that had dominated the industry for decades since their creation.

But Donald Trump beating Hillary Clinton was a wakeup call for the *Liberal Media Industrial Complex*, so they launched a bold new effort under the disguise of fighting "fake news" to completely reshape social media. While they first focused on Facebook and Twitter, eventually they stumbled upon a huge secret that was right in front of their nose for years. People like me were creating YouTube videos on a regular basis covering news and politics and we were getting enormous audiences rivaling or beating cable news. In the run-up to the 2016 election my YouTube channel was averaging around 700,000 viewers a day, about half of what CNN's primetime shows like Anderson Cooper and Don Lemon get on their best nights.[738]

But now the Establishment discovered the "fake news" problem was flourishing on YouTube, they said, and it had to be stopped by changing the algorithm to artificially favor mainstream media channels over videos posted by ordinary YouTubers. In October of 2017, sociologist and technology critic Zeynep Tufekci said, "YouTube is the most overlooked story of 2016," after realizing there was much more to YouTube than cat

---

[738] SocialBlade.com - Detailed Statistics for the Mark Dice YouTube channel October 2016

videos and pranksters.[739]   Traditional media outlets discovered the world of underground news and they were shocked at just how popular we were.

Slate pointed out that Twitter and Facebook had been receiving the brunt of criticism about spreading "fake news" but, "Now a series of controversies is forcing YouTube to address its responsibilities more directly and candidly than it has in the past."[740]

Soon YouTube would completely change the way the website had functioned for the previous ten years, and turned it from what was meant to be a place where anyone with an important message could post videos and build an audience, to mostly just another mainstream media site filled with brand name news channels and videos of familiar celebrities.

By mid-2018, as *Wired* magazine points out, YouTube was "ditching vloggers" in favor of Hollywood celebrities. "YouTube used to be all about young digital influencers who managed to threaten TV with their video blogs. Not anymore. It seems that YouTube is opting for traditional celebrities instead."[741]

Another blogger noticed the changes and ran with the headline, "YouTube is turning away from its creators to become a new MTV," and noted, "YouTube can't promise brand safety with volatile creators on the platform — advertisers don't want to be caught in a firestorm. The only move is to pivot, and YouTube is ready. Hollywood names like Will Smith and Demi Lovato are safe bets.

[739] https://twitter.com/zeynep/status/915608049141915648

[740] Slate "YouTube Is Realizing It May Be Bad for All of Us" by Will Oremus (March 14th 2018)

[741] Wired "YouTube's ditching vloggers, old-school celebs are back again" by Chris Stokel-Walker (May 8th 2018)

Same with music videos already vetted by major record labels."[742]

YouTube, which for over a decade was a place for independent content creators to upload their videos, even began producing shows themselves.[743] For the better part of ten years since its launch in 2006, Hollywood studios and mainstream celebrities didn't pay much attention to YouTube. They either were afraid of it because it threatened their monopoly on content distribution, or they were too blind to see how the new technology was revolutionizing media and helping to create new kinds of stars.

Right-Wing Channels Dominating

In March of 2018 *Vanity Fair* warned that right-wing "Dark-Web Trolls" were "taking over YouTube" because so many anti-social justice warrior channels were getting popular.[744] The *New York Times* then said YouTube was "radicalizing" people to the right, and claimed that if people started watching videos of Donald Trump speeches then YouTube will begin recommending videos of "white supremacist rants" and "Holocaust denials."[745]

The article declared that, "Given its billion or so users, YouTube may be one of the most powerful

---

[742] Polygon "YouTube is turning away from its creators to become a new MTV" by Julia Alexander (May 7th 2018)

[743] Bloomberg "With 40 New Original Shows, YouTube Targets TV's Breadbasket" by Lucas Shaw and Mark Bergen (May 4th 2017)

[744] Vanity Fair "Why the Right's Dark-Web Trolls Are Taking Over YouTube" by Maya Kosoff (March 1st 2018)

[745] The New York Times "YouTube, the Great Radicalizer" by Zeynep Tufekci (March 10th 2018)

radicalizing instruments of the 21st century," and that, "Its algorithm seems to have concluded that people are drawn to content that is more extreme than what they started with — or to incendiary content in general."[746]

The New York Times had previously complained that, "For the New Far Right, YouTube Has Become the New Talk Radio," saying, "They deplore 'social justice warriors,' whom they credit with ruining popular culture, conspiring against the populace and helping to undermine 'the West.' They are fixated on the subjects of immigration, Islam and political correctness. They seem at times more animated by President Trump's opponents than by the man himself, with whom they share many priorities, if not a style."[747] The Left became determined to paint the Right's rising stars as radicals, Islamophobes, and far-right extremists hoping to derail the spread of our videos.

One Leftist blog called "Right Wing Watch" founded by Jared Holt declared that, "White Supremacy Figured Out How To Become YouTube Famous," and whined that, "YouTube has served as an alternative media ecosystem apart from the mainstream where any person can contribute to national conversation and reach thousands of people overnight. But the Right's overt domination of the platform, in addition to political forums on Reddit and 4chan, has created an environment where white nationalists and right-wing extremists can easily inject

---

[746] Ibid.

[747] New York Times "For the New Far Right, YouTube Has Become the new Talk Radio" by John Herrman (August 3rd 2017)

hateful rhetoric and conspiracy theories into national political discourse."[748]

When BuzzFeed or CNN reported "breaking news" about the Trump administration or when something started trending on Twitter, us YouTubers could quickly publish videos giving another perspective and point out things the mainstream media was ignoring or lying about. Our subscribers would see the videos, but perhaps more importantly, people searching for information on YouTube about those issues could find our videos, and if they were popular with favorable ratings, those videos would be discovered by people seeking out information on the subject matter. But all that has changed.

"Authoritative Channels" Boosted to the Top

For over a decade the top search results on YouTube were the most popular videos associated with the search terms you entered in, regardless of whether the videos were posted by someone who had just opened a YouTube account, a full time YouTuber, or a mainstream media outlet. The algorithm that was originally in place worked very well, because instead of showing the most-viewed videos (which could have generated a large number of views by using misleading titles and thumbnails) YouTube surfaced videos with the most "watch time" up at the top.

This means that if people clicked on a video and found that the title and thumbnail were misleading or it wasn't a quality video, and then decided not to watch it by clicking away rather soon once it began playing, the

---

[748] Right Wing Watch "White Supremacy Figured Out How To Become YouTube Famous" by Jared Holt (October 2017)

algorithm would know that it wasn't what people were searching for because the average amount of time people spent watching the video would be low. But if the video had a high watch time average, the site (accurately) figured that people had found what they were looking for because they kept watching it, and those were the videos that ranked the highest in the search results.

All that mattered was that the video was uploaded to YouTube by someone—anyone. If it was good, and people watched it instead of clicking away after a few seconds, it would show up in the top of the search results. But all that changed in October 2017 when YouTube reconfigured the algorithm to favor videos from mainstream media outlets.[749]

They added internal tags on certain channels deeming them "authoritative sources," and overnight the top search results for most things were now videos from channels like CNN, NBC, Entertainment Tonight, etc. Most of these videos have only a tiny fraction of the views (and watch time) compared to countless other videos about the subject being searched for, but those videos are now buried under pages of content from channels that YouTube has deemed "authoritative" sources.[750]

They had manually intervened in the search results previously, but only for certain topics they deemed "extremist" material, like videos supporting ISIS. YouTube had been redirecting search results for these topics to curated videos and playlists they had specifically

[749] USA Today "YouTube alters algorithm after searches for Las Vegas shooting turn up conspiracy theories" by Jessica Guynn (October 5th 2017)

[750] Wall Street Journal "YouTube Tweaks Search Results as Las Vegas Conspiracy Theories Rise to Top" by Jack Nicas (October 5th 2017)

chosen in order to "confront and debunk violent extremist messages."[751] But now "the Jigsaw Method" as they call it, was rolled out on a massive scale and incorporated news, current events, and many other topics people regularly search for.

"We're continuing to invest in new features and changes to YouTube search that provide authoritative results when people come to YouTube looking for news," a YouTube spokesperson said in a statement.[752] "So far this year we have introduced new features that promote verified news sources when a major news event happens. These sources are presented on the YouTube homepage, under 'Breaking News,' and featured in search results, with the label 'Top News.' Additionally, we've been rolling out algorithmic changes to YouTube search during breaking news events. There is still more work to do, but we're making progress."[753] Soon it wasn't just videos from mainstream media channels boosted to the top during "breaking news" events, but almost anything having to do with news at all.

MSNBC's Chris Hayes rang the alarm about YouTube's algorithm because he didn't like the search results for videos about the Federal Reserve.[754] *Mother Jones* magazine joined in on the criticism, reporting, "If you search for 'Federal Reserve' on YouTube, one of the first videos to surface is titled 'Century of Enslavement.'

---

[751] YouTube Official Blog "An update on our commitment to fight terror content online" (August 1, 2017)

[752] Fortune "YouTube Responds to Criticism After Unverified Texas Shooting Reports Top Search Results" by Tom Huddleston Jr. (November 6th 2017)

[753] Ibid.

[754] https://twitter.com/chrislhayes/status/1037831504158646272

Using archival footage and the kind of authoritative male voice heard in countless historical documentaries, the 90-minute video espouses the idea the Federal Reserve was formed in secret by powerful, often Jewish, banking families in the early 20th century, causing America to spiral into debt."[755]

It continued, "The incendiary Federal Reserve video, flagged by MSNBC host Chris Hayes earlier this month, is just one of many examples of how political extremists have mastered YouTube's algorithms and monetization structure to spread toxic ideas ranging from conspiracy theories to white supremacy. The video 'Why Social Justice is CANCER,' for instance, appears after searching for 'social justice.'[756] That video was from Lauren Chen (formerly known as Roaming Millennial.)[757]

Soon the search results for "Federal Reserve" featured only videos from mainstream media channels, and the documentary Chris Hayes called out (*Century of Enslavement: The History of the Federal Reserve*—which was the top search result) was nowhere to be seen. I looked all the way through page 25 of the search results and it still didn't show up.[758] Other videos critical of the Federal Reserve, including one titled "Exposing the Federal Reserve," which is a high-quality 30-minute

---

[755] Mother Jones "Political Extremists are using YouTube to monetize their toxic ideas" by Tonya Riley (September 18th 2018)

[756] Ibid.

[757] "Why Social Justice is CANCER | Identity Politics, Equality & Marxism" by Lauren Chen (July 24th 2017)

[758] The video, which is an hour and a half long, is titled "Century of Enslavement: The History of the Federal Reserve" posted by the CorbettReport channel on July 6th 2014 and has nearly 2 million views.

cartoon,[759] and "The Federal Reserve Explained in 3 Minutes" also vanished.

A whistleblower later revealed to Breitbart that "Federal Reserve" had been added to the secret "Controversial Query Blacklist" file which causes "authoritative content" (i.e. mainstream media channels) to artificially rise to the top of the search results over other videos that actually qualify organically for those positions.[760]

My most-viewed video "Donald Trump's Funniest Insults and Comebacks," which has over 11 million views, is now buried on page three of the search results when looking for the exact title. All the top results for "Donald Trump's Funniest Insults and Comebacks" are videos from CNN, NBC News, ABC News, the Washington Post, HuffPost, etc, most of which are critical of President Trump and have far less views and watch time.

My channel had reached one million subscribers in May of 2017, and at the time had more subscribers than MSNBC's channel, NBC News, CBS News, and even Fox News.[761] And many of my videos far eclipsed theirs in the number of views, but since the algorithm changes my channel virtually stalled in growth while theirs all grew exponentially.

---

[759] While the YouTube video is titled "Exposing the Federal Reserve" the video itself is actually the film "The American Dream" by Tad Lumpkin and Harold Uhl

[760] Breitbart "New Whistleblower Allegation: YouTube Manipulated 'Federal Reserve' Search Results In Response to MSNBC Host's Complaint" by Allum Bokhari (July 30th 2019)

[761] SocialBlade.com Detailed Statistics for MSNBC, NBC News, CBS News, and Fox News' YouTube channels.

In the spring of 2019, YouTube changed the algorithm so when people searched for my own name, the top search results were *other people's videos* about me, with mine buried at the bottom of the page. When searching for almost any other YouTuber, however, their most recent videos were featured at the top of the page with a notification highlighting their latest uploads.

I had been calling YouTube out about this since I first learned of it in May 2019, thanks to people leaving comments on my videos giving me a heads up, but YouTube wouldn't respond to me. It was only after an uproar four months later when Steven Crowder became aware that none of his videos were coming up in the search results for his name either, and directed his lawyer to contact them about it while his fans bombarded YouTube with a flood of tweets denouncing them for what they had done.

They quickly made some adjustments, partially fixing the problem near the end of September 2019, but didn't publicly acknowledge the complaints or that they had reverted the algorithm back to the way it was. But at least my two most recent videos started showing up again at the top of the search results along with those of the other popular conservative channels that had been censored (Steven Crowder, Paul Joseph Watson, The Next News Network, Lauren Chen, and Breitbart News).

Shortly after a feminist writer for Slate.com, an online magazine, complained about many of the top search results for "abortion" being pro-life videos (including one that showed what a baby looks like in the first trimester—complete with arms, legs, fingers and toes), YouTube quickly changed the algorithm to feature various pro-abortion videos at the top. "I emailed YouTube Friday afternoon asking why anti-abortion videos saturated the search results for 'abortion,'" she wrote, adding, "By Monday morning…the search results had changed to include a number of news outlets among the top results."[762]

National Review pointed out that YouTube was happy to "airbrush away the reality of abortion," by artificially boosting pro-abortion videos after her complaint.[763] Now a search for "abortion" brings up videos from Vice News, the BBC, and BuzzFeed. In a leaked document given to Breitbart, one engineer admitted "We have tons of white and blacklists that humans manually curate."[764]

The document also first revealed the existence of the "Controversial Query Blacklist" file that contains a list of search terms that will bring up manually curated videos in the results or ensure the top results are videos from mainstream media channels.[765] The list includes "abortion," "Federal Reserve," and even people like anti-gun activist David Hogg, and Congresswoman Maxine Waters.

When *Captain Marvel* was released in March 2019 YouTube changed their algorithm in order to bury videos of people who were giving the movie negative reviews

---

[762] Slate "YouTube's Search Results for "Abortion" Show Exactly What Anti-Abortion Activists Want Women to See" by April Glaser (December 21st 2018)

[763] National Review "YouTube Changed 'Abortion' Search Results after a Slate Writer Complained" by Sanda Desanctis (December 22nd 2018)

[764] Breitbart "THE SMOKING GUN: Google Manipulated YouTube Search Results for Abortion, Maxine Waters, David Hogg" by Allum Bokhari (January 16th 2019)

[765] Ibid.

which were appearing as the top search results.[766]   The film's star Brie Larson had been insulting white men and promoting intersectional feminism on her publicity tour, angering many Marvel fans who took to YouTube to express their thoughts. Those videos, being very popular, surfaced at the top of the search results for "Brie Larson," but that soon changed.

A writer for *The Verge* posted two side by side screenshots showing the before and after top search results and noted, "This is kind of a fascinating discovery: YouTube seems to have changed the immediate 'Brie Larson' search results to News.   That pushes up authoritative sources and, in turn, pushes troll or MRA-style [Men's Rights Activists] video rants pretty far down the page."[767]

She went on to report that, "YouTube recategorized 'Brie Larson' as a news-worthy search term. That does one very important job: it makes the search algorithm surface videos from authoritative sources on a subject. Instead of videos from individual creators, YouTube responds with videos from *Entertainment Tonight*, ABC, CBS, CNN, and other news outlets first."[768]

YouTube has even experimented with disabling some of the search filters to make it impossible to do a more focused search when looking for something specific. In March 2019 they temporarily disabled the ability to filter search results by dates, in order to prevent people from finding recent uploads of the New Zealand mosque

---

[766] The Verge "YouTube fought Brie Larson trolls by changing its search algorithm" by Julia Alexander (March 8th 2019)

[767] https://twitter.com/loudmouthjulia/status/1103730622281994240

[768] The Verge "YouTube fought Brie Larson trolls by changing its search algorithm" by Julia Alexander (March 8th 2019)

massacre which was live-streamed by the shooter and was being uploaded to YouTube by various people who had gotten the footage from the perpetrator's Facebook page before moderators removed it.[769]

This way you couldn't narrow the search parameters by the date something was posted which is often the only way to find certain clips now because they're buried under countless other videos that are artificially pushed to the top even though they're not necessarily relevant to the search terms. Luckily this time, disabling the search filters was only temporarily, but who knows what the future holds.

Recommended Videos

Playing favorites with mainstream channels and serving their videos up as the top search results no matter how few views or little engagement they have wasn't good enough though. The *Wall Street Journal* complained, "YouTube's algorithm tweaks don't appear to have changed how YouTube recommends videos on its home page. On the home page, the algorithm provides a personalized feed for each logged-in user largely based on what the user has watched...Repeated tests by the Journal as recently as this week showed the home page often fed far-right or far-left videos to users who watched relatively mainstream news sources, such as Fox News and MSNBC."[770]

---

[769] CNBC "Facebook, YouTube and Twitter go to extraordinary lengths to take down mosque massacre videos" by Lauren Feiner (March 18th 2019)

[770] Wall Street Journal "How YouTube Drives People to the Internet's Darkest Corners" by Jack Nicas (February 7th 2018)

Their report continued, "After searching for '9/11' last month, then clicking on a single CNN clip about the attacks, and then returning to the home page, the fifth and sixth recommended videos were about claims the U.S. government carried out the attacks. One, titled 'Footage Shows Military Plane hitting WTC Tower on 9/11—13 Witnesses React'—had 5.3 million views."[771]

Others had been complaining about "conspiracy videos" too. As you can imagine, CNN piled on the criticism as well, reporting, "YouTube has long faced criticism for allowing misinformation, conspiracy theories and extremist views to spread on its platform, and for recommending such content to users. People who came to the site to watch videos on innocuous subjects, or to see mainstream news, have been pushed toward increasingly fringe and conspiracist content."[772]

NBC News also complained that, "YouTube search results for A-list celebrities [have been] hijacked by conspiracy theorists" and noted, "YouTube did not respond to a request for comment," [but] "Some conspiracy videos' rankings dropped after NBC News reached out for comment."[773]

In January 2019 YouTube issued a public statement saying that they will continue, "taking a closer look at how we can reduce the spread of content that comes close to—but doesn't quite cross the line of—violating our Community Guidelines. To that end, we'll begin reducing recommendations of borderline content and content that

---

[771] Ibid.

[772] CNN "YouTube says it will crack down on recommending conspiracy videos" by Kaya Yurieff (January 25th 2019)

[773] NBC "YouTube search results for A-list celebrities hijacked by conspiracy theorists" by Ben Collins (July 30th 2018)

could misinform users in harmful ways—such as videos promoting a phony miracle cure for a serious illness, claiming the earth is flat, or making blatantly false claims about historic events like 9/11."[774]

It went on to say, "This change relies on a combination of machine learning and real people. We work with human evaluators and experts from all over the United States to help train the machine learning systems that generate recommendations."[775]

YouTube now deciding what is and is not a conspiracy theory has dramatic implications. For example, mainstream media outlets claimed that people who thought "Empire" actor Jussie Smollett faked his "racist and homophobic attack" at the hands of Trump supporters were spreading a "conspiracy theory."[776] And since such "conspiracy theory" videos are now admittedly buried in the search results and kept out of the Recommended and Up Next sections, YouTube was actively hiding the truth about what actually happened, which later came out.[777]

A recent addition to YouTube's terms of service specifically bans, "Content claiming that specific victims of public violent incidents or their next of kin are actors, or that their experiences are false," which means that anyone who posted a video or did a livestream saying they thought Jussie Smollett faked the "attack" was in violation of their rules and at risk of having their videos

---

[774] YouTube Official Blog (January 25th 2019)

[775] Ibid.

[776] Mercury News "Is Donald Trump Jr. promoting a Jussie Smollett conspiracy theory?" by Martha Ross (February 1st 2019)

[777] NBC News "YouTube announces it will no longer recommend conspiracy videos" by Kalhan Rosenblatt (February 10th 2019)

taken down and issued a Community Guidelines strike or even having their entire channel banned if they had previous infractions.[778]

For many years about one-third of my total views were from "Suggested" videos, but then in April 2019 I and many other YouTubers noticed a quick and dramatic drop, which is detailed in our Channel Analytics. From that point on my total views from "Suggested" videos dropped to around five percent, a significant drop, most likely because my channel was identified as "borderline" and so my videos don't show up on people's homepages anymore or next to similar content.

The "Alternative Influence Network"

It wasn't enough to bury independent content creators' videos under piles of mainstream media channels when searching for various topics, or preventing our videos from showing up in the "Recommended" section or the "Up Next" sidebar. The *Liberal Media Industrial Complex* got upset that a bunch of YouTubers were collaborating with each other, and doing interviews with one another. In September 2018 a report from a "research institute" called Data & Society claimed to have identified what they called a network of "far-right" YouTubers who indoctrinate people through their videos by promoting right-wing "extremist" ideologies.

"Although YouTube's recommendation algorithms are partly to blame, the problem is fundamentally linked to the social network of political influencers on the platform

---

[778] YouTube Help "Harassment and cyberbullying policy"

and how, like other YouTube influencers, they invite one another on to their shows," the report reads.[779]

It includes an illustration looking like a collage on the wall of a detective's office linking together all the connections of an organized crime family and notes, "The graph is a partial representation of collaborative connections within the Alternative Influence Network (AIN)–a network of controversial academics, media pundits, and internet celebrities who use YouTube to promote a range of political positions from mainstream versions of libertarianism and conservatism to overt white nationalism. While collaborations can sometimes consist of debates and disagreements, they more frequently indicate social ties, endorsements, and advertisements for other influencers."[780]

The report basically recommends that YouTube forbid people from interviewing individuals who liberals deem unsavory or who talk about things they consider "offensive" or "hateful" which as you know includes almost everything from illegal immigration to the American flag. "The platform should not only assess what channels say in their content, but also who they host and what their guests say. In a media environment consisting of networked influencers, YouTube must respond with policies that account for influence and amplification."[781]

---

[779] The Guardian "YouTube's 'alternative influence network' breeds rightwing radicalisation, report finds" by Olivia Solon (September 18th 2018)

[780] The Alternative Influence Network on YouTube by Rebecca Lewis page 10

[781] The Alternative Influence Network on YouTube by Rebecca Lewis page 44

In an interview about the report, lead researcher Rebecca Lewis explained how most of the focus on "extremism" and "fake news" has been on Facebook and Twitter, but, "We don't have as clear a picture of what's happening on YouTube and Google. It is important to bring to the fore some illustrations of the problems that do exist on these platforms. I'm trying to show there are fundamental issues we need to be addressing [regarding the algorithms of] YouTube in the same way we have recognized fundamental issues with Facebook and Twitter."[782]

She went on to say, "I absolutely think reassessing the algorithms is one step that needs to be taken. Assessing what government regulation options are available is absolutely worthwhile, and then thinking about how YouTube monetization structures incentivize certain behaviors is something that needs to be done. It needs to be a multi-pronged solution."[783]

Five months after the Alternative Influence Network report was published a group of "researchers" calling themselves Digital Social Contract did a test to see how YouTube's "Recommended" videos section changed, and looked at over 80 different channels listed in the report and noted, "For the first two weeks of February [2019], YouTube was recommending videos from at least one of these major alt-right channels on more than one in every thirteen randomly selected videos (7.8%). From February

---

[782] Mother Jones "Political Extremists Are Using YouTube to Monetize Their Toxic Ideas" by Tonya Riley (September 18th 2018)

[783] Ibid.

15th, this number has dropped to less than one in two hundred and fifty (0.4%)."[784]

The Digital Social Contract report also highlighted that a video of actress Emma Watson promoting feminism had another video titled "How Feminism Ruined Marriage" queued in the "Up Next" autoplay section right beside it, which they claimed was "an anti-feminist video from an alt-right channel."[785]   That "alt-right" channel was Ben Shapiro's, who is a Jew, not an alt-right white nationalist, but instead is often a target of alt-right figures who hate him because he's Jewish.[786]

Censoring Videos

YouTube has always had a policy forbidding certain kinds of content from being uploaded like pornography, graphic violence, animal abuse, or blatant invasions of someone's privacy; which are very reasonable rules, but after the 2016 election they began removing videos critical of the radical Leftist agenda, including videos denouncing child drag queens, feminists, and for even reporting on anti-white hate crimes.

Those kinds of videos can now easily violate YouTube's "Community Standards" and result in getting channels issued a strike (and the video taken down), and if a channel gets three strikes within a three month period,

---

[784] Digital Social Contract "YouTube stops recommending alt-right channels" by Nicolas Suzor (February 27th 2019)

[785] Ibid.

[786] The Washingtonian "83 Percent of Anti-Semitic Tweets Against Journalists Targeted Just Ten People" by Benjamin Freed (October 19th 2016)

the entire channel and all its videos are completely deleted.

YouTube's senior leadership (and overall corporate culture) believes there are 58 different genders, and Christians are just old-fashioned superstitious bigots; so we're talking about godless liberal Silicon Valley standards, not Midwestern community standards. YouTube also teamed up with the Southern Poverty Law Center, who began searching for videos they recommend be taken down.   Soon all kinds of them were being removed under the banner of stopping "hate speech."[787]

I got a strike on a video I uploaded about a black man who opened fire inside a Tennessee church hoping to kill as many white people as possible.[788]   The video was appropriately titled "Black Man Shoots Up White Church - Media Ignores Anti-White Hate Crime" and didn't show any graphic images, but as you probably know by now, reporting on anti-white hate crimes is deemed "racist" by the Left.   The liberal media wants people to believe hate crimes are only committed by white people against blacks and don't want anyone talking about how such attacks are actually a two way street.

Black conservative Candace Owens even had a video removed from her channel that was critical of Black Lives Matter because it was deemed "hateful" against black people.[789]   A channel called High Impact Vlogs had a video removed and got a Community Guidelines strike for

---

[787] Daily Caller "EXCLUSIVE: YouTube Secretly Using Southern Poverty Law Center To Police Videos" by Peter Hasson (February 27th 2018)

[788] US News & World Report "State: Man in Church Shooting Aimed to Kill 10 White People" by Associated Press (May 20th 2019)

[789] https://twitter.com/RealCandaceO/status/903027170460803072

criticizing the parents of Desmond is Amazing, the 11-year-old "drag kid," after the boy was featured on *Good Morning America*.[790]

YouTube pulled a funny 2018 midterm election ad by a Republican running for governor of Florida in which he showed off his "Deportation Bus," which he used to promote his campaign, claiming his ad was "hate speech."[791] They later restored the video after their censorship began making headlines.

Tommy Robinson's entire channel has been "quarantined" with special restrictions that prevent any of his videos from ever showing up in the search results at all. This designation also causes all comments to be disabled on every video, and the view counts censored as well, so people can't gauge how popular they are in another attempt to suppress his message by hiding the number of people watching his videos.[792]

Hunter Avallone, a conservative millennial who makes fun of feminists and other SJWs, had his entire channel deleted in April 2019 for "hate speech" despite not having any current strikes. After a growing outrage about the

---

[790] YouTube "High Impact Vlogs" channel "The Two Videos YouTube Didn't Want You To See! (December 1st 2018)
The original video titled "ABC Just Promoted Something SO DISGUSTING & DISTURBING You Won't Believe It…Or Will You?" can be seen on BitChute here: https://www.bitchute.com/video/_1uEOgN41CU/ (Published November 26th 2018 on the HighImpactFlix BitChute channel.)

[791] Washington Times "Ga. gubernatorial candidate's 'Deportation Bus' ad deemed 'hate speech,' removed from YouTube" via Associated Press (May 16th 2018)

[792] The Independent "Tommy Robinson's YouTube videos restricted after internet giant refuses to delete channel" by Lizzie Dearden (April 2nd 2019)

censorship, YouTube restored his channel and once again claimed it was just a "mistake."[793]

The Prager University channel (stylized PragerU) sued YouTube after they discovered that almost all of their videos were hidden when YouTube was in Restricted Mode, which most schools and public libraries have it set on by default in order to filter out "sensitive content."[794] Many of my videos are also completely hidden to people who are browsing in Restricted Mode as well, even though my content is family friendly.

In December of 2017 YouTube hired 10,000 new human moderators to supposedly remove "extremist" content and videos containing "hate speech," and soon after they began taking down popular videos and entire channels that hadn't come anywhere close to actually violating the terms of service. As a result of the new moderators a major purge occurred a few months later in February of 2018. Jerome Corsi's entire channel was taken down, Mike Adams' "Natural News" channel was also removed, and many others.

YouTube even began issuing community guideline strikes and removing videos that criticized CNN's Town Hall on gun control following the Parkland school shooting in Florida.[795] Tim Pool had produced a video

[793] Hunter Avvalone YouTube Channel "I Got Banned!" (April 10th 2019)

[794] TubeFilter.com "Conservative Organization PragerU Sues YouTube Over Alleged Censorship Of Conservative Voices" by Sam Gutelle (October 24th 2017)

[795] Breitbart "YouTube is Shutting Down Conservative Criticism of CNN over Parkland Shooting" by Allum Nokhari and Charlie Nash (February 28th 2018)

where he debunked the conspiracy theories about the shooting, but his video was removed as well.[796]

After some channels and videos were restored due to a major outcry about this latest wave of censorship, Gizmodo reported that, "the usual whackos like far-right personality Mark Dice are going wild on Twitter claiming the admission of any mistake at all constitutes victory. Hopefully they're wrong and YouTube isn't walking back punishments on people like [Jerome] Corsi, whose prior best hits include a steadfast belief Barack Obama is secretly gay and also some kind of Muslim, though InfoWars claimed yesterday that it got YouTube to revoke one of the two strikes against it."[797]

"YouTube's New Moderators Mistakenly Pull Right-Wing Channels" was the headline at Bloomberg News.[798] It was just another "mistake," they said. YouTube deleted the entire channel of a gamer for posting a clip of him playing "Red Dead Redemption 2" which showed him "killing" a feminist NPC (non playable character) by lassoing her and then feeding her to an alligator.[799]

The game is a western and takes place in the late 1890s, and the character was just one of the townspeople who was hanging out in the street and happened to be promoting women's suffrage (right to vote) so he thought

[796] Gateway Pundit "YouTube Deletes Popular Journalist's Video Criticizing the Media Over Falling for 4Chan Florida Shooter Hoax" by Cassandra Fairbanks (February 17th 2018)

[797] Gizmodo "YouTube's New Moderation Team Stumbles Out the Gate" by Tom McKay (February 28th 2018)

[798] Bloomberg "YouTube's New Moderators Mistakenly Pull Right-Wing Channels" by Mark Bergen (February 28th 2018)

[799] Variety "YouTuber Temporarily Suspended For Video of Suffragette Killing in 'Red Dead 2'" by Stefanie Fogel (November 8th 2018)

it would be funny to feed her to the alligator, which the game allows players to do to any of the "townsfolk."

Professional gaming is a huge industry where people stream themselves playing various video games, which as you know, often include the main character "killing" a number of other characters in the game, but the YouTube moderators deemed feeding the feminist to the alligator "graphic content that appears to be posted in a shocking, sensational, or disrespectful manner." After others in the gaming community expressed outrage over YouTube censoring a clip of someone playing a popular game, they restored his channel.[800]

After the Covington Catholic incident involving the high school kid in the MAGA hat and the Native American man beating a drum in his face at the National Mall in Washington D.C., a retired Navy SEAL named Don Shipley posted a video about Nathan Phillips, the "Vietnam Veteran" Native American, calling him a fraud because Army records show he was never actually in Vietnam. YouTube soon terminated the Navy SEAL's channel, claiming he was "harassing" the old man.[801]

Infowars host Alex Jones was banned from YouTube in August 2018 in part for his criticism of a drag queen festival where adult drag queens performed simulated strip teases for an "all ages" show which included children in the audience brought there by their degenerate parents. He called it an "abomination" and a "freak show" and so his video was deemed "hate speech" and

---

[800] The Verge "YouTube reverses ban for streamer who killed Red Dead 2 feminist" by Patricia Hernandez (November 8th 2018)

[801] PJ Media "YouTube Deplatforms Retired Navy SEAL Who Exposed Tribal Elder Nathan Phillips' Stolen Valor" by Debra Heine (February 26th 2019)

"transphobic," resulting in YouTube removing the video and issuing him a community guidelines strike.[802]

The deleted video (titled "Shocking 'Drag Tots' Cartoon Sparks Outrage") can be seen on BitChute.com[803] and Infowars.com.[804] YouTube also cited another video of Jones as being "Islamophobic" because he was ranting about the increased crime in Europe due to the influx of Muslim refugees in recent years.[805]

He was given his second strike for that video, titled "Learn How Islam Has Already Conquered Europe,"[806] and soon a third (and final) strike for "circumvention" of YouTube's "enforcement measures" because he had promoted another YouTube channel that had taken the feed of his show from his website and was streaming it on their channel since Jones was under a 90-day live-streaming suspension from the previous strikes.[807]

The H3H3 Podcast channel then had their livestream taken down and were issued a community guidelines strike simply for talking about Alex Jones being

---

[802] Politifact "Why Infowars' Alex Jones was banned from Apple, Facebook, Youtube and Spotify" by Manuela Tobias (August 7th 2018)

[803] https://www.bitchute.com/video/WtAHuu0ycCY/

[804] Infowars.com "Watch These Videos YouTube Doesn't Want You To See" (July 25th 2018)

[805] Tech Crunch "Here are the platforms that have banned Infowars so far" by Sarah Wells (August 8th 2018)

[806] The video is still available to watch on Infowars.com, which hosts it and the other videos that led to the YouTube ban here: https://www.infowars.com/watch-these-videos-youtube-doesnt-want-you-to-see/

[807] Engadget "YouTube removes Alex Jones' official channel for violating guidelines" by Kris Hold (August 6th 2018)

banned.[808] They are a popular husband and wife duo with over a million subscribers (on their podcast channel) who were actually defending YouTube's decision to ban Alex Jones, and were repeating some of the crazy things he has said over the years which may have been flagged by the AI voice recognition systems that monitor livestreams. H3H3 co-host Ethan Klein later said, "How can I even sit here now and call Alex Jones a conspiracy theorist when our channel just got [a strike] for even fucking talking about him? I was criticizing him!"[809]

After BuzzFeed stumbled across a 14-year-old girl's channel who does comedy sketches mocking social justice warriors and deriding political correctness, they did what they always do and wrote a hit piece urging people to pressure YouTube to ban her for "hate speech."[810] The writer of the article (Joseph Bernstein) even labeled her an "extremist."[811]

Before the article came out, "Soph" as she goes by, had over 800,000 subscribers which terrified BuzzFeed that such a young, talented, and popular girl was pushing back against the liberal agenda, but shortly after it was published she got two strikes on her channel for previous videos which had been up for weeks with no problems.[812]

---

[808] https://twitter.com/h3h3productions/status/1028047008144080896

[809] H3 Podcast #77 "Alex Jones Stream Shut Down" (August 11th 2018)

[810] BuzzFeed "YouTube's Newest Far-Right, Foul-Mouthed, Red-Pilling Star Is A 14-Year-Old Girl" by Joseph Bernstein (May 13th 2019)

[811] https://twitter.com/Bernstein/status/1128308490047561728

[812] ReClaimTheNet.org "YouTube censors 14-year-old creator Soph after BuzzFeed hit piece" by Tom Parker (May 14th 2019)

The following week her entire channel was completely demonetized, dealing a crushing blow to her chances of turning YouTube into a career.[813] A month and a half later she received her third and final strike for "hate speech" after she posted a video critical of homosexuals, and her entire channel was completely deleted. [814]

In June 2019 Project Veritas released a 25-minute report which included an undercover investigation into Google which showed that the head of the Innovation Department said they were doing everything they could to prevent another "Trump situation in 2020" and was bragging about how Google had come up with a new definition of "fairness."

The Project Veritas report also included an interview with a current YouTube employee which was done in a silhouette to protect his identity. He explained how YouTube was actually preventing certain conservative and libertarian channels from having their videos show up in the "Recommended" section, confirming what most of us had already basically known since it was obvious. He also provided Project Veritas with leaked documents detailing their algorithm manipulation.[815]

Within hours YouTube deleted the video from Project Veritas' account, claiming it violated the head of Innovation's privacy even though it only showed her

---

[813] https://twitter.com/sewernugget/status/1131340929720147968

[814] ReclaimTheNet.org "YouTube deletes Soph's channel after her latest video was removed for 'hate speech' by Tom Parker (August 1st 2019) The video which caused the strike is titled "Pride & Prejudice" and can be seen on her BitChute channel here: https://www.bitchute.com/video/FNqiV8kL4cc/

[815] Project Veritas "Insider Blows Whistle & Exec Reveals Google Plan to Prevent 'Trump situation' in 2020 on Hidden Cam" by Staff (June 24th 2019)

talking at a restaurant and mentioned who she was. Most privacy violations are for publishing someone's home address or cell phone number. On CNN's official YouTube channel they posted the video of their reporter stalking and harassing the old woman in her front yard because she shared someone on Facebook that originated with the Russians. During part of the altercation her full street address, which is posted on the front of her house, was completely visible.[816] How is *that* not a violation of *her* privacy and YouTube's terms of service?

In October 2019, the channel Red Ice TV was completely deleted, despite having no current strikes against it. No specific reason was given, just that it had supposedly violated YouTube's policy prohibiting "hate speech." It had over 330,000 subscribers, and for over ten years was run by a husband and wife duo out of Sweden who focus on preserving European culture and exposing anti-white racism, so of course they've been smeared by the media as "white supremacists." They were the most popular Identitarian channel on YouTube.[817] Leftist groups like Media Matters, the Southern Poverty Law Center, and the ADL had been pressuring YouTube to ban the channel for years.[818]

---

[816] CNN's YouTube Channel "Some Americans unwittingly helped Russian trolls" (February 21st 2018)

[817] Identitarianism is a right-wing political ideology whose supporters believe European people are entitled to preserve their own cultures and territories, instead of becoming "melting pots" due to massive immigration from countries of other races.

[818] Media Matters "YouTube banned Alex Jones, but it's letting white supremacist content thrive" by Madeline Peltz and Talia Lavin (November 5th 2018)

No Conservative is Safe

Kara Swisher, the co-founder of Recode Media which hosted the historic joint interview with Steve Jobs and Bill Gates, said she wanted to "kill" YouTube CEO Susan Wojcicki after discovering that her 13-year-old son was watching Ben Shapiro's videos, and claims he is the "gateway drug" to "neo-nazi stuff."[819]   She made the comments while interviewing Susan Wojcicki at the "Lesbians Who Tech" conference in March 2019 (Kara Swisher is a lesbian who must have adopted her poor kid or used a sperm bank).

She added that her son is "lost" (meaning he's not infected with the liberal pathogen) and insinuated that YouTube was responsible. Susan Wojcicki responded, "I have a son too and I get some of these discussions also at the dinner table. I think what you're describing is — and the way we think about it too — look, there's a set of content that has to meet the community guidelines. Ben Shapiro is going to meet the community guidelines. I don't think you're suggesting that we remove him from the platform. Are you?"

Kara Swisher responded, "I would," and continued, whining "You know, last time I saw you, I was like, 'Get Alex Jones off that platform,' and you're like, 'Well the community guidelines,' and then [later] you got him off."[820]   She then changed the subject and went on to ask Susan if there was enough "diversity" in the company, particularly in management. "Diversity" is a code word

---

[819] Recode.net "Full Q&A: YouTube CEO Susan Wojcicki talks about child safety, the Google walkout, and AI on Recode Decode" by Eric Johnson (March 11th 2019)

[820] Ibid.

for "less straight white men," because Big Tech is concerned that there are too many of those kinds of people working in Silicon Valley.

Ben Shapiro is a huge nerd, he's not a right-wing extremist or a hateful bigot, and is about as mainstream of a political commentator as you can get, yet Kara Swisher, who holds tremendous power in Silicon Valley and has direct access to all of the major CEOs, is demanding that he be banned from YouTube because she thinks he's a right-wing extremist, proving that no conservative, no matter how moderate, is safe.

YouTube Gives Millions to Mainstream Media

Demonetizing us, censoring our videos, down-ranking them in the search results, and hiding them from the "Recommended" section while boosting mainstream media channels still wasn't silencing us enough, so YouTube decided to just give $25 million dollars to brand name news channels and provide them with special consulting to help them create more engaging videos and grow their audience on the platform.[821]

"We will provide funding across approximately 20 global markets to support news organizations in building sustainable video operations," they announced in July 2018. "Provided on an application basis to news organizations of all types, these grants will enable our partners to build key capabilities, train staff on video best

---

[821] AdWeek "The Google News Initiative Is Putting $25 Million Toward Fighting Fake News on YouTube" by David Cohen (July 10th 2018)

practices, enhance production facilities and develop formats optimized for online video."[822]

So people like me were able to figure out how to produce quality and engaging videos and built an audience all on our own, but since ordinary YouTubers came to dominate mainstream media, YouTube decided to just give them everything they need to emulate what we had come to learn through years of innovation and practice.

The largest "YouTube news channel" is the Young Turks, which was started by progressive Democrat Cenk Uygur in 2005, and over the years has gotten help from some very wealthy benefactors. In 2014 they got $4 million dollars from an investment firm,[823] and then later got another $20 million in 2017 from former Walt Disney Studios chairman Jeffrey Katzenberg.[824] That's *not* a typo —*twenty million dollars!*

It's interesting that their channel bears the same name as the insurgent group of Muslims who committed genocide against the Armenian people (who were Christians), killing 1.5 million of them between 1914 and 1923 in one of the first modern day genocides.[825] For years Cenk Uygur actually denied the Armenian Genocide until growing pressure caused him to change his position,

---

[822] YouTube official blog "Building a better news experience on YouTube together" (July 9th 2018)

[823] Politico "Buddy Roemer firm invests $4 million in Young Turks Network" by Hadas Gold (April 16th 2014)

[824] Business Insider "Progressive media outlet The Young Turks has raised $20 million in venture-capital funding and plans to double its staff" by Maxwell Tani (August 8th 2017)

[825] Encyclopedia of Human Rights by David Forsythe page 98 Oxford University Press

saying he will refrain from commenting on it because he doesn't know enough about it.[826]

Making things even more bizarre is that the Young Turks cohost Anna Kasperian is Armenian, and works for a "news" organization which appears to be named after the very group which committed genocide against members of her own family.[827] She's the daughter of Armenian immigrants and actually grew up speaking Armenian as her first language.[828]

While YouTube has a policy against allowing "extremist groups" on the platform, they have no problem with a channel that some interpret as paying homage to a group that murdered more than a million Christians.[829] Instead, YouTube CEO Susan Wojcicki enjoys hanging out with them and tweeted a photo of herself sitting down talking with Cenk Uygur at YouTube's headquarters, thanking him for his time.[830]

Young Turks host Hasan Piker even declared that "America deserved 9/11" in response to Congressman Dan Crenshaw doing an interview with Joe Rogan where he said that Osama Bin Laden attacked the U.S. because

[826] TYT Network "Rescinding Daily Pennsylvanian Article" by Cenk Uygur (April 22nd 2016)

[827] The Young Turks "Germany Acknowledges The Genocide" By Ana Kasperian on official YouTube channel (June 2, 2016) Around 3:20 timestamp in the video.

[828] The Young Turks "People Don't Trust Foreign Accents — Study" via The Young Turks YouTube channel (October 28th 2010) at the :20 mark, Ana explains she grew up speaking only Armenian.

[829] Paste "Why Cenk Uygur Is Getting Confronted about the Name 'The Young Turks,' and Why It Matters" by Monica Hunter-Hart (January 5th 2017)

[830] https://twitter.com/SusanWojcicki/status/890654400192028672

of our western values.[831] Piker also appeared to praise Al Qaeda for blinding Crenshaw (a retired Navy SEAL) who lost an eye while serving in Afghanistan in 2012.[832] He then mocked the disabled veteran for having one eye. Hasan Piker is allowed to host a show on the platform, but Alex Jones isn't. Piker has his own personal YouTube channel as well, that hasn't been demonetized.

In 2016 YouTube launched their "Creators for Change" program where they began funding and coaching various YouTubers to make videos denouncing "hate speech," "xenophobia," and "extremism."[833] These handpicked social justice warriors produce propaganda for the platform and some of them promote the latest degeneracy the Left is trying to convince people is normal.

At the end of every year YouTube produces a mashup of what they consider to be the year's top stars and it's always a bunch of SJWs and LGBT activists. Their 2018 "Rewind" video, as it's called, featured drag queens and highlighted Hollywood celebrities like Will Smith and John Oliver over ordinary YouTubers. It got so many thumbs down that overnight it became the most disliked video on YouTube *ever*.[834] Shortly after that, YouTube announced that they were trying to figure out how to

---

[831] Washington Times "Young Turks host Hasan Piker mocks Dan Crenshaw's war injury, says 'America deserved 9/11'" by Jessica Chasmar (August 22nd 2019)

[832] Ibid.

[833] The Verge "YouTube is investing $5 million in creators who 'counter hate and promote tolerance'" by Lizzie Plaugic (January 24th 2018)

[834] Vox "YouTube's 2018 'Rewind' is the site's most disliked video ever. The implications are huge." by Aja Romano (December 14th 2018)

prevent what they called "dislike mobs" from "weaponizing the dislike button" and considered removing it altogether.[835]

The Adpocalypse

Since I'm an old school YouTuber, I was posting videos for six years before my channel was monetized (at the end of 2012) opening the door for me to become a professional YouTuber. While it has always been difficult to make a living on YouTube because monetized videos only pay a small fraction of a penny per view, a few years after I started doing it full time, it became almost impossible, especially for smaller channels that aren't getting five to ten million views a month.

In April 2017 after the *Wall Street Journal* published a report about finding advertisements for major brands appearing on "racist" and "offensive" videos, all hell broke loose. Tons of companies pulled their advertisements from the platform entirely, kicking off what us YouTubers call the "Adpocalypse" (advertising apocalypse). YouTube immediately rolled out some new tools they had been testing to comb through the titles, tags, and descriptions of videos and automatically demonetize (strip advertisements from) ones that were about (*or even mentioned*) certain topics.

Every video uploaded is now immediately scanned by YouTube's voice recognition software which creates a transcript of everything that's said in the video. That transcript is then scanned for keywords that may indicate a video is about a "sensitive" or "controversial" topic and

---

[835] The Verge "YouTube wants 'dislike mobs' to stop weaponizing the dislike button" by Julia Alexander (February 1st 2019)

then demonetizes it if certain words or phrases are found. As a result of the Adpocalypse, almost half of all of my videos were demonetized, and from that point on making a living on YouTube became uncertain.

News channels like mine were hit the hardest, because news and politics are filled with "divisiveness" and controversial issues that YouTube wanted to shield advertisers from. For people who make cooking videos, or how-to videos about fixing cars, or doing home improvement projects, those kinds of videos aren't about anything that's particularly "non-advertiser friendly" like ones that talk about illegal immigration, climate change, political cover-ups, or exposing fake news.

Bloomberg News later reported, "In fact, 96.5% of all of those trying to become YouTubers won't make enough money off of advertising to crack the U.S. poverty line."[836] Their report continued bearing bad news, pointing out that, "Breaking into the top 3% of most-viewed channels could bring in advertising revenue of about $16,800 a year…That's a bit more than the U.S. federal poverty line of $12,140 for a single person. (The guideline for a two-person household is $16,460.) The top 3% of video creators of all time in [the research group's] sample attracted more than 1.4 million views per month."[837]

But even for those who never expected to be full-time YouTubers, it was still nice to make a few dollars every

---

[836] Los Angeles Times "Hey, star-struck. Making it on YouTube isn't easier than making it in on the silver screen" by Chris Stokel-Walker (February 28th 2018)

[837] Bloomberg "Success on YouTube still means a life of poverty. 96% won't crack the poverty line" by Chris Stokel-Walker (February 26th 2018)

month for the time and effort put into creating videos about things they're passionate about. Despite the loss of income caused by the increased scrutiny, a lot of the more popular YouTuber news channels were still able to get by, or at least kept making videos because it's about the message not the money, but we all have to pay the bills, so YouTube decided to make people's lives even harder by demonetizing entire channels instead of just certain videos.

In January 2019 Tommy Robinson's entire channel was demonetized.[838] A few months later in May 2019 Count Dankula was fully demonetized. What's particularly interesting is that he learned about it from an email from BuzzFeed asking for a statement about it. It appears they had lobbied YouTube to get him demonetized and then reached out to him for a comment immediately after their YouTube source confirmed they had done it.[839]

BuzzFeed learned about it before him, which speaks volumes about what's happening. Sargon of Akkad's channel was also completely demonetized because of a rape joke he had made three years earlier on Twitter, and —what a "coincidence"—BuzzFeed was the first to break that story as well.[840]

---

[838] BuzzFeed "YouTube Says Tommy Robinson Will No Longer Be Able To Make Money From His Videos" by Mark Di Stefano (January 17th 2019)

[839] BigLeaguePolitics "Count Dankula Demonetized on YouTube After Buzzfeed Hit Piece" by Tom Pappert (January 18th 2019)

[840] BuzzFeed "YouTube Has Downgraded Carl Benjamin's Sargon Of Akkad Account After He Talked About Raping A British MP" by Mark Di Stefano (May 10th 2019)

Another round of mass demonetization and channel bans occurred in June 2019 (dubbed the Vox Adpocalypse) occurred after a gay activist named Carlos Maza, who works at Vox, ranted nonstop on Twitter for an entire week about conservative comedian Steven Crowder making fun of him. Maza's rant, which was conveniently timed to coincide with the kickoff of gay pride month for extra leverage, was a rallying call for liberals to pressure YouTube to completely ban Crowder (the most-subscribed conservative channel on YouTube) for "hate speech" because he called Maza a "lispy queer" since he talks with a lisp, and he's a queer.

What do you think the "Q" stands for in LGBTQ? They call themselves queers, but normal people can't use the word now apparently because the Left is trying to claim that only gay people can say *queer*, similarly to the double standard most black people have about the n-word.

While YouTube didn't ban Steven Crowder from YouTube, or give him any community guideline strikes to take down any of his videos; they did demonetize his *entire* channel, not just the "offensive" videos in question, which were probably never even monetized to begin with, thus, preventing him from ever making another dollar from the pre-roll ads you often see before videos start playing.[841]

It wasn't just Steven Crowder's channel though. Dozens, perhaps hundreds, of others were hit at the same time, some of which were very popular with hundreds of

---

[841] Fox News "YouTube ends monetization of conservative commentator Steven Crowder's channel, several others after left-wing outrage" by Gregg R (June 5th 2019)

thousands of subscribers.[842]   YouTube said this was just the beginning of their latest crackdown, and vowed to purge more "hateful" right-wing channels.

The very next week the *New York Times* ran a front page story titled "The Making of a YouTube Radical" which included a collage of various (mostly) conservative YouTubers who have sizable followings, and told the story about how a lonely loser named Caleb Cain "fell down the YouTube rabbit hole" and it turned him into a "radical." How radical? The *Times* explained that, "He began referring to himself as a 'tradcon' — a traditional conservative," supported "old-fashioned gender norms," started dating a Christian girl, and "fought with his liberal friends."[843]

"Fought" meaning discussed politics and disagreed with the nonsense they were indoctrinated to believe. The man admits he never thought about doing anything violent and wasn't even a hateful person, but he was the new poster boy denouncing right-wing YouTubers and the "algorithm."

Other outlets immediately added more fuel to the fire and he was interviewed on CNN where he once again blamed "the algorithm" for "radicalizing" him.[844] He said the conservative YouTubers he used to watch warned of Cultural Marxists who "were trying to destroy Western

---

[842] Just a few of them include Jesse Lee Peterson, Press For Truth, Ford Fischer, Mr. Allsop History, SinatraSays, and many others.

[843] New York Times "The Making of a YouTube Radical" by Kevin Roose (June 8th 2019)

[844] CNN "It's YouTube's time in the hot seat" by Seth Fiegerman (June 11th 2019)

civilization and install some sort of socialist regime."[845] That's exactly what they're doing of course, but now if you just mention that, you're considered a right-wing extremist and at risk of having your entire channel demonetized or even deleted.

When the White House announced the Social Media Summit and invited dozens of the top conservative social media personalities to meet with President Trump to discuss the issues of censorship and liberal bias, the media freaked out saying that the attendees (which included me, as you probably know) were "trolls," "conspiracy theorists," and "extremists."[846]

President Trump addressed us by saying, "So this is a historic day. Never before have so many online journalists and influencers, and that is exactly what you are, you are journalists and you are influencers, come together in this building to discuss the future of social media...Each of you is fulfilling a vital role in our nation. You are challenging the media gatekeepers and the corporate censors to bring the facts straight to the American people...Together you reach more people than any television broadcast network by far."[847]

I knew once word got out that I was invited to the White House I would have a huge target on my back and just a few days later over 200 of my YouTube videos were demonetized, with about 100 of them manually reviewed by the moderators and deemed "non-advertiser friendly"

---

[845] CNN "Former alt-right follower calls radicalization a health crisis" posted on their YouTube channel (June 12th 2019)

[846] CNN "Trump invites right-wing extremists to White House 'social media summit'" by Oliver Darcy (July 11th 2019)

[847] White House Official Transcript "Remarks by President Trump at the Presidential Social Media Summit" (July 11th 2019)

despite not just being fully monetized for days, months, (and some for years) but many of them had been manually reviewed previously and *approved* for monetization.

YouTube moved the goal post again, and may be looking for a reason to demonetize my whole channel by deeming a "significant portion" of my content "non-advertiser friendly" like they had done to dozens of other channels a month earlier. Many of the videos were of me making fun of CNN hosts, Alexandria Ocasio-Cortez, Beto O'Rourke, and other members of Congress. Apparently it's okay for Stephen Colbert to do political comedy, but not a conservative YouTuber.

In January 2017 YouTube introduced what they call Super Chats, which is a creative way for a viewer to get their question answered by their favorite YouTuber while they're doing a livestream by tipping them a few bucks. Basically, viewers can choose a dollar amount anywhere from $5 to $500, and their question or comment will be highlighted in color and pinned up at the top of the chat box in order to catch the streamer's attention since comments in the chat can scroll by the screen so fast they're impossible to read.

In May 2018 BuzzFeed targeted Super Chats, claiming they were fueling racism and began pushing for them to be disabled because someone spent $100 on a Super Chat to post a message that said "WHITE PRIDE WORLD WIDE!" during someone's livestream.[848] A few months later the *Wall Street Journal* (which is responsible for setting off the first Adpocalypse in April 2017) also started complaining about people making money from

---

[848] BuzzFeed "How YouTube's 'Super Chat' System Is Pushing Video Creators Toward More Extreme Content" by Ishmael N. Daro and Craig Silverman (May 17th 2018)

Super Chats in a report titled, "Hate Speech on Live 'Super Chats' Tests YouTube."[849]

Just a few days later, KillStream, which was a free speech variety show that included debates about various issues, was completely banned from YouTube since the *Wall Street Journal* pointed out some of the viewers had been posting racist messages in their Super Chats.[850] A channel has no control over what viewers put in the comments or Super Chats, but now the media was blaming YouTubers themselves for what their fans (or trolls) were saying.

The Liberal Media Industrial Complex is targeting Super Chats because even fairly small channels can earn a significant amount of revenue from them, since fans tossing in $5 and $10 can add up pretty fast, whereas in order to earn the same amount of money from video views alone as they can make in a livestream could take hundreds of thousands or millions of views.

Because of the growing demonetization issues those of us on the politics and news side of YouTube have had to move to a more fan-funded business model instead of relying on monetized views. I now rely heavily on fans buying my books, shirts, and supporting me through Patreon and PayPal. By removing the financial incentives for people to make quality videos it was just another way for YouTube to discourage us from spending our time and energy producing news commentary and covering current events and has killed the dreams of one day becoming a full-time YouTuber for many.

---

[849] Wall Street Journal "Hate Speech on Live 'Super Chats' Tests YouTube" by Yoree Koh (November 2nd 2018)

[850] WhatsTrending "Killstream is KICKED OFF YouTube For Hate Speech SuperChat" by Alex Firer (November 6th 2018)

BuzzFeed reported, "The result of the YouTube crackdown is that prominent right-wing YouTubers are scrambling to find alternatives, setting up shop on YouTube wannabes, or even building their own video apps. It's all in preparation for what they see as the inevitable day when YouTube gives them the boot or forbids them from making money on the platform by demonetizing all of their videos."[851]

MCNs Dropping Channels

Many YouTubers join what are called Multi-Channel Networks, or MCNs, which are companies that take a percentage of their revenue in exchange for offering consultations on how to improve the performance of videos, grow their audience, and even give them access to "brand deals" or sponsorships like talk radio shows have when the hosts plug various products and services.

So even if YouTube's automated system demonetizes a lot of videos, MCNs can get the channel some sponsors who are okay with their product being promoted there, and that way the YouTuber can still earn a living. But since being a member of an MCN can be a way around demonetization, YouTube decided to order MCNs to drop certain channels, and they had to, because they're under contract with YouTube, and if they didn't then YouTube wouldn't do business with the MCN at all.[852]

---

[851] BuzzFeed "Right-Wing YouTubers Think It's Only A Matter Of Time Before They Get Kicked Off The Site" by Ishmael N. Daro (April 18th 2018)

[852] Polygon "YouTube networks drop thousands of creators as YouTube policy shifts" by Julia Alexander (April 24th 2018)

So first it was just certain videos getting demonetized, then entire channels (including the loss of Super Chats), and then YouTube went even further forcing MCNs to drop certain people so they couldn't acquire sponsorships for their videos.

One person who got kicked out of his network got an email reading, "The team here at Fullscreen is reaching out to let you know that your agreement with Fullscreen, Inc. has been terminated. Due to the nature of your uploads and because your uploads may potentially infringe on the rights of others or potentially violates applicable laws or regulations, including without limitation YouTube's Terms of Service and/or YouTube's Community Guidelines, we feel it is best that we part ways. Thank you for your understanding, and good luck with your YouTube channel."[853]

A friend of mine, Luke Rudkowski, who runs the "We Are Change" YouTube channel was kicked out of his MCN, and when applying to others he was told that he would have to delete several of his videos they deemed inappropriate before they would accept him. The videos in question had been automatically demonetized, but didn't violate YouTube's terms of service so they were not deleted. Various MCNs thought they were problematic, however, and could get them in trouble with YouTube for including Luke's channel in their network because he had posted certain content about various wars, military actions, and social unrest in parts of the world.

When a channel reaches 100,000 subscribers YouTube sends them a framed "Silver Play Button" plaque to celebrate their success, and if they reach a million subscribers, they get a gold plated one, but YouTube got

---

[853] https://twitter.com/ChiefCanuck/status/984921575471251456

upset that so many anti-social justice warrior, pro-free speech, conservative channels were reaching 100,000 subscribers, they started refusing to send out the plaques to certain channels once they reached the milestone because YouTube didn't want to appear as if they were endorsing their views.[854]

Patreon

Patreon is a service that allows artists to fund their work by having fans sponsor them with varying amounts of monthly support. While the site was created in 2013, it really took off in April 2017 after the "Adpocalypse" when YouTube rolled out their new guidelines and screening mechanisms to demonetize videos they deem "non-advertiser friendly."

Most YouTubers joined Patreon as a way to supplement the revenue they were losing from so many videos getting demonetized, and for most of them, especially small to moderate sized ones, Patreon is pretty much a standard part of being a YouTuber since earning money from ads has never been the same in the wake of the Adpocalypse.

But since many of them came to rely so heavily on Patreon for their revenue, this became a danger for conservatives who are now at risk of having their Patreon accounts shut down at any time for being "intolerant" of the liberal agenda by not supporting gay "marriage," or pointing out facts about illegal immigration and crime.

The first person to be banned from Patreon that made headlines because it was seen as a political decision was Lauren Southern (banned in July 2017), a Canadian YouTuber who became known for her criticism of multiculturalism and the mass immigration of people from the Middle East into Europe. She once even documented her visit to a doctor where she said she wanted to identify as a man and was given a doctor's note which she then took to Canada's "DMV" and got a driver's license legally declaring she was a "man" just to see how easy it was to get her gender legally changed.[855]

Lauren Southern's ban caused quite a stir online and Patreon's CEO Jack Conte appeared on Dave Rubin's "Rubin Report" YouTube channel to respond to the criticism. He said that Lauren wasn't banned because of what she had been saying about the "Islamization" of Europe, but that she had "put lives at risk" during a stunt she recorded involving refugee boats illegally bringing people across the Mediterranean Sea into Europe.

The CEO claimed they have a policy about what he called "manifest observable behavior," and if a creator does certain things, like commits crimes, then they will be banned, but, "The decision to remove a creator page has absolutely nothing to do with politics and ideology."[856] He also claimed that Patreon's policies about speech (not actions) only focused on what people said *on their Patreon page*, not on Twitter or anywhere else, and emphasized that Lauren Southern was banned for *actions*

---

[855] YouTube "Lauren Southern Becomes a Man" by Rebel Media (October 3rd 2016)

[856] The Rubin Report "Patreon CEO Jack Conte: Lauren Southern, IGD, and Free Speech (Live Interview)" (July 31st 2017)

not words, but soon this would be proven to be another lie.[857]

December 2018, Sargon of Akkod (who had over 800,000 subscribers at the time) was banned for using a "racial slur" that someone at Patreon discovered he said in an interview months earlier. The context in which it was said was actually while he was denouncing the alt-right, saying they were acting like a bunch of "white niggers," (trying to use their own insults against them) and so his entire Patreon account was disabled, causing him to lose thousands of dollars a month in income with no recourse.[858]

About a year after Lauren Southern was banned from Patreon, her friend and sometimes collaborator Brittany Pettibone was also banned for her support of Generation Identity, a right-wing identitarian movement in Europe working to preserve European culture from Islamization.[859]   The two girls have been smeared as "white supremacists" by the liberal media because they celebrate Western European culture and oppose mass migration of Muslim refugees into Europe.   Soph's Patreon was shut down one day after YouTube deleted her channel for the same enigmatic excuse of "hate speech" against homosexuals.[860]

---

[857] Ibid.

[858] Business Insider "Crowdfunding platform Patreon defends itself from protests by 'intellectual dark web,' publishes slur-filled posts from banned YouTuber" by Benjamin Goggin (December 18th 2018)

[859] Breitbart "Stripe, PayPal, Patreon: The Right Is Being Banned from Online Fundraising" by Allum Bokhari (July 24th 2018)

[860] ReclaimTheNet.org "Patreon suspends Soph's account one day after YouTube deleted her channel" by Tom Parker (August 2nd 2019)

Patreon now has a policy against even making "negative generalizations of people based on race [and] sexual orientation," so if you point out well-documented facts about crime in black communities or the HIV rate among gay men, that would be a violation of their terms of service because it's seen as casting them in a negative light.

Imagine a bank not letting someone cash a check that was written to them because the bank didn't like what the person was going to do with the money, or didn't like the kind of language the person uses when talking with their friends. That's exactly what Patreon has done here, and it's beyond Orwellian and is a dangerous precedent that's likely only going to follow with much worse actions in the near future.

Meanwhile, far-left individuals and groups are allowed on Patreon, including "Revolutionary Left Radio," a communist podcast which is run by an admitted "militant revolutionary Communist who wants to put every fascist in the world against the wall and violently expropriate the wealth and property of the owning class."[861] Before a Breitbart article was published highlighting violent Leftists using Patreon, the group's banner on their Twitter account featured masked militants holding guns.[862]

Another Communist account called the "Guillotine Podcast" had over 350 patrons (sponsors) donating monthly. The Patreon page itself said they are working to "inspire insurrection" and notes that they want to fire

---

[861] Breitbart "Patreon tolerates calls for violence from leftists while demonetizing conservatives" by Allum Bokhari (December 15th 2018)

[862] Ibid.

"massive .44 rounds at the heads of politicians and capitalists."[863]

Milo Yiannopoulos was banned by Patreon one day after he joined in December 2018. They released a statement saying, "Milo Yiannopoulos was removed from Patreon as we don't allow association with or supporting hate groups on Patreon."[864] He joined Patreon just days after widely circulated reports said he was $2 million dollars in debt from legal fees, employee salaries he hadn't been paying, and other expenses he racked up in his ascent to Internet infamy. So in a desperate attempt to try and raise money he joined Patreon, but was immediately denied access.

In some cases it's not necessarily Patreon that wants to ban someone, but Visa or MasterCard, who demands Patreon shut down people's accounts, or threatens to stop processing payments for Patreon all together which would completely put them out of business overnight.[865]

The Future of YouTube

For the first ten years of YouTube's existence it was an even playing field where anyone could upload videos and if people watched them and shared them, their message could be seen by millions of people. The search results were fair, and if you were looking something up the videos you would find were relevant to what you had hoped to find. The only videos that would be deleted

---

[863] Ibid

[864] https://twitter.com/Patreon/status/1070446085787668480

[865] Breitbart "Mastercard Forces Patreon to Kick Off Jihad Watch's Robert Spencer" by Charlie Nash (August 15th 2018)

were things any reasonable person could agree on, like pornography, animal abuse, calls to violence, etc.

People found themselves having great careers when their passion unexpectedly opened the door to huge audiences who shared their views. But the corporate conglomerates didn't realize how many people would use YouTube to counteract the mainstream media and nobody expected how popular conservative channels would become. So YouTube is scrambling to put the genie back in the bottle, and don't really care how obvious their liberal bias is, or even how much money they lose doing it. Conservative content must be reigned in or stamped out at any cost.

In the early years of YouTube only a few carefully chosen channels were monetized, but in 2012 they opened up the "Partner Program" as it's called, to anyone, allowing them to monetize their videos no matter how many (or few) subscribers or total views they had. You could start a channel, and immediately begin earning ad revenue from your videos if people watched them, but that has all changed.

Now they manually review every channel before it's allowed in the Partner Program, so their moderators look through the videos and see what kind of content someone is producing, and if they don't like it, none of the videos on the channel will ever be monetized no matter how popular they are.

Some wonder if YouTube is harming themselves financially with all these new restrictions and the mass demonetization crusade they've engaged in, but the fact is there are plenty of other "brand friendly" or pro-liberal agenda channels that they can get revenue from. After all, being a YouTuber is the number one dream job for most kids today. It's not being an astronaut, football player, or a movie star; it's literally being a YouTuber.[866]

They've also been moving away from the monetized view business model entirely. In 2017 they began offering television packages similar to a cable provider but through an Internet connection, calling it YouTubeTV. It started off in just five U.S. markets, but then in January 2019 they massively expanded to 195 markets, making their service available to 98 percent of U.S. households.[867]

They have also been slowly morphing into another Netflix by producing original content like the popular *Cobra Kai* series which is a spinoff from the 1980s *Karate Kid* movies and stars Daniel LaRusso (Ralph Macchio) and Johnny Lawrence (William Zabka). They rent a large library of popular movies and TV shows on-demand too, for just a few dollars per stream.

As one online media outlet put it, "The golden age of YouTube is over," and it will never be the same.[868] "The platform was built on the backs of independent creators, but now YouTube is abandoning them for more traditional content."[869] Countless videos once regularly discovered by curious minds are now lost in limbo. Voices opposing certain aspects of the liberal agenda have been systematically silenced. And Leftist propaganda has been

---

[866] USA Today "Forget astronaut: YouTube is a more intriguing work frontier than space for today's kids" by Dalvin Brown (July 18th 2019)

[867] CNBC "YouTube's bet against big cable announces nationwide expansion" by Jillian D'Onfro (January 23rd 2019)

[868] The Verge "The golden age of YouTube is over" by Julia Alexander (April 5th 2019)

[869] Ibid.

artificially amplified to give the impression that their view is the correct one.

For those of us who have seen the changes made in recent years, as we look back on what YouTube once was, it's like returning to the location of your favorite dive bar to find that it's been bulldozed and replaced by a strip mall filled with a bunch of trendy stores you would never step foot in.

Author's Note: Once you finish this book, please take a moment to rate and review it on Amazon.com, or wherever you purchased it from if you're reading the e-book, to let others know what you think. This also helps to offset the trolls who keep giving my books fake one-star reviews when they haven't even read them.

Almost all of the one-star reviews on Amazon for my last two books "The True Story of Fake News" and "Liberalism: Find a Cure" are from NON-verified purchases which is a clear indication they are fraudulent hence me adding this note.

It's just more proof that liberals are losers and can't play fair, so if you could help me combat them once you're finished with this book since you actually bought and read it, I would appreciate it very much!

Thank you!

The Future of Fake News

Once "fake news" consisted primarily of made-up stories posted on cheap websites nobody had ever heard of, or websites with similar URLs to brand name outlets publishing completely fake articles hoping they'll go viral through social media and generate a bunch of ad revenue from all the clicks. I'm sure you're familiar with people making fake screenshots on Photoshop and posting them on social media claiming they came from news articles, text messages, DMs, or someone's "deleted" tweet, but we're far beyond those primitive forms of fake news and are approaching something that was once only found in science fiction films.

In Arnold Schwarzenegger's 1987 film *The Running Man*, he was an innocent police helicopter pilot who was framed for the massacre of civilians looting a grocery store after an economic collapse, and with the help of some doctored video that aired on national television, the general public thought that he had been caught red handed murdering the people, when in fact he had refused orders to open fire on them. His face was also digitally placed onto the body of someone else at another point in the film to further sell the lie to the public.

While deceptively edited video has been a problem and can cast people in a false light and twist their statements or place them out of context, the video tricks we're now facing are far more sophisticated. They can make almost anyone appear to do or say almost anything —just like what happened to Arnold Schwarzenegger in *The Running Man.*

These fake videos are called "deepfakes" named after the deep learning of artificial intelligence algorithms that are used to create them. This same technology had been used dating back to the 1990s in order to make it appear that Forrest Gump shook hands with President John F. Kennedy, and made John Wayne look like he was handing off a six pack of Coors Light to someone in a commercial even though he had been dead for over ten years.[870]

More recently it was used to digitally impose Paul Walker's face onto another actor's body to finish *Fast and the Furious* part 7 after he died in a car accident before the film was done being shot.[871] But unfortunately this technology isn't just being used for entertainment anymore, and people are starting to realize that in the wrong hands it can pose a tremendous danger.

In April 2018 comedian Jordan Peele released a video showing Barack Obama appearing to warn that, "We're entering an era in which our enemies can make it look like anyone is saying anything at any point at time — even if they would never say those things." Obama went on to say, "So, for instance, they could have me say things like…President Trump is a total and complete dip shit."[872]

The video then cut to a split screen showing Obama on one side and Jordan Peele on the other, revealing that

[870] Hollywood Reporter "R. Lee Ermey and John Wayne Shared Screen Time Together — Kind of" by Ryan Parker (April 15th 2018)

[871] Hollywood Reporter "How 'Furious 7' Brought the Late Paul Walker Back to Life" by Carolyn Giardina (December 11th 2015)

[872] The Hill "'Obama' voiced by Jordan Peele in PSA video warning about fake videos" by Morgan Gstalter (April 17th 2018)

he was doing the voice for Obama since he does a pretty good impression, and he was also using real-time face mimicking software in order to match his lips and facial expressions onto a digitally recreated version of Obama. It was a clever PSA to bring this kind of technology to people's attention, since at the time most people hadn't heard of deepfakes.

Two years earlier, in 2016, researchers at Stanford University posted a video demonstrating their "Face2Face Real-time Face Capture" technology, showing how by using their software and an ordinary webcam they could map a person's facial expressions onto George W. Bush, Barack Obama, and Donald Trump.[873] This may have been the same software Jordan Peele used for his video.

The following year a different group of researchers from the University of Washington created another fake Obama video showing him saying things that he has actually said in the past, but the video was completely synthetic and showed him in a different setting while making the statements. They released a paper explaining how they were able to do it.[874] Deepfakes like this could easily change someone's reaction to seeing or hearing something, giving a false impression as to how they feel about a certain event or issue; but this is just the tip of the iceberg.

Technology to manipulate video in such ways was once extremely expensive and required teams of people to produce, but today deepfakes can be made by amateurs on their home computers. SnapChat filters and Facebook

---

[873] Standford.edu "Face2Face: Real-time Face Capture and Reenactment of RGB Videos"

[874] UW News "Lip-syncing Obama: New tools turn audio clips into realistic video" by Jennifer Langston (July 11th 2017)

messenger filters can now overlay different cartoon faces and other effects on someone's face in real time.

In January of 2018 someone took a video of actress Amy Adams singing "I Will Survive" and swapped her face for that of Nicholas Cage's.[875] Then in January 2019 someone made one by taking a segment of Jennifer Lawrence speaking with reporters backstage after the Golden Globe awards and put Steve Buscemi's face in place of hers. The video was so bizarre and realistic looking that it became the most viral deepfake video since Jordan Peele's Obama video, and introduced the term "deepfake" to a much wider audience.[876] A few days later Stephen Colbert had Steve Buscemi on as a guest and asked him if he'd seen the video. He joked that he had "never looked better," but underneath the laughs appeared to be a concern about what this technology was now capable of.[877]

In June 2019 a deepfake of Mark Zuckerberg was posted online showing him giving what looks to be an interview with CBS News, where he says, "Imagine this for a second: One man, with total control of billions of people's stolen data, all their secrets, their lives, their futures. I owe it all to Spectre. Spectre showed me that whoever controls the data, controls the future."[878]

---

[875] Washington Post "Here are the tools that could be used to create the fake news of the future" by Philip Bump (February 12th 2018)

[876] Fortune "What Is a Deepfake? Let This Unsettling Video of Jennifer Lawrence With Steve Buscemi's Face Show You" by Kevin Kelleher (February 1st 2019)

[877] Time "Here's Steve Buscemi's Reaction to That Haunting Fake Jennifer Lawrence Mashup Video" by Melissa Locker (February 7th 2019)

[878] CNET "Deepfake video of Facebook CEO Mark Zuckerberg posted on Instagram" by Queenie Wong (June 11th 2019)

It was a publicity stunt for a futuristic art and technology exhibit in the UK, but also was meant to serve as a warning for what problems technology may cause in the near future. CBS tried to get the video removed from Facebook because the deepfake was made from an interview Zuckerberg gave to CBS News and "violated their trademark."[879] Facebook wrestled with whether or not to remove the deepfake videos, but chose not to take any action, but their existence sparked a difficult conversation, which is what the makers intended.

The "Spectre" exhibit also commissioned the creation of a deepfake of Kim Kardashian which looked and sounded extremely realistic, unlike the Zuckerberg one which was an obvious fake. This one looked and sounded just like Kim Kardashian bragging about the power social media companies have over their users' data, and concluded, "I feel really blessed because I genuinely love the process of manipulating people online for money."[880]

Needless to say, she was not happy about it, and tried to have the video removed by filing copyright complaints against social media accounts that posted it.[881] But these kind of satire videos are the least of celebrities' concerns.

---

[879] CBS News "CBS News asks Facebook to remove 'deepfake' video of Mark Zuckerberg with unauthorized CBSN trademark" by Lex Haris (June 12th 2019)

[880] PC Magazine "Facebook Declines to Delete Fake Zuckerberg Video" by Michael Kan (June 11th 2019)

[881] Tech Dirt "Kim Kardashian Deep Fake Video Removed By Copyright Claim" by Timothy Geigner (June 19th 2019)

Deepfake Porn

Just like many early Internet entrepreneurs were quick to use the emerging new technology to share porn— allowing people to access it from their home computer instead of having to go out and buy magazines or VHS tapes from some seedy adult video store—one of the early uses of deepfake technology was to make fake porn videos depicting famous celebrities like Gal Gadot (*Wonder Woman*), Daisy Ridley (*Star Wars*), and Scarlett Johansson (*The Horse Whisperer*).

Celebrity deepfake porn videos were soon banned by PornHub[882] and Reddit where users were posting clips they had made of their favorite actresses.[883] While most of the videos weren't being passed off as actual sex tapes, their creation obviously caused concern for those actresses whose likeness is now appearing in realistic-looking porn videos.[884]

Another concern is that since the software to create such fakes is widely available online, people could make fake sex tapes of someone in attempts to extort money from them, threatening to post the fakes online if they don't pay up. Or scorned ex-lovers or those rejected by women could create deepfakes and post them online in order to "get back" at them.[885]

---

[882] The Verge "Pornhub is the latest platform to ban AI-generated 'deepfakes' porn" by Adi Robertson (February 6th 2018)

[883] CNET "Reddit cracks down on 'deepfake' pornography" by Erin Carson (February 7th 2018)

[884] Wired "Yes people can put your face on porn, no the law can't help you" by Emma Grey Ellis (January 1st 26th 2018)

[885] Engadget "AI-powered face swapping has taken a dystopian turn" by Richard Lawler (January 26th 2018)

Information Warfare

When the Bush administration was planning for the invasion of Iraq in 2003, the CIA reportedly came up with the idea to create a fake video appearing to be Saddam Hussein having sex with a teenage boy. "It would look like it was taken by a hidden camera. Very grainy, like it was a secret videotaping of a sex session," a CIA official later admitted to the *Washington Post*.[886]

The CIA also reportedly discussed making a fake video appearing as if Osama bin Laden and his lieutenants were sitting around a campfire drinking alcohol and talking about their "conquests with boys" as well, but another former CIA official with knowledge of the plan said, "Saddam playing with boys would have no resonance in the Middle East — nobody cares. Trying to mount such a campaign would show a total misunderstanding of the target. We always mistake our own taboos as universal when, in fact, they are just our taboos."[887]

He was referring to the practice of "bacha bazi" which is an Afghani term meaning "boy play" that refers to sexual relationships between older men and young boys who are from very poor families or orphans and used as sex slaves by wealthy and powerful Afghanis.[888] U.S. soldiers were reportedly told to ignore such abuse because

---

[886] The Washington Post "CIA unit's wacky idea: Depict Saddam as gay" by Jeff Stein (May 25th 2010)

[887] The Telegraph "CIA considered faking Saddam Hussein sex video" by Toby Harnden (May 26th 2010)

[888] BBC "The sexually abused dancing boys of Afghanistan" by Rustam Qobil (September 8th 2010)

it is part of the culture in regions of the Middle East.[889] This abomination is a whole other issue, but the point is the CIA actually proposed making a deepfake of Saddam Hussein as a pedophile thinking it would incite people to rise up and overthrow him, because if such a video were real, people in a civilized culture would do just that.

Fake Photos

Nvidia, a video graphics card company, has created an AI so powerful that it can automatically change the weather in video footage, making a clip of a car driving down a road on a sunny day appear as if it was actually shot in the middle of winter with a few inches of snow on the ground and the leaves missing from the trees.[890] The same technology can take photos of cats or dogs and change them to make them look like a different breed, and can change people's facial expressions from happy to sad, or anything in between.[891]

Nvidia's AI can even generate realistic pictures of people who don't actually exist by taking features from actual photos and combining elements of them together into a composite that is almost impossible to tell that it's fake.[892] The website ThisPersonDoesNotExist.com uses this technology to display a different fake photo every

---

[889] The New York Times "U.S. Soldiers Told to Ignore Sexual Abuse of Boys by Afghan Allies" by Joseph Goldstein (September 20th 2015)

[890] The Verge "Nvidia uses AI to make it snow on streets that are always sunny" by James Vincent (December 5th 2017)

[891] Ibid.

[892] CNET "This website uses AI to generate startling fake human faces" by Jackson Ryan (February 14th 2019)

time you visit it, most of them looking like HD photos of ordinary people.

AI can now create 3D models of people just from a few photographs, and while it may be fun to input a character in your favorite video game that looks just like you, the capacity for nefarious abuses of this technology are vast.

Fake Audio

In November 2016, Adobe (the creator of Photoshop) demonstrated what they called Adobe Voco, or Photoshop-for-voices, which can generate realistic sounding audio, making it sound like someone is saying something that they never actually said. The software works by inputting samples of someone's voice, and then can create fake audio files in that same voice saying whatever is typed onto the screen.[893]

Dr. Eddy Borges Rey, a professor at the University of Stirling, said, "It seems that Adobe's programmers were swept along with the excitement of creating something as innovative as a voice manipulator, and ignored the ethical dilemmas brought up by its potential misuse."[894]

He continues, "Inadvertently, in its quest to create software to manipulate digital media, Adobe has [already] drastically changed the way we engage with evidential material such as photographs. This makes it hard for lawyers, journalists, and other professionals who use

[893] BBC "Adobe Voco 'Photoshop-for-voice' causes concern" November 7th 2016)

[894] Ibid.

digital media as evidence."[895] Google has created similar software called WaveNet that generates realistic sounding human speech by modeling samples of people actually talking.[896]

In May 2019 a group of Machine Learning Engineers released an audio clip they created using their RealTalk technology which sounded like podcaster Joe Rogan talking about investing in a new hockey team made up of chimpanzees.[897] It wasn't perfect, but if you didn't know that it was fake before you heard it, you may be fooled into thinking that it's real. The researchers admitted, "the societal implications for technologies like speech synthesis are massive. And the implications will affect everyone."[898]

"Right now, technical expertise, ingenuity, computing power and data are required to make models like RealTalk perform well. So not just anyone can go out and do it. But in the next few years (or even sooner), we'll see the technology advance to the point where only a few seconds of audio are needed to create a life-like replica of anyone's voice on the planet. It's pretty f*cking scary," the creators wrote on their blog.[899]

They went on to list some of the possible abuses this technology may be used for, "if the technology got into the wrong hands."   These include, "Spam callers impersonating your mother or spouse to obtain personal

---

[895] Ibid.

[896] Medium "RealTalk: This Speech Synthesis Model Our Engineers Built Recreates a Human Voice Perfectly" by Dessa (May 15th 2019)

[897] Ibid.

[898] Ibid.

[899] Ibid.

information. Impersonating someone for the purposes of bullying or harassment. Gaining entrance to high security clearance areas by impersonating a government official," and "An 'audio deepfake' of a politician being used to manipulate election results or cause a social uprising."[900]

They raise some great points. What's to stop people from creating deepfakes of politicians, CEOs of major corporations, or popular YouTubers, and making them appear as if they're saying racist, hateful, or violent things, and claiming they got it from a coworker or a "friend" who secretly recorded it, or that the clip was from an old YouTube video once uploaded to someone's channel that they later deleted?

National Security Concerns

In July 2017 researchers at Harvard, who were backed by the U.S. Intelligence Advanced Research Projects Activity (IARPA), published a report titled *Artificial Intelligence and National Security* where they detailed the growing risk of deepfake forgeries, saying, "The existence of widespread AI forgery capabilities will erode social trust, as previously reliable evidence becomes highly uncertain," and details some of the horrific possibilities that are right around the corner.[901]

The report then quotes part of an article one of the researchers wrote for *Wired* magazine about these dangers, saying, "Today, when people see a video of a politician taking a bribe, a soldier perpetrating a war

---

[900] Ibid.

[901] The Belfer Center for Science and International Affairs - Artificial Intelligence and National Security by Greg Allen and Taniel Chan (July 2017) page 30

crime, or a celebrity starring in a sex tape, viewers can safely assume that the depicted events have actually occurred, provided, of course, that the video is of a certain quality and not obviously edited. But that world of truth —where seeing is believing—is about to be upended by artificial intelligence technologies."[902]

The article continues, "When tools for producing fake video perform at higher quality than today's CGI and are simultaneously available to untrained amateurs, these forgeries might comprise a large part of the information ecosystem."[903]

The *Artificial Intelligence and National Security* report goes on to warn that, "A future where fakes are cheap, widely available, and indistinguishable from reality would reshape the relationship of individuals to truth and evidence. This will have profound implications for domains across journalism, government communications, testimony in criminal justice, and of course national security...In the future, people will be constantly confronted with realistic-looking fakes."[904]

It concludes that, "We will struggle to know what to trust. Using cryptography and secure communication channels, it may still be possible to, in some circumstances, prove the authenticity of evidence. But, the 'seeing is believing' aspect of evidence that dominates

---

[902] Wired "AI Will Make Forging Anything Entirely Too Easy" by Greg Allen (July 1st 2017)

[903] Ibid.

[904] The Belfer Center for Science and International Affairs - Artificial Intelligence and National Security by Greg Allen and Taniel Chan (July 2017) page 31

today—one where the human eye or ear is almost always good enough—will be compromised."[905]

Elon Musk is funding a non-profit organization called OpenAI which is trying to ensure that the creation of artificial intelligence will be "safe," but they created an AI tool so powerful they won't release it to the public out of concern that it could create such realistic forgeries and fake news articles that they would be difficult to distinguish from real ones. "Due to our concerns about malicious applications of the technology, we are not releasing the trained model," the organization wrote on their blog.[906]

Others are equally concerned. Sean Gourley, who is the founder and CEO of a company called Primer, which data mines social media posts for U.S. intelligence agencies to track issues of concern and possible threats, warns, "The automation of the generation of fake news is going to make it very effective."[907]

Nothing may be safe from the weaponization of artificial intelligence. A group of researchers at the University of Chicago developed an AI system in 2017 that could write fake Yelp reviews and even though sites like Yelp and Amazon have machine learning algorithms designed to detect fake reviews written by trolls or bots, when they unleashed their Yelp review writer on the site

---

[905] Ibid.

[906] USA Today "Too scary? Elon Musk's OpenAI company won't release tech that can generate fake news" by Edward C. Baig (February 15th 2019)

[907] MIT Technological Review "Fake News 2.0: personalized, optimized, and even harder to stop" by Will Knight (March 27th 2018)

their safeguards had a hard time detecting the fake reviews.[908]

Ben Zhoa, one of researchers who worked on the project, said, "We have validated the danger of someone using AI to create fake accounts that are good enough to fool current countermeasures," and warned, "more powerful hardware and larger data for training means that future AI models will be able to capture all these properties and be truly indistinguishable from human-authored content."[909]

This makes the forged documents purported to be George W. Bush's service record in the National Guard or the infamous "Steele Trump-Russia Dossier" created by Fusion GPS seem like child's play. *The New York Observer* reported that there are already multiple fake "Trump sex tapes" circulating among those working in intelligence agencies and suggested that they were created in order to "muddy the waters" in the event that a "real" Trump sex tape surfaces, which some believe was made by the Kremlin when Trump visited Russia in 2013 for the Miss Universe Pageant, for what the KGB calls "kompromat" or compromising material.[910]

Trump has insisted that even before his trip to Russia he was well aware of hidden cameras in hotel rooms there and the government's attempt to gain blackmail material on high profile individuals like himself, and made sure

---

[908] Scientific America "Could AI Be the Future of Fake News and Product Reviews?" by Larry Greenemeier (October 16th 2017)

[909] Ibid.

[910] Observer "Spies Suspect Kremlin Is Pushing Dozens of Fake Trump Sex Tapes" by John R. Schindler (November 9th 2017)

not to get ensnared in their trap.[911]   His bodyguard testified that prior to the trip he and Trump had discussed that the Russians used such tactics and knew not to take the bait.[912]

So it's highly unlikely that a real Trump sex tape exists, but it is likely that Deep State operatives within our own CIA may have manufactured such fakes for the same reason they floated the idea of doing such a thing to Saddam Hussein and Osama bin Laden — to discredit Trump and use it as propaganda to fan the flames of an insurgency hoping to bring him down.

As Winston Churchill said, "A lie gets halfway around the world before the truth has a chance to get its pants on."[913] Nobody is safe from being smeared by deepfakes, whether they're an ordinary person who has been targeted by a jealous ex-lover, a disgruntled coworker or classmate, or whether they are the President of the United States whose political opponents or a foreign adversary want to bring down.

The other side of the coin is that if and when actual damning footage is shot of someone doing or saying something illegal or morally reprehensible, they could easily just claim the footage is fake. Perhaps half of the people would believe them, having reasonable doubt since the technology exists to actually fake it and people may have a motive to do it.   We're clearly not in Kansas

---

[911] New York Post "Russian offered to send prostitutes to Trump's hotel room" by Mark Moore (November 9th 2017)

[912] New York Daily News "Ex-Trump bodyguard testifies Russian operative offered to 'send five women' to future President's hotel room" by Leonard Greene (November 9th 2017)

[913] Brainy Quote - Winston Churchill

anymore and only time will tell just how pervasive and damaging deepfakes will become.

Conclusion

We're in the middle of a war — an information war. It's being waged by tyrannical billion dollar tech companies against those of us who use their products and services in ways they hadn't intended or imagined. They sold us tools thinking they were toys, but we saw the potential this new technology had to enable us to defend the Republic and spread our message across the country with a few clicks of a keyboard or taps on a touchscreen. In the marketplace of ideas, we were winning; so our opponents started cheating, and despite the metaphors this is not a game, this is our life.

They don't want to just silence us online, they want to repeal the First Amendment and arrest us for "hate speech" for disagreeing with them as they aim to overthrow the United States government and replace it with a Communist technocratic super-state that's a crossbreed between the regimes in George Orwell's *Nineteen Eighty-Four* and Aldous Huxley's *Brave New World*.

Syndicated columnist Joseph Sobran Jr. once stated, "Liberalism is really piecemeal socialism, and socialism always attacks three basic social institutions: religion, the family, and private property. Religion, because it offers a rival authority to the state; the family, because it means a rival loyalty to the state; and property, because it means material independence of the state."[914]

---

[914] AZQuotes.com - Joseph Sobran Quotes

They want to turn Boy Scouts into child drag queens, and are encouraging people to buy sex bots instead of engagement rings. They want people to denounce God and view Christians as the enemy, while the hordes of lazy and entitled degenerates live off the labor of those who get up and go to work every morning. Most people are too distracted to see what's actually happening and are slowly becoming part of the problem.

They know more about the history of their favorite football team than they do of their own country. They're more familiar with the names and statistics of the players than they are of the people who are in charge of running the government. Sports entertainment and the latest talent shows on TV are mostly modern day bread and circus events that distract attention and divert energy from things that really matter. Our culture, our economy, and our country is at stake.

If America falls, it will never be restored. It will be relegated to the history books like the Roman Empire and other great civilizations that have collapsed. To prevent our planned destruction it's going to take hard work, vigorous study, and unwavering dedication. You don't get physically fit by going to the gym once a year. Or once a month, or even once a week! You have to go on a regular basis, and keep going! Isn't the health of our society just as important as our own physical health?

Pay close attention to what you do with your time, your talent, and your money. Get involved in your local community. Get on the school board, or city council, or at least show up once in a while to give them a piece of your mind. Maintain regular face-to-face interactions with your friends and family so you don't get trapped in the downward spiral of living your life through a screen.

Do a regular digital detox on the weekends and holidays, and give yourself time for introspection by stepping away from the endless news cycle and social media feeds to get a bigger perspective of what's going on and what's important. Maybe we have been asleep at the wheel. Maybe we took the freedoms and prosperity of living in America for granted while the enemy quietly schemed behind our backs. Well not any more!

It's time to wake up. It's time to get focused on the long-term goals of what we need to do in order to preserve the freedom of speech, family values, Christian traditions, and our economic security. I hope this book has helped you become more media literate so you can see how the mechanisms of information distribution function in our modern age and what their effects are.

If you found this book valuable in your journey please rate it and write a brief review on Amazon or whatever ebook store you downloaded it from, if that's where you bought it, and tell your friends and family to checkout this book since I don't have a major publisher backing me (I self-published this) or their marketing team to promote it. I only have my social media accounts, and you. But that's all I need. And that's is exactly why they are so scared of us!

Also by Mark Dice:

-The True Story of Fake News
-Liberalism: Find a Cure
-The Illuminati in Hollywood
-Inside the Illuminati
-The Illuminati: Facts & Fiction
-The New World Order: Facts & Fiction
-The Resistance Manifesto
-Big Brother: The Orwellian Nightmare
-The Bilderberg Group: Facts & Fiction
-Bohemian Grove: Facts & Fiction

Connect with Mark on:

Facebook.com/MarkDice
Twitter.com/MarkDice
Instagram.com/MarkDice
YouTube.com/MarkDice
MarkDice.com

Made in the USA
Columbia, SC
11 November 2020

24262650R00183